
Nuclear Proliferation

Breaking the Chain

Edited by

George H. Quester

The University of Wisconsin Press

Published 1981

The University of Wisconsin Press
114 North Murray Street
Madison, Wisconsin 53715

The University of Wisconsin Press, Ltd.
1 Gower Street
London WC1E 6HA, England

First printing

Printed in the United States of America

ISBN 0-299-08600-3 cloth, 0-299-08604-6 paper
LC 80-53960

Contents

Contributors

George H. Quester is Professor of Government and Director of the Peace Studies Program at Cornell University.

Joseph S. Nye is Professor of Government at Harvard University.

Pierre Lellouche is Research Associate at the Institut Français des Relations Internationales in Paris.

Irvin C. Bupp is Associate Professor of Business Administration at the Graduate School of Business Administration at Harvard University.

Lawrence Scheinman is Professor of Government at Cornell University.

John R. Redick is Research Director of the Stanley Foundation at its research office in Iowa City.

Robert E. Harkavy is Associate Professor of Political Science at Pennsylvania State University.

Onkar Marwah is Assistant Director of the Program for Strategic and International Studies at the Graduate Institute of International Studies in Geneva.

Lewis A. Dunn is a Senior Professional Staff Member at the Hudson Institute in Croton-on-Hudson, New York.

Michael Nacht is Associate Professor of Public Policy and Associate Director of the Center for Science and International Affairs at Harvard University.

Preface

This volume collects a series of predictions on how the world's nuclear proliferation problem will unfold in the 1980s and 1990s. These predictions are meant to go beyond the conventional wisdom, or to contradict it, in a look across the horizon. The collection was commissioned with the expectation that 1980, an election year, would be a good time to take stock of U.S. policy in this area, but also more broadly to review whether greater pessimism or greater optimism might be in order on the prevention of further nuclear weapons spread. Early outlines and preliminary drafts of the papers were presented at a conference in Cambridge, Massachusetts in May of 1980.

The papers benefited importantly from comments each author drew from all the other authors. The review committee drawn from the *International Organization* board of editors — Stanley Hoffmann, Harold Jacobson, and Henry Nau, joined by Peter Katzenstein as incoming editor of the journal — also provided very valuable critical assistance. Wallis Ammerman deserves a great deal of credit for her editorial work in making all of the papers more readable. Important thanks must also be extended to the World Peace Foundation and its Director, Alfred Hero, for financial support and substantive suggestions throughout the project.

1
Introduction:
In Defense of Some Optimism

George H. Quester

As the 1980s begin, pessimists might question whether the prospects for preventing nuclear weapons spread (or even the prospects for world peace) are very good anymore. It must thus be noted that the authors in this collection largely resist this trend of analysis and are generally more optimistic than the conventional wisdom might have suggested.

Each of the authors would probably be quick to concede that nuclear proliferation is a serious problem in two important senses: the spread of nuclear weapons would make the world a less happy place, and such spread may be difficult to stop.

Yet they largely reject the conclusion that halting the spread of nuclear weapons will be impossible. At the very least, further proliferation may come much more slowly than the pessimists have predicted and may come in more ambiguous or diluted forms. In our analysis we will thus have to consider "quasiproliferation" cases where nations may stockpile bombs and never announce or detonate them, letting unconfirmed (and undenied) rumors carry the message around. We may also have instances where states detonate a token explosive to prove a point, and then detonate no more.

A world of more than fifteen nuclear weapons states may be a disaster. But what of a world which sees only eight or nine reach this stage by the end of the century, with some of the "memberships" in the nuclear weapons club being of the ambiguous varieties just noted? An important possibility to be explored, which most of the authors in this collection might indeed endorse as a working premise, is that the smaller number is livable (as compared with the larger), in terms of lower risks and costs of war, and lower stimulus to still further proliferation.

One indeed has to worry about "chains" of nuclear weapons spread, as each country acquiring bombs induces another to follow suit. Yet the possibility remains that proliferation can be contained, and that such chains can be broken.

Viewpoints not represented

We should first stipulate a number of viewpoints not represented among the authors collected here.

One is that nuclear weapons proliferation would actually be desirable for the world—that it would in some way reduce the likelihood of war or aggression, in the end increasing the total of human happiness and welfare. Examples of such a view can be found in the official pronouncements of some states in the past two decades (pronouncements not always to be taken so seriously), and in some academic analyses.[1] For reasons to be outlined a little later, each of the authors in this volume has really been working under an opposite premise.

Another viewpoint not really represented is that which concedes that nuclear proliferation is undesirable, but then concludes that halting it is hopeless. Such a perception is sometimes presented in terms of "the world must stop trying to stop nuclear proliferation, and learn to live with it."[2] None of the papers in this collection accepts this, or seriously contemplates how we could adjust to a world of many nuclear weapons states; consistent with the general opposition to further proliferation, most of us as authors simply view a proliferated world with unrelieved dread.

Yet a third unrepresented perspective is that which agrees that nuclear proliferation is bad, and still preventable, but which sees the requirements of halting proliferation as being quite total. This is a view that current steps are manifestly inadequate, but that a crash program of total commitment to nonproliferation would be adequate, and is indeed called for.[3] Sentiments that "it's high time we locked up this dangerous technology," or that INFCE represents a sell-out of nuclear arms control by the Carter administration, thus

[1] For a more elaborate presentation of arguments that nuclear proliferation may not be so undesirable, see Kenneth N. Waltz, "What Will the Spread of Nuclear Weapons Do to the World? in *International Political Effects of the Spread of Nuclear Weapons,* John Kerry King, ed. (Washington, U.S.G.P.O., 1979), pp. 165–97.

[2] A recent illustration of a resignation to nuclear proliferation as more or less inevitable can be found in John J. Weltman, "Nuclear Devolution and World Order," *World Politics,* XXXII, 2 (January 1980): 169–93.

[3] Such a view might fairly be ascribed to Albert Wohlstetter, et al., *Swords From Plowshares* (Chicago: The University of Chicago Press, 1979).

would be more typical of such a perspective. This is often presented as a "hawkish" view, that the United States should push nonproliferation very far ahead in priority, simply in terms of its own national interests, deploying our power, withholding technology as necessary, because nuclear weapons spread cannot otherwise be prevented.

Fourthly unrepresented is what might seem a logical variation on this theme—although it usually draws endorsement from an entirely different, more "dovish" group of observers—that nuclear proliferation cannot be halted unless substantial disarmament also occurs among the current possessors of nuclear arms, the superpowers.[4] It is unfair and unreasonable, according to this view, to ask for a stopping of "horizontal proliferation," unless there is also a halting of the "vertical proliferation" in the continuing increase in Soviet and American arms, indeed unless progress is made (in accordance with Article VI of the Nuclear Nonproliferation Treaty) toward "general and complete disarmament." This is an interpretation which requires an all-out surrender of national sovereign prerogatives as the price of stopping nuclear weapons spread, and it is basically unrepresented among our authors.

Compared with views that "all-out" actions and sacrifices are required to halt nuclear weapons spread, most of the collection's authors are inclined to believe that gentler and less total approaches have some chance of containing proliferation, and perhaps that any more total approaches might become counterproductive. They may disagree among themselves (as illustrated by the contributions of Nye and Lellouche) about what should and should not be included in an antiproliferation campaign, but none is convinced that only a "total effort" can succeed.

A part of this issue boils down to the opportunity costs of achieving nuclear arms control. To what extent are nations ready to surrender some political influence, or some economic material well-being, as part of an effort to prevent the spread of nuclear weapons? The tone of the volume must be characterized as "realistic," in that it does not assume that the entire world will be so eager for nuclear peace that it would make every sacrifice requested as a barrier to proliferation. But it also stops short of the absolutes of a realpolitik analysis which would see power as the only objective of foreign policy anywhere, which would thus preclude any of the sacrifices required to stop the spread of nuclear weapons.

Pessimistic possibilities

Aside from stipulating unrepresented perspectives, I feel obliged to outline possible changes in the international system that could affect the

---

[4] The tone of this view is clearly reflected in the analysis of William Epstein, *The Last Chance* (New York: The Free Press, 1976).

prospects for nonproliferation and upset any optimism. (The final chapter presents this editor's predictions about how a relatively successful resistance to nuclear proliferation might affect the international system. For the moment, however, we must first face a different question—how changes in the international system might indeed upset any resistance to proliferation.)

First, a major breakdown of Soviet-American relations, continuing the discouraging trends of 1978 to 1980, would surely put a strain on the effort to avoid nuclear weapons spread. The nuclear proliferation issue for the moment is unique in that superpower coordination seems to be continuing, while grain sales and Olympic sports and other forms of cooperative interaction have been mortgaged to the conflict over Afghanistan, as ratification of SALT II seems to have become very unlikely. In the extreme, however, if the Middle East or some other corner of the world were to see actual combat between American and Soviet forces (even if this were prayerfully kept at the conventional level), the approaches to preventing nuclear proliferation listed in this volume might not stand the strain.

A second source of instability and unpredictability in a nonproliferation regime stems simply from U.S. domestic politics. The American presidential election process has notoriously produced rapid changes in policy, on proliferation as on other issues, with the shifts from Johnson to Nixon and from Ford to Carter hardly being trivial. As one looked ahead in the summer of 1980, a reelection of Carter might have been forecast to produce relatively greater continuity in American policy in this realm in 1981 and 1982. The election of Ronald Reagan, whose off-hand statements have sometimes indicated a skepticism about whether nuclear proliferation was so undesirable, by contrast suggested something very different (although there were advisers in his camp, for example, Fred Ikle or Albert Wohlstetter, who might persuade him to come back to a more anti-proliferation position). John Anderson, running as a fresh-face and third alternative offering a change, similarly was not totally predictable on the nuclear policies he might adopt.

Third, the technological and economic background of nuclear matters has not been very much more predictable than its politics. If the world sees more nuclear accidents of the Three Mile Island variety, this may grievously delay nuclear power. But if Saudi Arabia were to fall to the same kind of domestic instability that reduced Iran's oil output, this might instead very convincingly increase the economic appeal of nuclear power, with complicated consequences for any nuclear nonproliferation regime. Well short of an upheaval in Saudi Arabia, the world finds it generally difficult to predict even the more "normal" price changes of the OPEC system.

It is fair to say that a dominant fear of the 1970s nuclear proliferation discussion was that such weapons would spread not because they were very much desired, but because a rapid growth in nuclear electric power production would make such bombs too cheap and easy to produce. In a twisting of economics jargon, commentators speculated that our problem would now be "supply-push" rather than "demand-pull." Albert Wohlstetter, attracting a fair amount of attention in his "Spreading the Bomb Without Quite Breaking the Rules" article[5] suggested that the spread of dual-purpose nuclear technology might be the bulk of the weapons proliferation problem.

In light of Pakistan's more recent attempt to acquire nuclear weapons (described in the Marwah chapter) by equipment and processes which are not really any spinoff from civilian purposes, this 1970s emphasis (which Pierre Lellouche argues gripped too heavily the Carter administration) has come under extensive criticism. Have we concentrated too much attention on one "barn door," leaving another unlocked?

The chapter by Irvin Bupp indeed presents a startlingly different prognosis of the growth of nuclear electrical production, not at all endorsing the conventional wisdom that nuclear power is destined to grow. Bupp concedes that predictions are hazardous, but notes that industry and government spokespeople have been tendentiously united time and time again in overstating probable growth. Bupp chooses to venture his own prediction, in face of the uncertainties, in light of the industry biases—that nuclear electric power production will instead grow very little in the next several decades, expanding far less than predictions would have it.

Such a prediction about the future of nuclear power can surely be wrong. Given that all the forecasts in the technological and engineering realm here have been surprisingly hazy and unreliable, one could hardly rule out the possibility of another dramatic upsurge in the installation of nuclear reactors, despite all the disappointments of the industry, despite the protests of the ecologists. Any resignation to the nongrowth of nuclear industry will surely be resented in economically underdeveloped regions, since a stagnation of nuclear power might simply dictate continued poverty for such countries.

In any event, it will not be easy to translate Bupp's pessimistic expectations about nuclear power growth into optimism or pessimism about nuclear weapons proliferation. Some of our proliferation worries would be eased, but others would be amplified or augmented.

To the extent that nuclear weapons worries were simply based on the enormous flows of plutonium and enriched uranium that would accompany a major growth in nuclear electricity production, the shrinking of estimates would have to be good news. Yet a new fear then emerges that some of these half-finished nuclear power reactor ventures will become bomb projects, simply because the project managers see this as an easy way—the only way—to redeem their investment, to protect their own reputations, or their national interests.

---

[5] Albert Wohlstetter, "Spreading the Bomb Without Quite Breaking the Rules," *Foreign Policy,* 25 (Winter 1976–77): 88–96, 145–79.

The decline of nuclear power might have been good news on the weapons proliferation front if the nuclear projects had never been begun. What has been begun and would persist in a half-finished state might be much more a mixed commodity.

There are other kinds of uncertainties about the nonproliferation environment that go beyond the three outlined. A coup in Saudi Arabia, or in Kuwait, or Dubai would be the kind of political upheaval most directly connected with the economics of the world, perhaps rekindling interest in nuclear power production, and then more rapidly spreading the "cheap byproduct" of nuclear weapons options. Yet as part of any list of pessimistic possibilities to be borne in mind, such coups and civil wars can occur as well in various non-oil-producing countries, in ways which upset regional stability and make nuclear weapons more attractive again (not just because they were too easily available, but because someone felt a real military need for them).

Returning to Soviet-American military interactions, even the current stalemate on SALT II is not particularly conducive to the avoidance of nuclear weapons proliferation. The strategic arms procurements which will follow may open still more of a Pandora's box, as "war-fighting" scenarios and procurements are taken more seriously by American strategic planners and political decision makers (in part because the Russians have at least pretended all along to take them seriously), as the apparent accuracies of new ballistic missiles and cruise missiles seem to offer counterforce targeting opportunities on each side. If the world sees the two superpowers seemingly treating World War III as less of a disaster and more of a military contest, this will not work to take the glamour off nuclear weapons for "nth" countries. (As will be noted in the concluding chapter, something less troublesome might arise if the superb accuracies of new missiles came to be increasingly married to conventional warheads.)

The apparent suspension of SALT may, however, be more than just a failure of arms control; a significant number of Americans may see it as a moment when the USSR moved beyond parity for the first time into a strategic superiority, as Soviet intercontinental missiles by 1985 might be able to disarm their American opposite numbers, while American missiles could not do the reverse. Skeptics about Soviet prowess will question whether this all could make much difference. Yet it is hardly to be denied that a Soviet superiority, if it were real, would be something truly new for the international system, such that many of our assumptions about that system might come into question, including those of any optimism about preventing nuclear proliferation. Michael Nacht's chapter offers an extended discussion of these linkages, including the impact on American alliance commitments.

As the examples of Pakistan and South Korea (and to a lesser extent, Taiwan and Israel) suggest, the United States from this point onwards will continuously have to weigh an interest in avoiding nuclear proliferation against some already mixed feelings about alliance commitments. Americans have to care about preventing proliferation, but they have to care about other considerations as well: discouraging armed aggressions against such countries, avoiding too close a coupling to nondemocratic regimes, and now reducing the flow of conventional weapons (a choice discussed in the chapter by Lewis Dunn).

American alliance commitments will probably thus remain in a state of uncertainty and flux in the aftermath of the Vietnam War and a more general reappraisal of the American role in a confusing and disappointing world. Is the Soviet move toward "parity" or "strategic superiority" any part of the explanation for these uncertainties about American alliance reliability? Will these uncertainties significantly upset the containment of nuclear weapons spread?

As Robert Harkavy's chapter outlines in detail, the world since 1945 has seen a new phenomenon evolve in the "pariah state," a state denied legitimacy by international organizations, while simultaneously being under military threat from its neighbors. If the tendency to impose such pariah status fades, this may ease the push toward nuclear proliferation (some forms of such proliferation can indeed be seen as the way out of such a status). If the tendency increases, adding rather than subtracting states from the pariah list, the problem of containing nuclear proliferation will again be worsened.

It is generally argued in this collection that international economic interaction ("interdependence") can be a force for good in slowing down separate national decisions to acquire nuclear weapons. If the volume of such interdependence no longer continues to grow, but now levels off (or even recedes, as part of some new drive toward mercantilist autarky), we would then again correspondingly have some bad news about the nuclear arms control we are seeking.

Any system to contain proliferation will, at the least, have to offer some cushioning against shocks—shocks quite specifically related to the nonproliferation theme. What if several states announce their withdrawal from the Nuclear Nonproliferation Treaty (NPT), or from some other legal commitment to renouncing nuclear weapons? What if one state, or more than one, procedes to violate its nonproliferation commitments, without having been so proper as to announce a withdrawal from the treaties involved?

What, moreover, if nuclear weapons spread beyond national control, so that such subnational groups as the FLQ, or IRA, or Breton Separatists get their hands on them?

The mere prospect of such nuclear terrorism may reinforce the global common sense that further national proliferation should be avoided, for as more countries acquire nuclear weapons, the chances that they will slip into such totally irresponsible hands will increase. Having nuclear weapons in one's own national nuclear arsenal is no protection against nuclear terrorism, for there is no hostage against which to threaten retaliation, no easy way to apply normal deterrence. If anything, having such weapons probably makes one's cities more prone to nuclear terrorist attack.

Yet, if any proliferation to subnational bodies were to occur, the state regimes of the world might still see this as a sign that the antiproliferation regime was generally failing, so that they should grab their own weapons before their neighbors grabbed theirs. It is such stampedes that amount to one of the worst nightmares for any advocate of nuclear arms control.

The undesirability of proliferation

Having stipulated systemic changes that could undermine a non-proliferation system, we may ask the sources that suggest any optimism that such a system can be maintained. The greatest base, it would be contended in this volume, is a common sense, which is increasingly affecting the world on the proliferation issue, that such proliferation would simply be bad.

The final chapter describes what the international system might look like if further nuclear proliferation can be avoided, due precisely to the prevalence of common sense and some good fortune. Instead here, I shall present a brief prediction of what the world may look like if proliferation occurs. It seems to this editor, as to all the authors, that such a future would be decidedly unpleasant. The diplomats and political leaders of the world may not always be ready to admit this fully, but the best guess is that they see it in very much the same way.

Is it really so very hard to conclude that any extensive further spread of nuclear weapons would be bad for the international system? As with most questions of arms control, the outputs to be watched are the likelihood of war, and the costs of war if it were to happen.

Some of the concern about nuclear proliferation would be derived from the first consideration, since current political conflicts among the nations of the world might be exacerbated and amplified to the point where they would break into violent exchanges.

As noted, a few analysts might suggest instances where the spread of nuclear weapons would have a beneficial effect; this is, after all, the argument on behalf of nuclear deterrence in general, and it translates into an assumption that "pariah states," states imminently threatened with extinction by their neighbors, might be able to escape this by brandishing nuclear weapons. A vow that "even if you totally defeat us and push us into the sea, we will destroy your cities and dams and cultural monuments as our last gasp of retaliation" may indeed be an effective threat. Assured-second-strike forces may stabilize political and military confrontations between the superpowers; why should this not work also, à la Gallois, between minor powers?[6] Issues which seem burning and uncompromisable may become otherwise when the object of our hatred admits to having nuclear weapons. It can hardly be denied that the tremendous increase in costs associated with nuclear war may decrease the likelihood of some kinds of war. The seriousness of any recourse to arms is emphasized and enhanced, and some old grudges may have to be suspended or forgotten.

Yet what if, as is entirely possible, the first generation of nuclear weapons for each of these new countries is not typically assured-second-strike, but rather very vulnerable and tempting for the preemptive attack of neighbors? Would this not again lead to great exacerbations of preexisting political conflict, since the temptation to "strike now for it may be our last chance" might turn out to be overwhelming? We must, thus, accept a mixed, somewhat more pessimistic conclusion about whether nuclear proliferation would increase or decrease the irritations of international conflicts and increase or decrease the likelihood of wars.

It follows, in a depressingly easy analysis, what the impact of proliferation will be on the *costs* of any war once it has begun. If nuclear weapons are to be found in the arsenals of two states, they are likely (albeit not certain) to come into use. As a matter of the logic of limited warfare, two nuclear powers could surely manage to hold such forces in reserve, in effect applying a policy of "no first use" to each other, but the assurance of this is not great, especially where the fear or temptation of preemptive attack might emerge on either side. The world has not yet seen an example of a shooting war between two nuclear powers, so no proof for the likelihood of restraint exists.

For nuclear weapons to come into use in a war between Pakistan and India, or between Israel and the Arab states, or anywhere else in the globe, would be to impose levels of human suffering and material destruction infinitely higher than any we have seen before. The world has not had to contemplate any human images of nuclear devastation since Hiroshima and Nagasaki; those were indeed horrendous, but they are removed enough in time so that they are largely repressed. A future "local nuclear war" could, however, easily include many more than two nuclear attacks, and these might involve warheads of considerably greater explosive power and radioactive after-effect than the bombs of 1945.

As a piece of political fallout from such events, use of nuclear weapons in battle would end the current global taboo on the use of these weapons in anger—a taboo which has developed and persisted ever since 1945 and remains one of our most valuable assets for the limitation of warfare and the advancement of arms control. For Pakistan to use such a weapon in actual

---

[6] Pierre Gallois, *The Balance of Terror* (Boston: Houghton Mifflin, 1961).

combat would make it ipso facto more likely that the United States or the USSR would do so in the future, if only because the stigma and psychological barrier of being "the first" would have been lifted.

Analysts differ on whether a widespread further horizontal spread of nuclear weapons would weaken alliances or strengthen them. Where an ally of one of the two superpowers had defied its leadership to acquire nuclear weapons, one might indeed anticipate a "washing of hands" as the alliance link was severed, in part as punishment. In some cases, however, the offender might get away with such defiance, and even profit thereby, as Washington or Moscow became desperate to maintain a moderating influence over the new possessor of nuclear warheads, and thus offered all kinds of concessions to keep the alliance intact. Nations neighboring an "nth" nuclear power might feel entitled to much more in the way of a renewal of alliance coverage, and in some cases could receive it. In other cases, however, by the perverse justice of the system, they would find their own alliance coverages attenuated because of their neighbor's transgressions.

If a great many nations came to possess weapons with the attendant risk that they will come into use and break the nuclear taboo, the major alliance leaders might well then shrink back into a protective isolation, fearing the consequences and negative linkages of any active foreign policy. On the strategic level, one could anticipate an elementary investment again in anti-aircraft defenses and rudimentary antimissile defenses, and in civil defense programs, for both the United States and the Soviet Union. It could be hoped that such investments would never look effective enough to blunt the retaliatory capability of the opposite superpower, but instead might be effective only against the crude delivery system used by an "nth" nuclear power. Despite such defenses, however, the probability will remain that an "nth" power could always somehow still get one or two of its bombs through, against targets in the United States or the USSR.

Summarizing what may be a complicated set of tendencies: continued proliferation of nuclear weapons would be politically undesirable (1) because it will make all alliance structures look tenuous and unstable, (2) it will leave individual states relatively unsure of themselves, and (3) it might (in a further "multiplier effect") lead some to seek nuclear weapons to cover themselves against the vagaries. The alliance leaders in the process may be driven into a continuous series of threats against their followers, threats causing crises when the bluffs are called. As often as not, the "innocent party" would suffer more than the "guilty."

The alliances on both sides will always be in a dilemma; the policies which are best for discouraging nuclear proliferation before it happens are not ideal for encouraging moderation in the use of such weapons once they have been acquired after the nonproliferation policy has failed for any particular case. The current Soviet and American policy toward India illustrates this dilemma.

Rather than punishing India for its decision to acquire what amounts to a nuclear weapon or making a last-ditch attempt to induce New Delhi to surrender these weapons, the more pressing concern may be to keep India on a moderate course on whether it brandishes or tests such explosives and on whether it shares the technology with any other aspiring nuclear weapons state. The previous object of an unsuccessful antiproliferation effort may thus have to be enlisted to join a patched-up antiproliferation effort, intended to keep everyone else from following on in through the open door; the last culprit may have to be aided as much as punished. The injustice of all of this would be particularly grating to a nonoffending country bordering the state that had "gotten away with it."

There is undeniably some logic of chain-sequence in the proliferation issue, whereby for any particular country to acquire these weapons increases the particular likelihood that one or two other designated countries will do the same thing. But one should not make the mistake of exaggerating the inevitability of such chain reactions. The grand hope of the antiproliferation effort is that such reactions can be slowed down and that the chains can be broken.

What seems clear is that the chances of breaking these chains will become slimmer once we move into a world of fifteen or more nuclear weapons states, as compared with the current situation of less than eight. The kind of mass psychology is not yet upon us whereby everyone contemplating the prospect of nuclear proliferation decides that the only appropriate response is to join in. This is an important part of what we still hope to head off.

It is commonplace to predict that further nuclear proliferation will constrict the freedom of action of the superpowers. This is sometimes inserted into the more polemical criticisms of the nonproliferation effort as being the alleged primary motivation for Moscow and Washington. Yet the grander prediction must be that proliferation will constrict the freedom of action of all the states in the system. The additional states that have acquired nuclear weapons since the first two—Britain, France, China, and India (and perhaps Israel?)—have not been distinguished by great emboldenings of behavior since these weapons were added to their arsenal. If anything, they have seemed to be tiptoeing, where they might have otherwise walked more boldly.

Some of the American commentators who profess to be less worried about nuclear proliferation occasionally question the sincerity of the Soviet commitment to the question, concluding that the Russians "cooperate" only because nonproliferation is mainly in Moscow's interest.

How many of the potential "nth" countries would be aiming their new warheads at the United States? And how many at the USSR? The same commentators suggest many of the latter, and none of the former. West Germany, Japan, and Italy were the original worry list on this subject. Sweden, Romania, and India also voiced strong objections to the Nuclear

Nonproliferation Treaty when it was drafted in 1968. Israel, South Africa, Brazil, and Argentina were also opposed, doggedly refusing to sign the treaty ever since. Of these states, only India could be described as being other than generally anti-Russian in political alignment (not more worried about Soviet than U.S. attack), and India (because it has actually exploded a bomb) may no longer be a "proliferation worry."

If one adds in the fundamentally anticommunist political motives of possible nuclear proliferation in South Korea and Taiwan, and the likely political inclinations of Pakistan, one then can grasp the outlines of the American "hawkish" indifference to nuclear proliferation.

Yet the holes in this kind of reassuring argument are too large for it to have any soothing impact for long. Countries sometimes change political complexions fairly rapidly, before and after acquiring nuclear weapons, as illustrated by events in Iran, and by the ins and outs of Mrs. Gandhi's regime in India. The abruptness of the change in the Chinese world outlook has been a blessing for the United States, but an equally abrupt change could always occur in the opposite direction.

If Brazil and Argentina get nuclear weapons, they will regrettably be aimed at each other, but can one really be sure, apart from this, that they will always be aimed more at Russian targets than at American? And what of Libyan or Iraqi nuclear weapons or Pakistani weapons, after some abrupt change of regime?

The French gift of logical clarity was magnificently illustrated in the "all-azimuth" strategy, whereby the French nuclear forces (in the interest of fairness?) were for a time presumably aimed at targets not only in Russia, but in every other direction. If New Yorkers and Washingtonians somehow never became nervous about the Force de Frappe's threat to their safety, it was because this threat could be passed off as logical abstraction more than real policy. Yet the genuine future of the nuclear weapons proliferation possibility is that it may truly be "all-azimuth," directed just as probably at the United States as at the Soviet Union and directed, perhaps, at all at once.

Pessimism and optimism

We began with a short presentation of the pessimistic view prevailing among most observers on the subject, that nuclear weapons spread may be impossible to prevent. We then outlined an even gloomier picture of what the world would be like if nuclear proliferation is not stopped.

Pessimism about the consequences of nuclear proliferation may, of course, not be an antidote to pessimism about whether it can be halted. The two can be reconciled logically by simply concluding that the human race is doomed. (Optimists about the consequences of proliferation, a view that has also been outlined, have it easier, of course, since a failure to hold back nuclear weapons spread is, in their view, no real human failure at all.)

In most of the world, however, the grim picture of continued nuclear weapons spread may indeed be a source of hope that the spread can be prevented. While the details are debatable, the general inclination is not really so much thought to be in doubt. The consequences of widespread nuclear proliferation are indeed very likely to be bad for the world—in terms of political cooperation and security, material well-being, and the likelihood and costs of wars.

Perhaps any nation in the world could convince itself that proliferation would be desirable, if one and only one more member could join the nuclear-weapons club—that nation itself. (Even here, there would be many exceptions; would not Denmark, Costa Rica, Italy, or the Ivory Coast find nuclear weapons much more of an embarrassment than a blessing?) The important point is for each, however, that such a unique entry into the ranks of the nuclear weapons states is not really a salient option; at best one could rather contemplate entry in tandem with a number of other states.

Nuclear proliferation, to repeat, is seen as a two-fold problem by the authors collected here. It would be bad if it takes place; it will not be easy to keep it from occurring. Yet the first problem helps us somewhat with the second. Because the ramifications of nuclear proliferation will be exponential if it proceeds further, the world has more support for preventing it. This support, which is by no means a unitary thing, will have to be pulled together at many levels and woven in a complicated variety of ways if arms control is to be achieved. The fabric will not be a single piece.

That nuclear weapons will not be procured may remain no more certain than that they were destined not to be used after 1945. Yet much of the same logic may apply. Weapons have been held out of use, for fear that other nations might use theirs. Weapons potential may go unexploited for fear that other nations might otherwise exploit theirs.

A proliferation chain reaction, whereby number fifteen would surely be followed by number sixteen, etc., threatens to take hold in the future if proliferation is not stopped. But we can hope that such a chain reaction is not yet in effect—that the current five or six or seven do not have to induce the emergence of another five or six or seven. With patience and luck, we may be able to avoid becoming ensnarled in these chains in the future. We can in effect break any chain connection with the spread of nuclear weapons thus far.

The mix of issues

The essays which follow are thus intended to piece together an overview of the nuclear proliferation issue as it emerges at the beginning of the 1980s.

The analyses by Joseph Nye and Pierre Lellouche usefully emphasize the tension which arose in the 1970s between American and European views of the problem, but they at the same time stipulate a great deal of agreement within the developed world.

The next two papers, by Irvin Bupp and Lawrence Scheinman, continue with specific policy discussions on the peaceful nuclear industry, which (quite aside from any weapons possibilities) might be stimulated simply by the world's desire for energy.

John Redick's discussion of the Latin American case then provides a valuable transition, considering the nuclear energy policies of Brazilian and Argentinian purchases of sensitive equipment from West Germany, and discussing also, on the arms control side, the first serious attempt to negotiate a regional zone free of nuclear weapons.

Robert Harkavy, Onkar Marwah, and Lewis Dunn then move into analyzing situations where the felt need for weapons may count for considerably more than the need for electricity.

Michael Nacht's paper offers an analysis of how the military confrontations of the superpowers interact with the problem of halting nuclear proliferation.

The final essay represents an attempt by this author to pull the strands of any moderately successful nonproliferation regime together into a prognosis on the overall shape of international politics.

2

Maintaining a Nonproliferation Regime

Joseph S. Nye

From one point of view, nonproliferation policy looks like the most frustrating effort since the tidal policies of King Canute. "Unless the system of states undergoes a revolutionary transformation, any suggestion that further proliferation can be stopped borders on the absurd."[1] Such an international millennium is improbable, but the spread of nuclear technology to an increasing number of nations is a certainty. The result, according to this conventional wisdom, is a hopeless situation.

But whether the policy prospects are hopeless or not depends upon the policy objective. If the policy objective is defined as preventing another explosion of a nuclear device, then the prospects are indeed gloomy. If the policy objective is to reduce the rate and degree of proliferation in order to be able to cope with the destabilizing effects, then the situation is by no means hopeless.

What is remarkable from this second point of view is that the rate of proliferation has not been faster. Of the score or more of states that could probably have exploded a device if they had chosen to do so, less than a third so chose in the past three decades. From a broader perspective, the policy objective is to maintain the presumption against proliferation. The great danger is

As a Deputy Undersecretary of State, the author (now professor of Government at Harvard) was responsible for much of the policy discussed. He wishes to make readers aware of this possible barrier to objectivity in judgments, though every effort has been made to assure that the statements in the article are accurate. For their comments he wishes to thank (but not implicate) McGeorge Bundy, John Deutch, Leonard Ross, Peter Cowhey, Barry Steiner, Reinhard Rainer, Randy Rydell, David Deese, Michael Mandelbaum, George Quester, Kenneth Waltz, and others.
[1] J. J. Weltman, "Nuclear Revolution and World Order," *World Politics* XXXII (January 1980): 192.

the exponential curve of "speculative fever"—an accelerating change in rate. In such a situation, general restraints break down and decisions to forebear are reconsidered because "everyone is doing it." Such scrambles have occurred in international politics—witness the rapid partition of Africa in the third quarter of the nineteenth century or the rapid extension of coastal states jurisdiction in the oceans during the past decade. Preventing the development of such a situation with regard to nuclear proliferation provides a long-term objective for a policy that will not end with a bang. It is a feasible objective and there have been some successes in its pursuit over the past four years. Ironically, these gains are currently threatened on one side by those who pursue a broader anti-nuclear agenda and assert it as antiproliferation policy, and on the other side, by those whose satisfied view of the past leads them to belittle the risks of proliferation in the future.[2] This essay will assess the central gains and mistakes of the last few years and outline the major problems of maintaining a nonproliferation regime in the future.

Building the nonproliferation regime: 1950s and 1960s

It has been said that the ultimate success of a national policy occurs when a country is able to elevate its interest to the level of a general principle. In that sense, American nonproliferation policy over the years has been surprisingly successful. The United States has helped to foster an international regime that establishes a general presumption against proliferation. International regimes are the sets of rules, norms, and procedures that regulate behavior and control its effects in international affairs.[3] Regimes are seldom perfect. They vary in coherence and degree of adherence. We measure their existence in the acceptance of normative influences and constraints on international behavior. For nonproliferation, the main regime norms and practices are found in the Non-proliferation Treaty (NPT) and its regional counterparts like the Treaty of Tlatelolco; the safeguards, rules and procedures of the International Atomic Energy Agency (IAEA), as well as in various UN resolutions. While there are a few important exceptions, the large majority of states adhere to at least part of this set of norms.

It is often the case in international politics that the strong make the rules, and many regimes can be traced back to the interests of the most powerful state. But regimes do not necessarily have a one-to-one relation to the position of the most powerful state. When the United States was the only nuclear

---

[2] See, for example, Amory Lovins, L. Hunter Lovins, Leonard Ross, "Nuclear Power and Nuclear Bombs," *Foreign Affairs* 58 (Summer 1980); and Kenneth Waltz, "Toward Nuclear Peace," Adelphi paper forthcoming. Both articles make a number of good points. In my judgment each would be destructive as a guide to policy for reasons spelled out in this article.

[3] See Robert O. Keohane and J. S. Nye, *Power and Interdependence* (Boston: Little Brown, 1977), Ch. 1. Also Oran Young, "International Regimes," and Ernst Haas, "Why Collaborate? Issue Linkage and International Regimes," *World Politics* XXXII (April 1980).

power, its first efforts at regime creation, the Baruch Plan of 1946, foundered because the USSR refused to accept the effort to legitimize the American monopoly. And today, given the subsequent diffusion of nuclear technology, the nonproliferation regime can no longer rest primarily on American power. The beginnings of the current nonproliferation regime date from December 1953, when President Eisenhower launched the Atoms for Peace Program. The idea of the Atoms for Peace approach was to assist countries in their development of civilian nuclear energy, in return for their guarantees that they would use such assistance for peaceful purposes only. Ever since 1945, policymakers had realized that the distinction between peaceful- and weapons-use of the atom was primarily a question of politics rather than physics. Many technical capabilities could support both purposes, but some more than others. In addition, technology could be used as an inducement for the building of institutions. The opportunities and dangers of deliberately transferring technology were questions of timing and degree, not absolutes. That degree provided a basis for diplomacy.

The Atoms for Peace approach has been correctly criticized for promoting nuclear energy in instances before it was economically justified. In addition, guarantees of "peaceful use" were sometimes too loosely written and gave rise to subsequent misunderstandings and recriminations. Nonetheless, the basic philosophy of the Atoms for Peace Program provided the foundation for a second attempt at establishing an international regime. Realizing that the technology was spreading anyway, the United States offered to share the fruits of its then long technological lead at an accelerated pace, in return for the acceptance by other countries of conditions designed to control destabilizing effects from such sharing. The policy was oversold, and poorly thought through in its execution at a time when too little was known about the pace and cost of peaceful nuclear development. But it did serve to create an initial consensus on which to build. Essentially, the most powerful state in the nuclear issue area used its power to attract others to a normative framework.

Specifically, the central accomplishment of the Atoms for Peace Program was the creation of a system of international safeguards and an institutional framework in the form of the International Atomic Energy Agency, established in Vienna in 1957. Under the IAEA safeguards system, nonweapons countries agree to file with the Agency regular detailed reports on nuclear civilian activities, and agree to allow international inspectors to visit their nuclear facilities to verify the reports and to ensure that there has been no diversion of materials from civilian to military purposes. The safeguards system is central to the basic bargain of the international regime in which other countries are assisted in their peaceful nuclear energy needs in return for their accepting the intrusion of safeguards and inspection.[4] The initial acceptance of

---

[4] Contrary to some opinions, safeguards need not be perfect to deter diversion and have a significant political effect. The necessary probability of detection is debatable, but thus far I am unaware of significant diversion of IAEA safeguarded materials.

such intrusion was slow and halting, but the idea was successfully implanted in the 1950s.

The next step in regime development was the formulation of the NPT over the course of the 1960s. Building on an Irish proposal at the United Nations in 1961, the United States and the USSR pursued their interests in limiting the spread of nuclear weapons by using a mix of bilateral and UN procedures to formulate a relatively simple treaty under whose first two articles nations undertook not to develop or to aid development of nuclear weapons or explosives. In addition, under the third article, nonweapons states agreed to put *all* their peaceful nuclear facilities under safeguards, thus closing the loophole in the safeguards system which rested on an artificial distinction between imported and domestic technology. In addition, under the fourth article, nonweapons states were promised access to technology; under the fifth, access to the potential benefits of peaceful nuclear explosions; and under the sixth, weapons states promised to take serious steps to control the "vertical" nuclear arms race.

Eight significant states have refused to sign the NPT, most frequently on the grounds that it is a discriminatory treaty. But among the eight, France indicated that it would not undercut the purposes of the Treaty, and in Latin America, a regional treaty limiting nuclear weapons helps to fill the normative gap. Skeptics have dismissed the treaty as a modern equivalent of the Kellogg-Briand pact, since any state can quit on three months notice. Other detractors have argued that the treaty is imperfectly drafted and involves promises that cannot be fully kept. Nonetheless, by establishing a normative presumption against proliferation and by creating procedures for verifying intentions, the NPT has helped to build confidence and a degree of predictability in states' behavior. Like its regional counterparts, such as the Treaty of Tlatelolco, it helps to strengthen the international regime by symbolizing a common interest. The NPT is not, as some enthusiasts tended to believe in the 1960s, sufficient or the same as the international nuclear regime, but with 111 adherents, it has certainly become a central part of the regime.

Threats to the regime: early 1970s

By the early 1970s, a degree of complacency existed about the non-proliferation regime that had been constructed. Such complacency was shattered, however, by three events in 1974 and 1975. One was the Indian explosion of a "peaceful" nuclear device using plutonium derived from a Canadian-supplied research reactor with U.S.-supplied heavy water—an event viewed in Canada and the United States as cheating on the basic bargain of the nuclear regime. Even if it was a violation of the spirit and not the letter of the poorly written early bilateral agreements, the ensuing reactions and recriminations in U.S. public and Congressional opinion (in contrast to an initially relaxed executive branch response) led to reverberations that spread throughout the international nuclear supply system and are still not fully settled. The Canadian embargo of uranium that even included its allies, and the U.S. Nonproliferation Act of 1978, whose stringent conditions aroused resentment abroad, can both be traced back to the Indian explosion.

The second event was the oil embargo and fourfold increase in oil prices, which created widespread insecurity in energy supply. Problems with oil led to a sudden surge of exaggerated expectations about the importance of nuclear energy and raised questions about whether there would be sufficient uranium to fuel all the reactors that suddenly appeared on the drawing-boards. The net effect was to accelerate governments' plans for early commercial use of plutonium fuel, which unlike the low enriched uranium currently used as fuel in most reactors, is a weapons-usable material. The IAEA projected that some forty countries might be using plutonium fuels by the end of the 1980s. At the same time, safeguards and institutions for dealing with such a flood of weapons-usable materials had not been adequately developed. As one careful observer reported in 1976, the existing IAEA safeguards system was workable, but there was little hope that it would be able to cope if nuclear expansion plans proceeded at their expected rate.[5] The pace of technological change appeared to be outstripping the pace of institutional development.

The third set of events that shook the regime in the mid-70s was the proposed sale of facilities for producing weapons-usable materials without regard to their economic justification or proliferation implications. In some cases, reprocessing plants were offered to countries that were building their first power reactors and lacked any serious economic justification for reprocessing. Subsequently, it was disclosed, in at least two cases, that the recipients were attempting to develop nuclear weapons programs, and that there would almost certainly have been violations or abrogation of safeguards. Under such circumstances there was grave danger of the collapse of the international regime that had been so laboriously constructed over the previous decades and a further weakening of public support for nuclear energy (not to mention exports) in many advanced countries. The international regime had entered a period of crisis and possible collapse arising from a series of events related to the development of the peaceful uses of nuclear energy.

The threats to regime stability originating from the ambiguities of "peaceful" uses were reinforced by trends in the power positions of the United States inside and outside the nuclear issue area. Outside the nuclear issue, the United States had suffered its disastrous defeat in Vietnam, with an accompanying inward turn in its cycle of foreign policy attitudes. This heightened the sense of insecurity felt by a number of former client states,

---

[5] Personal communication, Henry Jacoby, MIT, August 1976.

particularly in Asia, and weakened the credibility of security guarantees as an instrument that could be extended to less-developed countries. While the U.S. Congress showed strong concern about proliferation (for example, passing the Symington Amendment in 1976 which mandated a cut-off of military or economic aid to a country which imported a reprocessing plant), simultaneous Congressional restrictions on aid and arms transfers emptied such sanctions of much of their supposed clout. The sticks were shrinking and the carrots weren't growing.

Inside the nuclear issue area, the overwhelming preponderance of U.S. influence had begun to diminish. America's share of world exports began to decline as strong industrial competition for the sale of light water reactors developed in Europe—as might have been expected. Equally important, however, was the erosion of the American near-monopoly on provision of enrichment services, which had previously provided a significant source of leverage over nuclear fuel supplies. Long-term contracts at advantageous prices created an American umbilical cord to reactors operating overseas. Disputes over the role of private industry in enrichment, and a precipitous closing of the order books for contracts by the AEC in 1974 shook the faith in the reliability of American supply and accelerated the already existing inclinations towards independence. By the late 1960s and early 1970s, France, Germany, Britain, the Netherlands, Japan, and South Africa had all begun projects to build their own enrichment capacity—well before the more stringent nonproliferation policies of the late 1970s. Furthermore, the Soviet Union had begun to sell enrichment services to the world market. Thus by the mid-1970s, U.S. leverage over other countries' nuclear policies had begun to erode, because of changes both inside and outside the nuclear arena. The United States was still the most important state in the peaceful nuclear arena, but it no longer held a hegemonic position. Thus in any efforts to refurbish the regime, American leadership would be a necessary but not a sufficient condition for success.

Fuel cycle measures: the late 1970s

1976 and 1977 saw a series of American initiatives in response to the fuel cycle events that had threatened the regime. A number of private studies were raising doubts about the economic need for rapid introduction of plutonium fuels.[6] Congressional hearings and draft legislation called for a more stringent approach to exports. The election campaign accentuated public and press attention to the nonproliferation issue.

[6] Pan Heuristics, "Moving Toward Life in a Nuclear Armed Crowd" (Los Angeles, 1977); Spurgeon Keeney, ed., *Nuclear Power Issues and Choices* (Cambridge, Mass.: Ballinger, 1977); "Report to the American Physical Society by the Study Panel on Nuclear Fuel Cycles and Waste Management," *Review of Modern Physics* (January 1978).

Two important steps were taken by the Ford administration. First, the Nuclear Suppliers Group was established in London. Seven (later fifteen) major suppliers came together to discuss guidelines for nuclear commerce that would prevent commercial competition from undercutting safeguards obligations. While the guidelines were not finally agreed to until September 1977 and published through notes to the IAEA in January 1978, much of the basic work was done in 1976.

Second, in October 1976, President Ford announced a more cautious policy toward the use of plutonium in the U.S. nuclear program. Reprocessing was to be deferred pending a solution of proliferation and economic problems. The exact meaning of this deferral and how it was to be implemented was to be studied in a somewhat ambiguous Reprocessing Evaluation Program. Thus some of the main lines of response later identified with the Carter administration actually preceded it, and one of the basic policy choices faced by the Carter administration was what to do with the legacy of past policies. While the eventual choices stressed continuity with the past, there were strong pressures for more radical departures.

One set of suggestions came from antinuclear groups, who felt that proliferation could be stopped by stopping nuclear energy or nuclear exports. They argued that the transnational demonstration effect of an American renunciation of nuclear energy would also bring foreign nuclear energy programs and proliferation to a halt. They were correct in pointing out the unfortunate effect of exaggerated projections of nuclear growth. But the basic technology was too widely spread and the U.S. preponderance too diminished for a unilateral total moratorium policy to be effective. The momentum behind the French nuclear program, for example, would not be stopped by such a U.S. decision. And if some countries failed to follow suit (or did so with a ten-year lag), the problem would not be solved, but the United States would lose influence on those governments that persisted with nuclear programs. Moreover, while it was important to obtain changes in the way the nuclear fuel cycle was envisaged and organized, the fuel cycle was only part of the proliferation problem. If proliferation were more a technical than a political problem, this option might have been more attractive. On the contrary, its net effect would further weaken an existing multilateral regime for the sake of a new unilateral American alternative based on a series of wishful political assumptions.

Another suggestion not taken was to formally require the location of sensitive facilities only in weapons states, where diversion from civil to military purposes could not lead to any further proliferation. But such an approach would also have weakened the regime—because it would have been regarded as intolerable by key allies and NPT parties, such as Germany and Japan, who would have seen it as a violation of the treaty.

A third suggestion was to center U.S. diplomacy upon the London Suppliers club. But resentment had already risen about the Nuclear Supplier

Group. A number of important nonweapons states such as Yugoslavia were calling it a cartel and charging that it was inconsistent with the NPT. Suggestions of formal market sharing among suppliers would have exacerbated such reactions. Germany and others were arguing that technology denials and supplier restraints would simply cause resentment and destroy the existing regime. Their continued participation and agreement to guidelines was by no means assured.

A fourth approach was to try to coerce other supplier and consumers into accepting our nonproliferation approach by working with Canada and Australia to control uranium sources. While the United States had lost its monopoly of the enrichment market, these three countries had a large share of the natural uranium market. On the other hand, that share was not complete, and political manipulation would speed its erosion. Moreover, such an effort would again undermine rather than reinforce the existing regime without a clearcut replacement for it.

The approach that was chosen was designed to reinforce the existing regime, but not to accept the eroding status quo. It was important to shake others so that attention and action would be focused on refurbishing the regime, but to do so without coercion and with as little overt discrimination as possible.

Indeed, one of the basic problems in the design of nonproliferation policy is the discrimination issue. By its very nature, nonproliferation involves a degree of discrimination. Yet the way in which that discrimination is handled can spell the difference between success and failure in a policy of regime maintenance. Thus the Carter administration deferral of reprocessing at home was not expected to lead all other countries to follow suit. But it was felt that exaggerated projections of nuclear growth and spurious economic calculations were fueling decisions in the United States and other countries. U.S. diplomatic efforts to persuade others to look more carefully at their calculations and at the problems associated with plutonium would have been undercut if U.S. domestic programs did not defer plans for thermal recycle and stretch out the timing of breeder R&D. Since the United States could not unilaterally impose its will on others concerning how the nuclear fuel cycle should be constructed, six of the seven points in President Carter's 7 April 1977 nonproliferation statement dealt with issues within U.S. domestic jurisdiction. (The seventh point called for an international evaluation that will be described in this essay.)

Contrary to some accounts, most people in the administration recognized that there was no single technological fix that would create a safe fuel cycle, but rather sought to move discussion towards a series of technological and institutional steps that would lessen proliferation risks while allowing legitimate energy needs to be met. To gain the time necessary to develop technological and institutional arrangements, the administration urged that premature commercialization of fuel cycles utilizing plutonium be avoided and announced that the United States, for its part, would defer its own plans for commercial reprocessing and recycle of plutonium.

The strategy was to focus strongly against the recycle of plutonium in thermal reactors as a clear and present proliferation danger that promised at best marginal economic and supply assurance gains. Breeder reactors, however, had a greater potential long-term energy significance. Moreover, certain key governments such as France, Britain, Japan, and Germany were heavily committed to breeders. France, in particular, was well-placed to lead a coalition that could defeat U.S. views. With its strong nuclear program and domestic political support, France was a leading country in the nuclear field. French leadership would be essential in any refurbishing of the international regime. U.S. views on plutonium use had to be expressed in a manner that encouraged France to play a central part in supporting the regime. Thus the Carter administration did not oppose all breeder research and development programs at home or abroad. It expressed reservations about their commercial deployment before proliferation-resistant technological and institutional alternatives had been explored.

While this strategy eventually provided a basis for avoiding isolation and creating a coalition to refurbish the regime, initially the Carter administration had internal divisions over the question of where such a compromise might be struck. The most divisive issue was granting permission for the reprocessing of U.S.-origin spent fuel. The purists focused on the dangers of plutonium and tended toward a restrictive and coercive approach to granting permission. The pragmatists focused on the dangers of proliferation and using permissions to coax forth support for restrained export behavior and refurbishing the regime. In some early statements on foreign reprocessing of American origin fuel, the purist position put the United States in an unduly rigid position. It was not until mid-1978 that a position was stated which was to serve as a basis for key compromises with France and others later in the year, which assured that the strategy described above could be implemented.[7]

Needless to say, the process of policy formulation did not merely advance through debates over abstractions. In January 1977, the White House called for the completion of a Presidential Review Memorandum on Nonproliferation by March, While the formal interagency review process ground forward, events also forced policy ahead.

For example, although a Carter State Department transition-team paper had suggested a slow quiet approach to the French-Pakistan and German-Brazilian deals, the German government sent a special emissary to call on the new Vice President even before the inauguration. The result was to trigger

[7] See J. S. Nye, "Balancing Nonproliferation and Energy Security," Speech to the Uranium Institute, London, 12 July 1978.

prematurely a round of high level and highly visible diplomacy that gave a confrontational tone to the issue as well as diverting much precious time from the formal Presidential Review Memorandum (PRM) process.

Similarly, budgetary deadlines on energy issues drove decisions on large expenditures planned by the previous administration. Thus the Clinch River breeder-reactor decision advanced on a separate track from the generic nonproliferation policy, although it was announced as a nonproliferation measure. Other energy steps such as deployment of gas-centrifuge enrichment technology were also poorly coordinated with nonproliferation policy. Additional pressures came from U.S. Congressional groups eager to hold hearings on their recently reintroduced legislative proposals. Industry and environmental groups complained that insufficient attention and time was being given to their views. Delegations arrived from other countries in order to press for answers on pending export cases before the Nuclear Regulatory Commission; asking for permission to reprocess American-origin spent fuel; asking about the status of the Suppliers Group, the Reprocessing Evaluation Program, and so forth.

Amid this pressure of events it became clear to me that some device was needed to introduce a longer-term thrust into international nuclear policy. Maintaining and refurbishing the international regime would require a general approach around which a broad group of nations could rally. The process of rethinking the conditions of the regime had to be shared beyond the United States alone. The confrontational approach that was driven by events threatened to isolate the United States and further disrupt the regime. It was important that nuclear diplomacy should not polarize different groups focused on London and Vienna.

The device we designed to meet these various policy needs was the International Nuclear Fuel Cycle Evaluation Program (INFCEP until May 1977 when the French declared the word "program" redundant but made the acronym INFCE almost unpronounceable). The idea of INFCE was to expand the existing Reprocessing Evaluation Program to include the whole fuel cycle and to make participation international.

INFCE has been described as a pioneering effort at international technology assessment. Bertrand Goldschmidt has called it a technico-diplomatic compromise in a sort of giant scientific happening."[8] Officially, INFCE provided a two-year period in which nations could reexamine assumptions and search for ways to reconcile their different assessments of the energy and nonproliferation risks involved in various aspects of the nuclear fuel cycle. While officially INFCE was given a predominantly technical rationale, this was a means of attracting broad participation into what was really part of a political process of stabilizing the basis for the international regime. The sixty-

---

[8] Harvey Brooks and Eugene Skolnikoff, NATO paper, 1977; Bertrand Goldschmidt, *Le Complexe Atomique* (Paris: Fayard, 1980), p. 429.

six countries and organizations that came together in Vienna included consumers and suppliers, rich and poor, East and West, and a dozen countries that had not signed the NPT. In all, 519 experts from 46 countries participated in 61 meetings of 8 working groups, and produced 20,000 pages of documents. The common denominator of this diversity was the Final Plenary Conference finding that INFCE had "strengthened the view that effective measures can and should be taken to minimize the danger of proliferation of nuclear weapons without jeopardizing energy for peaceful purposes. . . . The participants were determined to preserve the climate of mutual understanding and cooperation in the nuclear energy field that is one of the major achievements of INFCE."[9]

As a diplomatic device, INFCE helped to reestablish a basis for consensus on a refurbished regime for the international nuclear fuel cycle. The very process of engaging in international technology assessment helped to heighten awareness of the nonproliferation problem and the threats to the regime. In that sense, INFCE helped the United States to set the agenda for other governments. Moreover, it affected the process inside other governments. Foreign offices rather than just nuclear energy agencies became more involved. Most important, attention to the problem and to regime maintenance was spread beyond the United States. While the United States did not always agree with all the details of INFCE's answers, the most important point was that INFCE focused other countries' attention on a U.S. question—nonproliferation. It was generally agreed, by diplomats in Vienna, that no country "won" and nearly all countries gained some of their position, including, for the United States, the core points against the recycling of plutonium in the current thermal reactors.[10] In turn, France and others won exaggerated statements of probable demand for breeder reactors, but this was qualified by statements denying the value of breeders to countries with small electrical or nuclear grids.

Although the final report was a massive body of negotiated language— some of which differed from purist versions and some aspects of the U.S. positions on plutonium—the technical conclusions lent support to the evolutionary approach as a potential point of political compromise to be developed in diplomatic forums.

While no single fuel cycle emerged on its technical merits as indisputably more proliferation resistant, a general basis was laid for more caution in introducing weapons-usable fuels. Working Group 1 agreed upon a range of projected demand for uranium by the end of the century that was less than one-half to one-third of the internationally accepted figures before INFCE started. This helped reduce the acrimony that characterized disputes over

[9] "Communiqué of the Final Plenary Conference of INFCE," 27 February 1980, p. 5.

[10] See, for example, *Nucleonics Week,* 28 February 1980; and the *Energy Daily,* 16 June 1980. "The conclusion . . . that recycle in thermal reactors is uneconomic, unnecessary, and for most countries, unwise . . . is seen as the U.S.'s main victory there."

uranium resources, since it had the same effect as doubling uranium reserves. In addition, Working Group 8 identified modest improvements (15 percent) that could relatively easily be made in the efficiency of uranium consumption. The net effect was to reduce by more than half the pressure for premature separation of weapons-usable fuels that had been created by exaggerated projections of nuclear demand.

As for the use of plutonium, Working Group 4 found that recycle in thermal reactors is not likely to have large economic advantages, and Working Groups 6 and 7 found that safe storage or disposal of spent fuel does not require reprocessing. Working Group 5 concluded that plutonium will be needed for breeder reactor programs, but that successful breeder programs will be based upon large nuclear energy programs where important economies-of-scale can be achieved. The net effect of these findings is to reduce the pressures for the widespread and premature use of plutonium that posed a clear and present danger to the international safeguards system. Instead, INFCE laid a basis both in time and institutional suggestions for a cautious introduction of plutonium use that could be guided by realistic development needs rather than wasteful and dangerous imitation based on a spurious conventional wisdom and exaggerated projections.

To the extent that countries are guided by realistic energy concerns, the INFCE technical findings combined with an evolutionary approach provided a valuable seed around which a restored consensus could crystallize. For example, the INFCE technical findings help to reduce the tensions between Article 7 of the Suppliers Guidelines, which urges restraint in sensitive exports, and NPT Article IV, which calls for "further development of the applications of nuclear energy for peaceful purposes, especially in the territories of the non-nuclear weapons states party to the Treaty, with due consideration for the needs of the developing areas of the world."

Because the criterion of economic justification that is part of the evolutionary approach allows for change, it does not constitute a denial of the right of nonnuclear weapons states to the peaceful uses of nuclear energy on their territories. Given the technical findings described above, a degree of restraint on sensitive exports at this time is not necessarily in basic conflict with Article IV or with the larger bargain of the NPT. After all, a certain tension is built into the language of the NPT (which says Article IV must be read in light of the obligations in Articles I and II not to foster the spread of weapons), and a common security interest in nonproliferation is the real basis of the Treaty.

This is not to say that there will not be disputes about supply policies and the NPT, but with a reasonable amount of goodwill, the INFCE findings mean there *need* be no breakdown over Article IV. Indeed, at the 1980 NPT Review Conference, it was Article VI rather than Article IV which hindered efforts to achieve a final communiqué.

If INFCE was generally successful as the central thrust of a policy designed to broaden concern for regime maintenance with relation to fuel cycle problems, other aspects of policy relating to the fuel cycle issues were less successful. The following are areas in which policy fell short:

1. *Incentives.* In 1977, President Carter announced incentives to help countries manage their fuel cycles in ways that would support nonproliferation interests. At the front end, the United States was willing to contribute to an international fuel bank to provide security of supply for countries fulfilling their nonproliferation obligations. At the back end, the United States offered to store limited amounts of foreign spent fuel, and to help explore sites for international spent fuel storage.

Both these initiatives proceeded extremely slowly. Diplomatic responses to the fuel bank were lukewarm. Fears of shortage eased somewhat as exaggerated nuclear growth projections began to decline. In addition, confidence in supply could not be so easily restored when large differences still existed over basic conditions governing the use of the fuel. Efforts to implement the spent fuel storage offer went forward, but were slowed by domestic political differences over the development of nuclear energy, and the disposal of nuclear wastes.

2. *Export Legislation.* Whatever its substantive merits or faults, the timing and tone of the Nonproliferation Act of 1978 had an unfortunate effect on efforts to restore consensus over fuel cycle measures.[11] It was widely regarded as a unilateral prejudging of the outcomes of INFCE, and an intrusion into other countries' nuclear programs. Both the procedural role of the Nuclear Regulatory Commission and the various guillotine clauses threatening to cut off supply created a sense of confrontation and insecurity. Ironically, in the process of executive-legislative bargaining that preceded passage of the act, the Carter administration had assured that most of the cut-off provisions were "rubber guillotines" which would be waived back before severing supply, but such nuances of the American domestic political process were generally lost on foreign audiences. The efforts required to soothe the European resentment and prevent the paradoxical outcome of embargoing U.S. allies represented political capital that should have been spent on more important issues.

Subsequent compromises and understandings with Japan and France that sufficient permissions for reprocessing of U.S. origin spent fuel would be allowed during the INFCE period in order to avoid disruption of their programs alleviated but did not totally remove some of the tensions created by the legislation.

3. *Domestic breeder policy.* In trying to direct world attention to the problems that must be created by too rapid a movement toward weapons-usable fuels, the Carter administration altered the U.S. domestic program so that it stressed a more gradual transition. This involved deferral of

[11] For a sample of such reactions, see *International Security* 3 (Fall 1978).

commercial reprocessing and cancellation of the Clinch River Breeder Reactor, which had been oriented toward demonstrating early commercialization. In terms of Carter's 7 April statement, the idea was not to halt the breeder program, but to restructure it to emphasize development of a safer fuel cycle over a longer time horizon rather than early commercialization. Or as the point was expressed in October 1977, "We are not antibreeder. We believe that a breeder program is an important energy insurance policy. Indeed, even without the Clinch River Breeder, President Carter proposed to spend some $450 million in this fiscal year on breeder research. What we do oppose is premature movement toward a breeder economy."[12]

There were a number of technical and budgetary reasons other than non-proliferation for opposing the Clinch River project. Indeed, the initial decisions arose in the budgetary context and the basic advice on cancellation came from White House staff concerned with energy matters. Subsequently, the Department of Energy Fission Strategy pointed out that early commercialization of the breeder could not be justified on economic grounds and that this technology should be developed for comparison with fusion (and solar) as a potential successor to current sources of electricity generation well after the turn of the century.[13] In terms of nonproliferation, the Clinch River decision indicated that the early development and spread of reprocessing was not required by early breeder commercialization. Unfortunately, too much of the decision was publicly attributed to nonproliferation reasons, thus obscuring the intrinsic economic weakness of the project, and implying a false trade-off between energy needs and nonproliferation concerns. Moreover, the nonproliferation argument became grossly oversimplified: "Bombs are made from plutonium; breeder reactors use plutonium; Ergo, let's not have any breeder reactors."[14] Since there are other ways to get plutonium and bombs, it was not hard for breeder proponents to make a mockery of the caricatured argument rather than dealing with the real questions of whether and when the uncertain breeder economics would justify additional degrees of risk from widespread flows of weapons-usable fuels.

In part, this reflected deliberate distortions by opponents of the Carter administration's actions; but in part it reflected internal divisions within the administration about the role of nuclear energy in general. The nuclear industry at home, and a number of foreign governments saw the administration as antinuclear and the Clinch River decision as destroying the future. Clinch River became a rallying point for a massive industry lobbying effort. The net effect was that the annual Clinch River debates in Congress became highly distorted symbolism that trivialized the real argument at home and abroad and were enormously wasteful of money and

---

[12] J. Nye, "Nuclear Power Without Nuclear Proliferation," Speech in Bonn, Germany, 3 October 1977, *Department of State Bulletin,* 14 November 1977.

[13] Office of Energy Research, "The Nuclear Strategy of the Department of Energy" (September 1978).

[14] *Energy Daily* (Washington), 11 February 1977.

time. In retrospect, while the decision may have made sense on its merits, the divisive effects and the difficulty in maintaining a clear argument proved to be politically unmanageable and costly.

Maintaining the regime: problems for the 1980s

The role of the fuel cycle

The policy responses of the late 1970s focused heavily on fuel cycle questions. Obviously there were other measures as well—for example, efforts to strengthen adherence to the NPT and Tlatelolco, efforts to negotiate a Comprehensive Test Ban, and specific diplomatic responses in particular problem cases.[15] But the charge that policy focused on fuel cycle questions is largely correct. This was not because policymakers regarded the fuel cycle as the only source of proliferation. Rather it was because some of the most immediate threats to the regime arose out of fuel cycle questions, and because in the post-Vietnam period, other nonproliferation instruments were often difficult to use.

One of the problems for the 1980s will be keeping fuel cycle questions in a reasonable perspective. One might say that fuel cycle questions were half the source of the proliferation problems of the 1970s and that the policy responses of the late 1970s provided half a solution to those fuel cycle problems. By any political arithmetic, to ameliorate a major social problem by one-quarter is not a trivial point. But it is not the solution to the whole problem. In my political judgment, Lovins et al. overstate when they say that nuclear power is "the main driving force behind proliferation."[16] Important steps remain to be taken in the fuel cycle area, but they must not monopolize attention or create frictions with other key nations that will interfere with the overall maintenance of the nonproliferation regime.

After INFCE, a number of steps will be necessary to strengthen the fuel cycle aspects of the regime.

Safeguards

INFCE helped to build agreement that safeguards improvements are feasible and necessary if the basic bargain of the nuclear regime is to be kept and nuclear commerce to proceed. Safeguards have moved from the category of "necessary evil" to one of "beneficial necessity." The next steps are both technical and institutional. Of the latter, the most important is the agreement

---

[15] See J. S. Nye, "Nonproliferation: A Long-Term Strategy," *Foreign Affairs* (April 1978).

[16] Lovins et al., op. cit, p. 1138 (though they are correct in its limited effectiveness in displacing oil).

by the handful of states with unsafeguarded facilities to join in the comprehensive safeguards regime.

Plutonium and highly enriched uranium management

The INFCE discussion helped to build acknowledgment that weapons-usable fuels are not like other fuels and require special procedures. New developments in fuel technology are reducing the need for weapons-usable uranium fuels in most research reactors. Equally important for the future are the IAEA discussions of plutonium storage. But storage regimes must be more than fig leaves and must encompass flows as well as stocks, with release criteria at the storage points and special guarding and monitoring procedures for all movements of unirradiated plutonium. Lovins et al. argue that international management cannot affect how reexported plutonium is used.[17] This may be true physically, but it is not necessarily true politically. A continuous international presence could reduce proliferation risk by raising the political costs of seizure or diversion. On this international basis, it may be possible to reconcile current divergences in national procedures for transfers of nuclear fuels.

International spent fuel storage

In the discussions over the past few years, it has become clear that a good deal of planned reprocessing was being driven by the excess supply of spent fuel rather than the demand for plutonium. Given the evolving consensus on the reservation of plutonium for breeders, this premature separation of plutonium from its radioactive protection would be both uneconomic and dangerous. A balance should be struck between reprocessing to meet demands for plutonium according to the slow and gradual pace of breeder programs and safe storage of excess spent fuel. Although spent fuel storage has been likened to plutonium "mines," radiation barriers remain and such sites are more amenable to international monitoring than are prematurely reprocessed plutonium "rivers." Internationally monitored national spent fuel storage could also be reinforced by the availability of international sites for spent fuel storage. In this way the evolutionary regime would be reinforced by a balance between a modest amount of breeder demand-oriented reprocessing and safer storage alternatives for excess supplies of spent fuel.

Fuel assurances

The period of turmoil in nuclear commerce that followed the events of 1974–75 created insecurities in fuel supplies that added to incentives for premature use of plutonium. A useful way of strengthening the regime would

---

[17] Ibid., p. 1140.

be to reinforce national stockpile measures by an international institutional arrangement to insure vulnerable countries against interruptions in bilateral supplies. For large programs in countries meeting nonproliferation standards, this might take the form of special agreements for long-term supply. For small programs, modest, internationally controlled stockpiles of low-enriched uranium could be helpful and are still worth further exploration.

Cooperation in R&D

An evolutionary approach to weapons-usable fuels is a common interest of all countries. Nonetheless, countries with small nuclear energy programs must be assured of equality when their programs have grown to a size that economies-of-scale might justify breeder reactors. As their programs grow, they will need to begin research and development in advance of the point where the economies-of-scale have been reached. Thus in an evolutionary-developmental regime, countries with large nuclear energy programs will have to make provisions for the energy R&D needs of the smaller programs. Although this presents some risks from a proliferation point of view, it is preferable to the alternative of a chaotic nonregime where all countries use (often spurious) R&D justification for unnecessary weapons-usable fuels. An international evolutionary regime under the IAEA would present clearer criteria for cooperative programs whether in national or international facilities.

The steps mentioned above represent modest but important ways to strengthen the fuel cycle aspects of the international regime begun in the 1950s and focused on the IAEA. They will not by themselves solve the problem of nuclear proliferation, in part because the fuel cycle is only part of the proliferation problem, and in part because there is always a temptation for some to remain outside the regime. Nonetheless, the norms of the regime create a strong presumption against misuse of the fuel cycle and the institutions provide mechanisms that help ascertain that the norms are being observed.

The problem of priority

Nonproliferation is not a foreign policy; it is part of a foreign policy. Foreign policy always involves the adjustment of partly conflicting objectives in order to achieve as much as possible within the constraints of a refractory world. How nonproliferation fares in that adjustment process depends on the priority it receives. One of the effects of the attention given to the issue in the late 1970s was to raise the priority of the issue for a number of governments. Higher priority means higher costs, including the prospect of sanctions inscribed in U.S. law and in the Supplier Guidelines. A number of governments which might otherwise have been tempted to keep the weapons option open were deterred by the prospective high political costs of such actions.

On the other hand, it is often costly to *impose* sanctions as well as to suffer them, and this is particularly true for sanctions that extend beyond an issue area and cut broadly across several domains of foreign policy. After the invasion of Afghanistan, for example, the United States found its foreign policy tightly bound by the legislated curtailment of military and economic assistance to Pakistan.

More generally, as the 1980s open, a number of skeptics inside and outside the bureaucracy urge a general lowering of the priority given to nonproliferation on the grounds that its negative effects are exaggerated. Proliferation may be disastrous for the particular countries that become involved in a regional nuclear arms race, but they argue that such a race would have little effect on the rest of the world. In particular, it would not affect the global balance of power, since the nuclear superpowers could always technically outrace the new entrants. From this point of view, it is not worthwhile for the large nuclear weapons states to invest much political capital in preventing the erosion of the nonproliferation regime.

Another group of analysts goes even further and argues that proliferation would have beneficial and stabilizing effects on world politics.[18] Just as nuclear weapons have produced prudence in U.S.-Soviet relations, they argue, so might nuclear weapons stabilize regional balances. This might be true if political conditions were similiar. But the transferability of prudence assumes governments with stable command and control systems, the absence of serious civil wars, the absence of strong destabilizing motivations such as irredentist passions and discipline over the temptation for preemptive strikes during the early stages when new nuclear weapons capabilities are soft and vulnerable. Such assumptions are unrealistic in many parts of the world. On the contrary, rather than enhancing its security, the first effects of acquiring new nuclear capability in many circumstances may be to increase a state's vulnerability and insecurity. And even a local use of nuclear weaponry would be a serious breach of a thirty-five-year global taboo.

The destabilizing aspects of proliferation are further complicated if one thinks of possible roles of nonstate actors. Whatever the prospect of successful acquisition of a nuclear device by a terrorist group, even threats of such action may create severe civil difficulties. Moreover, the possible theft of weapons-usable materials and black market sale to maverick states means that the problems posed by nonstate groups do not depend solely on their technological capabilities. Nor would the superpowers necessarily remain isolated from the effects.

Equally important is the way that the wide or rapid spread of nuclear capabilities could affect both the central strategic balance, and prospects for the gradual evolution of a peaceful and just world order. To illustrate both

---

[18] See, for example, Kenneth Waltz, "What Will the Spread of Nuclear Weapons Do to the World," in *International Political Effects of the Spread of Nuclear Weapons,* John Kerry King, ed. (Washington: G.P.O., 1979); and Adelphi paper forthcoming.

points, take the case of the Federal Republic of Germany and Japan. One of the striking and constructive features of the world since 1945 is that those two great powers of the prewar period have been reintegrated into world coalitions and institutions as the third and fourth most powerful states, in economic terms, without their feeling it necessary to develop equivalent nuclear military power. This makes the central strategic balance more calculable and contributes to the stability of Europe and Asia. It also presents examples of countries achieving significant status in world politics without nuclear weaponry. At a certain point—especially if it were to call into question the basic decisions hitherto maintained by Germany and Japan—widespread proliferation would surely have profound consequences which even the most sanguine superpower strategists could not ignore. Over the long term, if countries are able to achieve their goals of security, status, and economic well-being without the necessity of developing military nuclear power, the prospects improve for the evolution of new forms of effective power, coalitions, and institutions.

Unfortunately, there can be no decisive answer in the debate over the effects of proliferation. Particular outcomes may differ. Some cases may start a disastrous chain of events; other may turn out to have benign effects. At the same time, a great power, particularly one that plays a critical role in maintaining a regime, must take a prudent and cautious approach to the assessment of risks both inside and outside a region. The consequences of guessing wrong about effects are not the same in both directions; a stable outcome may be a happy regional surprise; an unstable outcome that triggers a chain of proliferation events could have a disastrous effect on the global regime.[19] In the debates about priority that are bound to occur in this decade it is important to remember the difficulty of maintaining a regime.

Rate vs. degree of proliferation

Even if there is a high priority given to nonproliferation, difficult policy choices exist in relating the rate and degree. Proliferation is sometimes conceived in simple terms of a single explosion. Indeed that concept is enshrined in the NPT. But it can also be conceptualized as analogous to a staircase with many steps before and after a first nuclear test. A first explosion is politically important as a key landing in the staircase, but militarily, a single crude explosive device does not bring entry into some meaningful nuclear "club." The very idea of a nuclear club is very misleading. The difference between a single crude device and a modern nuclear arsenal is as stark as the difference between having one small apple and having an orchard. While the rate of proliferation refers to the politically symbolic event of a first explosion, the degree of pro-

---

[19] In my judgment these considerations are not adequately dealt with by Waltz, cited above.

liferation refers to the size, military quality, and deliverability of a country's nuclear arsenal.

As technology spreads and proliferation occurs, the United States will have to direct more attention to these questions of advanced proliferation. Controls on information about laser fusion devices, technology with advanced weapons uses, launchers, and other delivery systems will require more systematic analysis. Strategic and arms control policies will also require attention from this perspective. Formulating sanctions that deter a quickening rate while creating firebreaks after a first explosion will be a delicate balancing act.

Obviously there is a trade-off between the attitudes and measures that are taken to deter first explosions—the events that politically symbolize the rate of proliferation—and the measures taken to limit the degree of proliferation after the first explosion. Yet clearly there is a difference, for example, between a South Asia in which India and Pakistan engage in an escalating nuclear arms race, and a situation which stabilizes around the fiction of one-time "peaceful nuclear explosions." Measures to deal with the degree of proliferation will be difficult to announce in advance, but will need advanced thought.[20] That thought must balance the effects of rate and degree; and of any measures both on the region and on the general regime. And the regime tends to be defined in terms of rate alone.

Relations among regimes

International regimes coexist in different issue areas with a degree of autonomy from each other. Nonetheless, they also exist within an overall political context and can have a net strengthening or weakening effect on each other. In one direction the nonproliferation regime interacts with other nuclear weapons and arms control regimes, in the other direction with international energy and economic regimes. A successful nonproliferation policy in the 1980s will require attention to the connections in both directions.

The relation between nonproliferation and other arms-control regimes is not as simple as it first appears. The usual connections are made by provisions like Article 6 of the NPT, and by various UN Disarmament Committee resolutions calling for a halt to the "vertical proliferation" of the arms of the superpowers.

This gives rise to certain paradoxes in nonproliferation policy. Ironically, calculability and stability of deterrence between the United States and the USSR has occurred over time and at high levels of weaponry. By historical evolution this pattern has produced prudence in their relationship and

---

[20] See Lewis Dunn, "After INFCE: Some Next Steps for Nonproliferation Policy," *Hudson Institute Paper* 33 (Autumn 1979).

extended deterrence to their allies who have thus been able to eschew the development of nuclear weaponry. Changes in the balance which are perceived as weakening the credibility of deterrence threaten not only the stability of the central relationship, but reduce the sense of security that permits allied states to foreswear proliferation. It is paradoxical but true that under many circumstances the introduction of a single weapon in a new state may be more likely to lead to nuclear use than the introduction of an additional thousand each by the United States and the Soviet Union.[21]

On the other hand, to profess indifference to the superpower nuclear arms relationship can weaken the nonproliferation regime in two different ways. First, a disdain for the arms control institutions and concerns expressed by nonweapons states can exacerbate the discrimination issue that is the central dilemma in nonproliferation policy. Second, nuclear doctrines and deployments which stress the usefulness of nuclear weapons in warfighting situations may help to increase the credibility of deterrence, but they also tend to make nuclear weapons look more attractive to others. If states that have deliberately eschewed nuclear weapons see them treated increasingly like conventional defensive weapons, they may one day reconsider their decisions. In short, the relation between nonproliferation and the general nuclear arms control regimes will require a sensitivity to both horns of the dilemma, during what promises to be a difficult period in the superpower relationship.

An analogous problem arises in relation to efforts to control conventional arms. Too often in the late 1970s, U.S. policy was unwilling to come to terms with the "dove's dilemma" of chosing between conventional or nuclear weapons. Conventional weaponry is an alternative to nuclear weaponry in providing a sense of military security in situations of extreme threat. On the other hand, conventional arms can be complements as well as alternatives to nuclear weapons. Arms transfers that provide effective delivery systems for nuclear weapons are no solution to the "dove's dilemma" nor to the problems of limiting advanced proliferation. Again, the need to balance the relations between security policies will be critical in the 1980s.

In the realm of energy and economic regimes, it is important that the moderate restrictions of an evolutionary approach to the nuclear fuel cycle not appear as a general posture of technology denial by advanced countries. Threats that poor countries will go nuclear to turn the terms of the North-South dialogue are not particularly credible because nuclear weapons are so ill-suited to such a purpose. But indifference to the energy and economic concerns of poor countries can weaken the nonproliferation regime. A forthcoming posture on energy and technology transfer including the development of nonnuclear energy alternatives, and other measures to deal with energy in-

---

[21] George Quester, "Nuclear Proliferation: Linkages and Solutions," *International Organization* 33 (Autumn 1979).

security, can help take the edge off of confrontations which may generate a spiteful dynamics over status and attention rather than security.

While national security concerns are the dominant reason for most states to preserve and strengthen the nonproliferation regime, at the same time, it is important not to neglect the status/prestige interests that nations have. Above all, it is important on prestige grounds that overt discriminatory solutions be avoided. Justifiable temporary differentiation and permanent discrimination are not the same thing. The United States must be careful not to reinforce the illusion that being a nuclear weapons state provides unusual privileges or position in international affairs. The weight of a state's voice in international forums, how it fares in the Law of the Sea, the exchange rate for its currency, or in resource transfers really does not have much to do with whether it possesses a nuclear weapon or not. There are other more usable and directly effective forms of power. The nuclear weapons states must be careful not to try to use nuclear status to threaten in other areas. And their general posture in international energy and economic regimes is bound to have an effect on their ability to manage the acceptability of the degree of discrimination that is inherent in the nonproliferation regime.

Conclusion

Three-and-a-half decades have passed since the energy of the atom was used in warfare. Yet rather than nuclear doom, the world has seen a surprising nuclear stability, thus far. Equally remarkable is the fact that while over the same period nuclear technology has spread to more than two-score nations, only a small fraction have chosen to develop nuclear weaponry. A third notable point about the period has been the development of an international nonproliferation regime—a set of rules, norms, and institutions, which haltingly and albeit imperfectly, has discouraged the proliferation of nuclear weapons capability. Can this situation last? Obviously there will be changes in political and technical trends, but the prospects that proliferation may be destabilizing in many instances, that nuclear weapons need not enhance the security position of states, and that superpowers cannot fully escape the effects provide the common international interest upon which the nonproliferation regime is based. Under such conditions some inequality in weaponry is acceptable to most states because the alternative anarchic equality is more dangerous. So long as countries can be made better off without a bomb than with one, then a policy of slowing the spread of nuclear weapons technology rests on a realistic formulation of common interests, and there are serious prospects for maintaining a legitimate and stable international nuclear regime.

Realistically, an international regime does not need perfect adherence to have a significant constraining effect, any more than deviant behavior means the irrelevance of domestic legal regimes. Nevertheless, there is a tipping point beyond which violations lead to a breakdown of normative constraints. The police function is traditionally the domain of the great powers in international politics, but if their preponderance in the nuclear issue area erodes, and they become diverted by other issues, there is a danger that the gradual historical curve of proliferation could approach such a tipping point.

Given the natural decline in American preponderance in the nuclear issue area, it was important that the burden of leadership in regime maintenance be more broadly shared. To a considerable extent, INFCE and the other initiatives of the late 1970s helped to accomplish this spreading of the burden. The United States persuaded others to share its agenda. For example, in sharp contrast to attitudes three years ago, key figures in Japan warn against asserting only "our own position and lacking the wider perspective of antiproliferation."[22] Or as one long-term French official noted wryly and privately in Vienna near the end of the INFCE, "we may encroach on your markets, but somehow we seem to have inherited your nonproliferation policy in the process." Changed attitudes are reflected in many decisions such as the June 1977 German policy of no further exports of reprocessing plants, or the agreement about sanctions in the 1978 Suppliers Guidelines, or the French pressure on South Africa and restrained response to Brazilian inquiries about breeder technology, and other examples not yet public. As important as the specifics is the general convergence that Lellouche describes elsewhere:

> The 1946 Baruch Plan, the Atoms for Peace Plan of 1953, the creation of the IAEA in 1957, the Test Ban Treaty of 1963, the Nonproliferation Treaty of 1968, the formation of the London Suppliers Group in 1974 and the launching of INFCE in 1977—each of these landmarks in the history of nonproliferation has been the product of U.S. policy. However the conditions which once made it possible for the United States to control proliferation unilaterally are no longer present. This in turn requires a change in mentality on the part of American leaders. Indeed the greatest achievement of the Evaluation would be to help change this mentality within the United States itself just as the Evaluation has helped to develop in Europe and elsewhere a greater awareness of the security implication of nuclear power development.[23]

To a very considerable extent, leadership in the job of maintaining the nonproliferation regime is now shared. But collective leadership is difficult to manage. The United States still has to adjust to sharing the process. The wrong policies in the 1980s could still sacrifice the current modest success in regime maintenance on the altars of either purism or cynicism. The best is sometimes the enemy of the good. So also is short-sighted blindness to the possible conse-

---

[22] *Asahi Shinbun*, editorial, 25 February 1980.
[23] Pierre Lellouche, "International Nuclear Politics," *Foreign Affairs* (Winter 1979/80): 347–8.

quences of the worst. Unfortunately, there is no simple solution to the political problem of proliferation. But given the difficulty of constructing international institutions in a world of sovereign states, and the risks attendant upon their collapse, political wisdom begins with efforts to maintain the existing regime with its presumption against proliferation.

3

Breaking the Rules Without Quite Stopping the Bomb: European Views

Pierre Lellouche

In a sense, writing about nonproliferation issues, in the aftermath of the Soviet invasion of Afghanistan, may seem totally irrelevant as compared with the gravity of the current East-West crisis and the subsequent European-American differences on détente, arms control, and defense policies.

At the time of this writing (June 1980), nonproliferation has definitely fallen out of fashion and the center of attention has shifted back to the more traditional East-West security issues. Nonproliferation, which was a top priority concern of the Carter administration only three-and-a-half years ago, is now nearly forgotten. The fact that America has reversed its earlier embargo towards India and has recently decided to deliver nuclear fuel to the Tarapur Power Station has gone practically unnoticed except by some experts. Similarly, the convening of the second NPT Review Conference in Geneva in August 1980 is scarcely attracting the public's attention.

Yet the problem of checking the spread of nuclear weapons remains. Technology, equipment, and fissionable materials are being transferred to many nations, some of which are known to be actively seeking nuclear weapons more or less openly, especially in the Near East and northwest Asia, thus adding to the already dangerous instability of key regions in the world. Similarly, the nuclear issues which have divided the United States and its European allies over the last seven years have yet to be resolved. Nonproliferation issues may, therefore, attract less attention today, but they remain of fundamental importance to international security in the years to come.

For this reason, it is perhaps useful to reflect on the events of the past decade and to analyze how nuclear policies of the United States and of the European suppliers have interacted.

The transatlantic nonproliferation quarrels in perspective

One of the most striking paradoxes of the nonproliferation controversy of the last seven years is that while the target of proliferation concerns was clearly centered on a series of unstable Third World countries, the main battle was fought between allied Western nations of Europe and America.

It may be too early to assess whether this transatlantic quarrel will eventually bring a positive contribution to the goal of nonproliferation. One thing is certain, however: the quarrel over nonproliferation and nuclear energy has helped to create profound and long-term damage to the overall climate of U.S.-European relations and particularly German-American relations.

The Carter administration's nonproliferation policy gave rise to the first major quarrel with the Europeans (and Germany in particular) in a series of transatlantic troubles which, over the past four years, gradually included economic and energy issues, strategic problems (including the neutron bomb episode, the handling of the SALT II Treaty ratification process, and the Theatre Nuclear Force modernization program), as well as political issues (Iran, the Middle East, the policy towards the USSR in the aftermath of Afghanistan).

Looking back at this distressingly long list of troubles, it is clear that the nuclear nonproliferation quarrel did play an important role in shaping what was going to become the standard European perception of the Carter administration's record in foreign policy—namely, a mixture of incoherence, reversals, poor management of the Alliance, misplaced priorities, coupled with an overreliance on quasireligious principles.

This being said, the recent transatlantic quarrel over nonprolifertaion cannot be fully understood without reference to earlier events.

It is well-known that Euro-American relations in the field of nuclear energy and nonproliferation have never been altogether smooth. Indeed, when looking at the history of international relations since World War II,[1] one finds that nonproliferation has been a constant source of strain in transatlantic politics. The 1940s were the decade of aborted cooperation among the Allies with respect to the Manhattan Project. In that decade, the United States breached the 1943 Tripartite Quebec Agreement signed with Great Britain and Canada and later sealed off its nuclear know-how from the rest of the world behind the walls of secrecy of the 1946 McMahon Act.

Similarly, the 1950s created new strains between the United States and continental Europe, and particularly France, over the extent of U.S. assistance

---

[1] See Bertrand Goldschmidt, *Le Complexe Atomique* (Paris: Fayard, 1980).

to the newly formed EURATOM and the birth of the French military nuclear program.

During the 1960s, while progress was made towards the establishment of an international nuclear safeguards regime, Europe and America were again at odds with respect to both the relationship between EURATOM and the IAEA–NPT safeguards and the issue of nuclear sharing within NATO (the MLF plan).

All of these issues and strains in one way or another revolved around the risks of proliferation and the policies which the United States was trying to implement at the time.

Though often overlooked in America, this historical background has played an important role in shaping European reactions to the U.S. policies of the 1970s. From a European standpoint, the nonproliferation debate of the 1970s constitutes the latest episode in a Euro-American rivalry that has lasted some forty years! There are some crucial differences, however, which go a long way in explaining the intensity and duration of the current quarrel.

1. Contrary to earlier periods, in the 1970s, the Europeans committed themselves on a very large scale to nuclear power programs, in the hope of reducing their very great dependence on imported fossil fuels. For the Europeans, therefore, nonproliferation was no longer a cost-free objective (as it was in the 1950s and 1960s), but one that entailed a great deal of sacrifice both in economic and energy terms and, though to a lesser degree, foreign policy objectives.

2. The second major change involves the "balance-of-power" between American and European industrial and technological capabilities in the field of nuclear energy. The 1970s saw the end of the long-held U.S. monopoly in the reactor manufacturing as well as in fuel cycle services.[2] Early in this decade at least two major suppliers of nuclear reactors had fully emerged on the international market in the FRG and in France; moreover, Europeans managed to free themselves to a large extent from the dependence on U.S. enriched uranium fuel, after the URENCO facilities and the EURODIF plant at Tricastin became operational. Finally, the Europeans had developed an impressive technological edge over the U.S. in reprocessing and fast breeder technology. The results of this new situation have been of fundamental importance in shaping both the substance of the nonproliferation quarrel and its outcome.

For their part, the Europeans discovered early in the debate that their own energy security interests and to a lesser extent foreign policy objectives were directly threatened by the new policies put forward by the United States. But even though they were in a defensive position, they realized that, contrary to earlier periods, this time they held the technological and industrial means

---

[2] Thomas Neff and Henry D. Jacoby, "Nonproliferation Strategy in a Changing Nuclear Fuel Market," *Foreign Affairs* (Summer 1979); Paul L. Joskow, "The International Nuclear Industry Today: The End of the American Monopoly," *Foreign Affairs* (July 1976).

necessary to defend these interests and to effectively resist American pressures. At the same time, these industrial achievements brought new problems. Having established themselves, because of the very success of their industries, as key actors in international nuclear relations, the Europeans also had to learn, often reluctantly, to live with the political responsibilities that came with that new role. This has been a slow and somewhat difficult realization and it is still unclear whether the Europeans are willing to pay the political and economic price that is inherent in nonproliferation policy.

Similarly, the United States, which was accustomed to treating nonproliferation unilaterally as its own "special responsibility" (to be shared at best with the other superpower), took a very long time before realizing the magnitude of the changes that had taken place in international nuclear relations. Not only did the United States have trouble recognizing the legitimate energy preoccupations of the Europeans, but it discovered very late in their relations that, henceforth, nonproliferation was to be negotiated with—rather than imposed upon—the European allies, and that in any case, such a policy could not succeed without the full cooperation of the European suppliers.[3]

In essence, therefore, the Euro-American nonproliferation quarrel of the 1970s constitutes one particular aspect of a wider ongoing structural transformation of transatlantic relations, which is characterized by: (1) a sharp decline in the ability of the United States to directly shape events and policies in Europe in accordance with U.S. objectives and (2) an increasing ability on the part of the Europeans to assert and defend their own interests against those of the United States.

What makes this structural problem even more difficult and apparent in the case of nonproliferation is that both sides are in essence condemned to cooperate. Not only does Third World proliferation constitute an objective security threat to both the United States and Europe, but the continued development of nuclear power in Europe also requires the restoration of a stable climate in international nuclear politics. This entails the need to reconcile the respective energy and military security concerns of Europe and America in mutually agreed-upon policies; this also means that a more balanced form of cooperation must replace the unilateral American policies of the past.

In essence, the painful quarrel of the past seven years reflects precisely this evolution—from an initial situation of open conflict to one in which both sides increasingly realize the need to establish a new cooperative relationship aimed at jointly managing proliferation in the future.

The present paper offers an analysis of this evolution from a European perspective, with particular emphasis on the policies of the two main European actors in this area—France and Germany.

[3] See Pierre Lellouche, "International Nuclear Politics," *Foreign Affairs* (Winter 1979).

This article is not, however, intended to provide yet another account of the various events that took place over the past seven years. An impressive literature has already been devoted to most of these events, ranging from the "sensitive" contracts signed by France and Germany in the early 1970s, to the London Suppliers Group, the new Carter policy, the Nuclear Nonproliferation Act of 1978 (NNPA), as well as the International Nuclear Fuel Cycle Evaluation (INFCE).[4]

Rather, it is more useful in my view to assess the extent to which European attitudes toward nonproliferation have evolved as a result of U.S. policies, in order to provide some guidelines as to what needs to be done to reach a settlement in the still unresolved transatlantic nonproliferation controversy.

Viewed from a European perspective, recent U.S. nonproliferation policies have confronted European supplies with two separate, though interconnected issues: (1) the question of nuclear transfers to the Third World and its impact on European exports policy; (2) the question of the future of the "plutonium economy" and its consequences on European breeder and reprocessing programs. Each of these questions will be addressed separately.

Nuclear exports and safeguards: impact of U.S. policy on European suppliers

In retrospect, perhaps the single most important achievement of the Ford and Carter administrations' foreign nuclear policies has been the triggering of an awareness in Europe of the fact that the exporting of nuclear materials and equipment is a special business and that nonproliferation is a policy for which Europe should also be responsible.

Although European policy has evolved considerably in this direction since the mid-1970s, disagreement persists with the United States in at least two areas: (1) the type of export controls and safeguards which should be established to deal with Third World proliferation from commercial fuel cycles and (2) the economic and political price that Europe should pay in order to implement such a policy.

Nonproliferation and nuclear exports as a European responsibility

Until the mid-1970s, when the controversy erupted with the United States, Europeans scarcely thought of themselves as responsible for or indeed involved in implementing nonproliferation policy. The latter was typically seen as "superpower business," which one should either oppose (as France did when it sought to acquire nuclear weapons against the wishes of both the United States and the USSR), or submit to more or less reluctantly (as Germany did when it signed the NPT in 1968).

---

[4] A good summary of all these events is to be found in B. Goldschmidt, op. cit., pp. 411–80.

As far as the FRG was concerned, nonproliferation had been settled with the Treaty of Paris in 1954. As a result, the question was seen in the FRG from a purely economic angle—i.e., in terms of nondiscriminatory access of the FRG to fuel cycle technology and to the international market. This preoccupation was central in delaying their ratification of the NPT until 1975. The French, on the other hand, viewed the problem from a purely political angle. Having themselves "proliferated" under de Gaulle, they conveniently chose an ambiguous position. On the one hand, they refused to oppose the right of every nation to acquire atomic weapons with its own means; hence, France's refusal to join the NPT. But on the other hand, France announced that it would conduct itself as if it were a party to the Treaty. . . .[5]

Another important element explaining this general attitude of aloofness with respect to nonproliferation policy was that France and Germany achieved a large-scale industrial capability in the nuclear area only in the early 1970s. During the 1960s, both nations had played a very marginal role as exporters of nuclear reactors in a market totally dominated by the United States,[6] where in addition, safeguards rules were either purely bilateral or nonexistent. As a result, neither France nor Germany had felt the need to set up a procedure for the political control of nuclear exports, although Germany did participate, in the early 1970s, in the discussions of the Zangger Committee.

The irony of this situation was that France and Germany were drawn into the nonproliferation issue, not because they intended to be politically (indeed, they were caught totally unprepared by the new U.S. policies), but because they emerged as alternative nuclear suppliers to the United States precisely at the time when America was having second thoughts about the efficiency of the NPT–IAEA system (which Washington had been instrumental in creating only a few years earlier).

In essence, the Europeans soon found themselves caught between three conflicting forces: (1) pressures from the United States, which had "discovered" the loopholes in the NPT–IAEA regime after the Indian nuclear test of 1974 and was demanding stronger nonproliferation rules; (2) a series of demands for nuclear assistance from developing countries triggered in part by the 1973 oil shock; and (3) the pressures from their domestic nuclear industries which needed export outlets in order to minimize the cost of the large domestic nuclear programs which were being launched at the same time in Europe.

Nuclear and industrial bureaucracies in both countries, which at the time enjoyed full control over exports, simply decided to treat their expanding business on a "business as usual" basis—that is, according to the international rules in force at the time. And in fact, none of these rules prevented the transfer of "sensitive" fuel cycle technologies (i.e., enrichment and

---

[5] See Pierre Lellouche, "France in the International Nuclear Energy Controversy: A New Policy under Giscard d'Estaing," *Orbis* 22, 4 (Winter 1979).

[6] France sold a single power Gas Graphite to Spain, in addition to the Dimona research reactor exported to Israel; the FRG had managed to export only one PHWR to Argentina.

reprocessing). Indeed, the general assumption then, as derived from the NPT, repeated statements by U.S. officials as well as from the Zangger Committee's trigger list, that "the whole field of nuclear science associated with electrical power is accessible now . . . including not only the present generation of power reactors, but also that advanced technology. . . . of fast breeder power reactors."[7] When combined with the other provisions of the NPT relating to nuclear exports to nonweapons states remaining outside the Treaty, the "normal" rules at the time were that (1) national access to the entire fuel cycle was implicitly guaranteed to nonnuclear weapon states party to the Treaty (as per Article IV), while (2) even nonparties could also benefit from this liberal regime to the extent that they accepted limited safeguards when dealing with a supplier nation party to the NPT.

In effect, several nations in the early 1970s had already used their then legitimate right to acquire sensitive technologies. In Europe this was the case with the establishment of URENCO and the construction of a centrifuge enrichment plant in Almelo (Holland), and was also the case with Japan, which obtained a demonstration-size reprocessing plant (Tokai Mura) from France. Similarly, nothing prevented Korea (a party to NPT) and Pakistan (a nonparty) from obtaining French cooperation in the reprocessing field or Brazil from asking for similar assistance from the United States and Germany.

In the meantime, the United States had changed its mind about the viability of such a liberal system (which, it must be emphasized, the United States had itself established). According to the new American approach, the nonuniversal, noncompulsory safeguards regime valid under NPT–IAEA norms had to be "improved" in order to prevent countries from coming "three months away" from the bomb and getting it "without quite breaking the rules."[8] Thus, the traditional deterrence function of safeguards through *detection* was no longer thought to be fulfilled under the "old" regime: safeguards should now be made compulsory and universal in order to ensure effective prevention. The second major change in U.S. thinking was that certain fuel cycle activities (i.e., enrichment and, in particular, plutonium reprocessing) were now considered to be too dangerous to be exported, even under safeguards. After having promoted full nuclear cooperation under its Atoms for Peace Plan of 1953, the United States was reverting twenty years later to the policy of denial of the immediate postwar period.

From a European perspective, these changes were seen as an attempt to rewrite valid international norms and agreements. Implied in this criticism was the notion that the "old" IAEA–NPT regime had been "good enough" as long as the United States was the dominant actor on the world market. The

---

[7] Statement by Arthur Goldberg, American Ambassador to the United Nations in May 1968, quoted in Karl Kaiser, "The Great Nuclear Debate—German-American Disagreements," *Foreign Policy* 30 (Spring 1978).

[8] See Albert Wohlstetter, "Spreading the Bomb Without Quite Breaking the Rules," *Foreign Policy* 25 (Winter 1976–1977).

prevailing view in Europe then was that the United States was simply trying to eliminate its European competitors by changing the political rules of nuclear trade. (Ironically, Americans were convinced of exactly the same thing on the part of the Europeans when they looked at the technological "sweeteners" willingly sold by Europeans in order to eliminate U.S. firms from Third World markets).[9]

While perhaps partly founded and certainly understandable given the history of U.S.–European rivalry in this field since the 1950s, these suspicions about American commercial objectives were also, in part, self-serving. There can be no doubt that both the French and German nuclear-industrial complexes (or bureaucracies) were fully aware of the loopholes in the NPT–IAEA regime in force at the time and that they used them in order to establish their respective industries on the world market. Hence, the tendency of European suppliers to respond to American political pressures by overplaying legal arguments[10]—i.e., by insisting that all the controversial nuclear deals signed in the mid-1970s were fully consistent with established international norms. One should note, however, that these practices were not new. The United States had employed similar "carrots" in the 1950s and 1960s, particularly in the safeguards area when it sought to establish its own industry in the European market.[11]

Beyond these immediate commercial objectives, the behavior of both European suppliers revealed an analysis of proliferation risks different from that of the United States. Europeans tend to view proliferation as a purely political problem. To a large extent, therefore, the connection with the commercial fuel cycle, including sensitive facilities, is considered irrelevant, for if a state really wants to acquire nuclear weapons, it will do so with or without safeguards or other technical obstacles.[12] In this context, embargo and denial policies, while perhaps useful in delaying proliferation in certain countries, will also reinforce tendencies of nuclear autarchy, thereby depriving the supplier states of any form of control over such national programs.[13]

In spite of these suspicions about American objectives, in spite also of the

---

[9] Parenthetically, it is important to note that this situation of mutual suspicion about the other side's commercial motivations runs throughout the entire controversy: as noted, such suspicion was evident in the mid 1970s with respect to nuclear exports to the Third World, but it also reappeared later in the plutonium controversy which we shall analyze in the following section.

[10] Kaiser, op. cit., p. 89.

[11] In this connection, it is useful to recall that the United States did conclude an unusually liberal safeguards agreement with EURATOM (as compared with its overall policy at the time) in order to promote the "penetration" of the U.S. nuclear industry in Europe in the late 1950s. (See Warren H. Donnelly, "Commercial Nuclear Power in Europe: The Interaction of American Diplomacy with a New Technology," U.S. House of Representatives, *Science Technology and American Diplomacy* (Washington, D.C.: GPO, 1977).

[12] See Horst Mendershausen, "International Cooperation in Nuclear Fuel Services: European and American Approaches," P - 6308, (Los Angeles: The Rand Corporation, December 1978).

[13] While this reasoning is often perceived in the United States as a convenient justification for European nuclear exports in the Third World, it is important to note that (1) such reasoning is widely shared in Europe and (2) it has been proven correct by history (recall for example the failure of U.S. attempts to prevent the Europeans from acquiring an autonomous enrichment industry).

Europeans own commercial motivations and their different views of proliferation risks, the European suppliers did gradually evolve toward the recognition of their own responsibilities in the nonproliferation area. A first step was made with the participation of France in the London Suppliers Group following the Martinique Summit between Presidents Ford and Giscard d'Estaing. France, it is important to recall, had previously boycotted the Zangger Committee meetings. Moreover, its participation in what might appear as a suppliers "cartel" was not without political cost, since France claimed to promote a *mondialiste* policy in which it intended to be a link between North and South. A second important step was made with the agreement on the Suppliers Group's Guidelines in September 1975. Although both France and Germany had opposed the U.S. concept of "full scope safeguards," as well as the notion of denying exports of "sensitive" technologies as contrary to the sovereign rights of nations, the two European suppliers did agree upon a set of international rules aimed at strengthening the nonproliferation regime, including one providing for suppliers' "restraint" in exporting sensitive facilities.

While this evolution was not considered to be sufficient in the United States (particularly during the 1976 presidential campaign), in both France and Germany, it was interpreted as a major step towards the U.S. position. Indeed, in France, this "concession" to U.S. pressures gave rise to a series of political attacks from the Gaullists against President Giscard's foreign nuclear policy, which they felt was too "close" to that of the United States.

Another positive sign of a greater awareness of proliferation issues came in September 1976 when France decided to establish a high-level political organ entrusted with the task of elaborating and implementing French nonproliferation policy. This was the first time France had announced such a policy and imposed direct presidential control over nuclear exports. In December 1976, this decision was followed by the announcement of an embargo on further sales of plutonium reprocessing facilities. Although the plant promised to Pakistan was implicitly excluded from the decision, the latter still represented a further rapprochement between France and the United States.

One interesting result of the French embargo was that Germany remained totally isolated in the nuclear exports controversy as the only country still willing to export reprocessing facilities. As a result, Bonn was now perceived by the United States as the chief obstacle to the development of a common nonproliferation policy by all supplier nations. In fact, partly to offset new pressures from the newly-elected Carter administration, Germany did modify its policy six months later, by adopting, in June 1977, an export embargo phrased exactly like France's.

Evolution of European attitudes during the Carter administration

Looking back over the experience of the past four years, it is somewhat difficult to evaluate precisely the influence of the Carter administration nonproliferation policy on the behavior of European suppliers. Part of this difficulty stems from the fact that Europeans had already evolved considerably, before Carter was elected. This is particularly true in the case of France, which joined the London Group and adopted in late 1976 a much more restrictive nuclear export policy. But the major part of the difficulty is due to the way in which the Carter administration chose to handle the nonproliferation question. Though not substantially different from that of its predecessor, Carter's nuclear export policy was considerably more confused and its "style" was quite different. The confusion was due, above all, to internal factors: the administration took many months (if not years) before it only began to control the various centers of authority in the nuclear exports area, which included a whole series of organs in the Executive and regulatory branch (not to mention various conflicting offices in the State Department, the White House and the newly created Department of Energy) and an equally large number of decision makers in the Congress. To any foreign government, the administration spoke with many voices, all different and at times openly contradictory, a situation which goes a long way towards explaining many of the misunderstandings and quarrels of that period. To a certain extent, this regulatory mess or "meltdown" was dealt with, somewhat by the 1978 Nonproliferation Act, but the sheer complexity of that legislation, coupled with the severity of its provisions, largely offset this benefit. To this administrative confusion, the Carter administration added a confusion of substance, as it diffused the export issue as such—though central to Third World proliferation—by opening a new debate on the "plutonium economy," which raised an entirely new set of problems.

Another characteristic of the new Carter policy, which also contributed to intensifying the quarrel with the Europeans, was the way in which the administration chose to deal with some of the issues outstanding from the Ford government and in particular the 1974 German-Brazilian Agreement. While the Ford administration proved effective in working through discrete multilateral channels (the London Suppliers Group), the Carter administration chose a "high visibility" posture which proved totally counterproductive. Instead of obtaining the "cancellation" of the Agreement, the Carter administration antagonized both Brazil and the FRG, and made compromise on the part of the Germans even more politically difficult as a result of the publicity given to the affair.

On the whole, the successes of the Carter administration in the nuclear exports area are not altogether obvious. Not only did it fail to convince Germany to renounce its controversial deal with Brazil (or the "sensitive" parts of it) but Carter also failed to prevent the FRG from signing in 1979–1980 another contract with Argentina which includes the transfer of a "Swiss"-made large-scale heavy water plant. As to the other outstanding cases left over from the mid-70s, the French-Korean contract had been cancelled before Carter was elected and the French-Pakistani contract was cancelled by

France in 1978 as a result of various internal events in Pakistan (the execution
of Prime Minister Bhutto, and the accumulation of evidence showing that his
successor, General Zia, clearly intended to produce nuclear weapons by all
available means). Moreover, U.S. pressures failed to prevent certain oil-
starved European suppliers from intensifying their nuclear cooperation with
Arab oil producers (notably France and Italy with Iraq).

Disagreement still persists on the full scope safeguards issue, despite the
inclusion of this requirement in the Nuclear Nonproliferation Act of 1978 and
the discussion of the concept in INFCE. The Carter administration insists on a
formal acceptance of the concept by both France and Germany. By contrast,
the latter argue that de facto full scope safeguards are already in force in all
but five nonweapons states, and that a formal inclusion of the full scope
concept in an international document (i.e., in the IAEA safeguards
regulations) could only worsen the emerging North-South controversy about
nuclear transfers. Given this background, when looking at the record of
European behavior in the nuclear exports area over the past four years, it is
interesting to note that this behavior seems to have been less influenced by the
Carter policy per se than by the respective situations of the world nuclear
market and of the European industries. The dominant factor is the virtual
paralysis of nuclear growth throughout the world since the mid-1970s as a
result of a combination of societal, economic, technical, and political
reasons.[14]

Interestingly enough, the impact of this situation has been substantially
different in the case of France from that of Germany, as well as that of the
lesser European suppliers. Thus far, France has managed to maintain and even
increase its domestic nuclear program. As a result, French nuclear industry is,
for the moment, less dependent than its German counterpart on nuclear exports. Framatome's order books are filled for many years to come by EDF's
domestic contracts—a fact which considerably reduces exports incentives and
the willingness to transfer sensitive "sweeteners." As for the latter, the French
have discovered that it is financially much more lucrative to provide services
from large plants located in France (i.e., La Hague and Tricastin) than to
export small-scale facilities at relatively low prices with the additional
drawback of weakening the French situation on the world enrichment and
reprocessing markets.[15] For the time being, therefore, France enjoys a unique
position among Western nations—its nonproliferation policy coincides with
the economic interests of its nuclear industry. History has shown that such a

---

[14] Pierre Lellouche and Richard Lester, "The Crisis of Nuclear Energy," *The Washington
Quarterly* (Summer 1979).
[15] This economic element has played an important part in the decision announced in September
1978 to cancel the contract signed with Pakistan. Politically, this cancellation was also useful in
terms of U.S.-French relations: by behaving in a "responsible" manner in the exports area, the
French could demand in return more consideration on the part of the United States for France's
plutonium program.

coincidence of interests is crucial to the successful implementation of a state's foreign nuclear policy.

The one exception to this situation is the case of the Osirak research reactor sold to Iraq in 1975. Following a long series of events, including the sabotage of the initial reactor core and many diplomatic exchanges with Baghdad, the French government has announced recently that it would sell Osirak according to the original terms of the contract (i.e., with a fuel core using 93 percent enriched uranium) rather than with the new low enriched "caramel" fuel developed by the CEA. While French officials insist that all the necessary precautions will be taken in order to prevent diversion of the HEU (through a variety of technical means), some lingering suspicions persist as to the proliferation potential of the Osirak reactor.[16] However, France's enormous dependence on Iraqi oil[17] would make the price of cancellation in this case too exorbitant to be contemplated. Moreover, following the events in Afghanistan, Iraq has become a key strategic asset for the West as a whole: this perhaps explains why the United States has apparently stopped complaining about various Iraqi deals in recent months.

The situation in Germany is profoundly different. While highly successful in the booming nuclear market of the early 1970s, KWU has suffered considerably from the depression of the world market in recent years, and more importantly, from the paralysis of the domestic nuclear program. Until the recent Argentinian contract, German industry had not had an order since 1975; by contrast, during the same period Framatome has signed contracts for some twenty-one plants, seventeen of them for the French domestic program. Although KWU's production capability is in the order of eight reactors a year, the firm now has work on six contracts (not including the Argentinian one). By comparison more than thirty-three reactors are currently being built in France. Given the situation of the domestic nuclear program, exports have, therefore, become a matter of survival for German nuclear industry. This is fully understood by the German government, which remains committed to atomic energy despite the current environmental problems, and it is thus determined to keep its industry alive until domestic conditions eventually allow a relaunching of the domestic program. In this context, the recent contract signed with Argentina provides another illustration of the price that European suppliers are not willing to pay for nonproliferation. Although the German bid was considerably higher than that of Canada's AECL (in the range of 300 million dollars), KWU secured the contract because Bonn did not insist on full

[16] Interestingly enough, these proliferation risks are not limited to the HEU itself, but to the plutonium to be produced by Osirak. Here, the matter is further complicated by the interference of another European supplier, namely, Italy, which is currently building a large plutonium "hot cell" in Iraq and is training a large number of Iraqi technicians in Italian facilities in reprocessing technology. In so doing, Italy also hopes to sell a large commercial reactor to Iraq and to secure stable oil deliveries.

[17] Iraqi oil represents 20 percent of total French oil imports, ranking second behind imports from Saudi Arabia.

scope safeguards (while Ottawa did) and KWU's contract was linked with a separate deal signed with a "Swiss" firm providing for the transfer of a heavy water production plant to Argentina.[18]

While technically not a violation of the London Suppliers Group Guidelines, the Argentinian deal offers a disturbing sign of what could become a new phase of savage competition among suppliers—one that could turn out to be even more dangerous than that of the early 1970s, given the desperate position of some nuclear industries.

In this connection, one should recall similar disturbing signs in Italy's behavior,[19] as well as the case of Switzerland, which is involved in the German-Argentinian deal. Similar pressures could also appear in Britain as well, should that country decide to go ahead with its plan to introduce LWR in its domestic program. In such a case, a new British industry would have to be established, which might in turn require export outlays in order to be cost-effective. Such trends might even worsen in the future since other smaller European suppliers will emerge in an already highly competitive world market. This is the case in particular with Sweden, Finland, which is becoming active in Libya in connection with the USSR, and, perhaps at some future date, Czechoslovakia, which also is becoming involved in Soviet nuclear exports.

Thus after years of a bitter nonproliferation quarrel with the Carter administration, the behavior of European suppliers does display some disturbing trends. The record of the Carter policy points to much incoherence and confusion and certainly to a series of failures in changing European behavior; many of the outstanding issues left over from the Ford administration remain open and new ones have been added.

Disagreement still persists as to the definition and substance of nonproliferation policy and, more fundamentally, as to the price that Europeans are willing or able to pay in the name of such a policy. In this respect the cases of Iraq and Argentina are extremely revealing. Both point to the enormous vulnerability of Europeans to their particular energy status and to the link between the situation of their respective domestic nuclear programs and their behavior on the export market. In the final analysis, this means that contrary to a belief widely held within environmental movements, antinuclear objectives and antiproliferation ones are in fact mutually exclusive, rather than complementary. The most effective way to promote a more responsible response on the part of the European supplier is to facilitate the growth of their domestic programs, rather than the opposite. To a large extent, this lesson has not been learned by the Carter administration, whose policy has in fact helped indirectly, if not willingly, European antinuclear groups (in particular in Germany), thereby making matters even worse in the nonproliferation area.

---

[18] See *Nucleonics Week,* 31 May and 27 September 1979.
[19] Ibid.

Despite these failures, the balance sheet of the Carter policy in the nuclear exports area should not be seen as entirely negative. A positive note deserves to be introduced in that the Carter administration by making nonproliferation a top-priority item in its foreign policy (at least until 1979) helped to generate in Europe a new awareness of the political and strategic risks associated with hasty nuclear exports.

To be sure this awareness has not always had much effect, and it is somewhat difficult to predict how long such a constraint will remain active in Europe, particularly when the United States seems to be shifting its priorities once more, and giving much less importance to nonproliferation. This is all the more true when the Europeans suppliers involved, in trying to save their nuclear programs, have to compete for a very tight export market, and as a result, have to pay a high economic and political price for the sake of nonproliferation.

The plutonium controversy: European energy interests versus U.S. nonproliferation policy

As seen from Europe, the decision by the Carter administration to launch a major offensive against the "plutonium economy" in April 1977, opened a second proliferation issue, distinct from the earlier controversy about nuclear exports. In essence, the new American antiplutonium crusade represented a much more direct threat to European energy policies than did the earlier Ford policy on nuclear exports. In the first place, the Carter policy threatened the fast-growing and very costly breeder and reprocessing programs under way in Europe, and, particularly, in France, which held a leading position in the world in both technologies.

This European commitment to the breeder was in part based on economic considerations (i.e., the fear that uranium resources were becoming very scarce),[20] but also on political reasons; of all energy technologies, the FBR was seen as the one "miraculous" source of autonomous energy for the future— the single most effective solution to the problem of Europe's tragic dependence on imported fuel. For the United States to go against this technology was perceived not only as a selfish and irresponsible "luxury," which only the United States could afford given its large domestic energy resources, but also as a political attempt to keep Europe in its current state of vulnerability vis-à-vis foreign supply sources.

---

[20] For example André Giraud, then head of the French CEA, assessed the breeder's contribution to the uranium issue in 1978 in the following terms: "France owns estimated natural uranium reserves of 100,000 tons. While these reserves are not large, consumed in light water reactors, they nonetheless represent 800-Mtoe, or one-third of the North Sea oil reserves. Through the use of breeder reactors, this uranium can produce 50,000-Mtoe, the equivalent of all the Middle East oil reserves." A speech before the Conference of the Japanese Atomic Industrial Forum, 8 May 1978, CEA, *Notes d'Information* 4 (April 1978).

More importantly, perhaps, the Carter policy seemed to run counter to the very logic of nuclear power development per se, thereby encouraging a logic, ironically, which had first been promoted by the United States in the 1960s and later became the law of European energy planners. It held that the present generation of thermal reactors simply constituted a transitory phase in the development of atomic power, to be followed by an era of "plentiful" self-generated energy produced by second-generation breeder reactors using reprocessed fuel.[21] Thus to oppose that transition, as President Carter did in April 1977, was to undermine the very rationale of the long-term nuclear programs launched in Europe in the aftermath of the 1973 oil crisis.

In this context, it is not surprising that the Europeans perceived the Carter approach as fundamentally antinuclear and that they opposed it even more firmly than the earlier Ford policy on nuclear exports. The fundamental disagreement was less about proliferation risks per se than about the actual contribution of nuclear power to the world energy problems—i.e., either as a short-term parenthesis in the history of mankind or as a major long-term energy source for the planet.

What lessons can be derived from this quarrel?

Although the plutonium controversy is still without a solution four years after it began, the interactions between the main actors (essentially the United States, France, and Germany) have brought to light many interesting, if not altogether positive results. Two of these results merit some attention: (1) In reacting to U.S. policy, France and Germany have tended to defend their own national interests rather than "European" interests. Given the differences between the two states (both in weapons status and in the industrial level achieved in the breeder and reprocessing areas), this has led to a great deal of tension rather than to a united policy against the U.S. antiplutonium stand; (2) While the Europeans were partly successful in bringing about a gradual modification of the original Carter administration policy, making it more compatible with European interests, this success is largely offset by the many uncertainties surrounding the future development of nuclear power.

European behavior: national interests versus European cooperation

One of the most interesting aspects of this transatlantic plutonium controversy has been the amount of tension which it has generated in intra-European nuclear relations.

The main reason for this lies in the differences between France and Germany with respect to nuclear weapons as well as the situation of their

---

[21] Alvin M. Weinberg, "Nuclear Energy: A Prelude to H. G. Wells' Dream," *Foreign Affairs* (April 1971).

respective nuclear programs (particularly in the breeder and reprocessing areas).

These tensions, however, have emerged only gradually, in parallel with the evolution of U.S. policy.

During the period immediately following the announcement of the Carter antiplutonium policy, European reactions pointed to unity and cohesion against what was perceived as an unprecedented threat to European energy programs. Political unity was evidenced first during the London summit meeting of May 1977. It was soon followed by a demonstration of technological and industrial unity in the breeder area, one that was most threatened by the U.S. policy, with the signing of the SERENA Agreement in July 1977 between France and Germany with the participation of Italy, Belgium, and the Netherlands.[22] A further example of European unity was given in the period immediately following the enactment of the NNPA in March 1978. Under French leadership, EURATOM as a whole decided not to comply with the requirement of the Act whereby a "renegotiation" of the 1958 U.S.-EURATOM Agreement had to be initiated within one month from the enactment of the NNPA.

These demonstrations of unity were not without *arrière pensées,* however, from the main European actors. France, in particular, promoted the SERENA Agreement because it reinforced French leadership in breeder technology. The Agreement also had the advantage of turning the French breeder program into a "European" one, thereby increasing its defenses against further American aggression. Similarly, although France had never been particularly eager to cooperate with EURATOM in the past, it found it very useful to encourage a joint response to the NNPA as a means to protest against the unilateral revision by the U.S. Senate of a valid international agreement. The main French motivation in this case was not only "European," however. Rather, the French feared that the inclusion of the right of "prior consent" for reprocessing in the 1958 U.S.-EURATOM Agreement would jeopardize the expanding and very lucrative reprocessing business of the COGEMA facilities at La Hague.

However, when it became clear to the French in the course of bilateral consultations with the United States in the summer and fall of 1978 that the United States had evolved towards a more pragmatic approach[23]—that the NNPA had "grandfathered" La Hague, and that as a result, the French breeder program was not directly threatened by the U.S. legislation—then the French tended to look for a separate arrangement with the United States in

---

[22] For an analysis of the SERENA agreement, see Pierre Lellouche, *Internationalization of the Nuclear Fuel Cycle and Non-proliferation Strategy* (New York: Praeger, forthcoming, spring 1981).

[23] In this respect, the turning point was the Uranium Institute speech "Balancing Non-proliferation and Energy Security," by Joseph Nye in July 1978 in London. (See Mr. Nye's article in this volume for a discussion of this evolution as perceived in the United States.)

order to prepare for the post-INFCE world. Suddenly, several areas of convergence appeared between the two countries: cooperation was established in R&D work in the area of proliferation and resistant fuel for research reactors; the United States also showed interest in the French chemical exchange enrichment process, while the French reacted favorably to President Carter's concept of an international fuel bank, as well as to the possibility of a plutonium repository scheme. Moreover, the French offered more conciliatory gestures when they cancelled the Pakistani reprocessing deal in July 1978 and when they announced their opposition to thermal recycling.

This Franco-American *rapprochement* triggered a great deal of anxiety in the FRG and finally caused a very serious strain in the French-German "couple" for several months in late 1978 and early 1979. The greatest German fear was that Franco-American "détente" in the nonproliferation area would lead to a post-INFCE deal concluded between the Western nuclear weapons states (the United States, the United Kingdom and France) at the expense of the nonweapons states in the industrialized world—with the latter being deprived of the right to own commercial reprocessing plants. In particular, the Germans worried about the future of their planned Gorleben reprocessing center, which, contrary to La Hague, did not benefit from the Grandfather clause of the NNPA. In addition, the FRG opposed both France and the United States by insisting on its need for thermal recycling, and by rejecting the concept of an international fuel bank. Finally, in firmly maintaining the agreement signed with Brazil, Germany added to the tension with Washington and further isolated itself from France. These tensions between France and Germany culminated in late 1978 and early 1979 during the highly secret bilateral negotiations on the status of the plutonium obtained after the reprocessing of German fuel at La Hague. The Germans, fearing discrimination by France, demanded immediate return of the plutonium to Germany (presumably for recycling purposes). The French, on the other hand, insisted that the plutonium should be kept in France until Germany could use it in breeder reactors. The dispute revived old fears of German proliferation in France and of French domination and discrimination in the FRG and was actively exploited in both countries. Gaullist and Communist spokespersons in France accused Germany of making a bomb "with the help of Giscard" (the latter having agreed to return the plutonium). Meanwhile, the German press accused the French of taking advantage of their quasimonopolistic situation in the reprocessing market in order to extract political concessions from the FRG. Further differences among the two countries surfaced after the European Court of Justice ruled in November 1978 that the EURATOM Treaty had to be applied fully by all members and without discrimination, which meant the revival of the supranational provisions of Chapter VI of the Treaty to which France, as a nuclear weapons state, had always refused to comply. One of the consequences of this ruling was that the EURATOM Supply Agency was henceforth entitled to exert direct control over the plutonium reprocessed at La Hague. While satisfying the German "non-discrimination" doctrine, this possibility was obviously unacceptable to the French. As a result, in 1979 France announced its intention to ask for a revision of the EURATOM Treaty. Thus, while presumably allied against the U.S. policy, France and Germany spent the better part of the last two or three years fighting their own internal plutonium battle.

Après la bataille

Although in the aftermath of the INFCE's final conference in February 1980, neither of the two sides claimed "victory" as to the outcome of the Evaluation, it is fair to say that, on balance, the Carter administration has been unable to convince the Europeans (as well as the rest of the world) to forego the "plutonium economy." Essentially, the key European actors maintain exactly the same policies in the reprocessing and breeder areas that they had established prior to 7 April 1977. To be sure, the European suppliers have developed an awareness of the special proliferation risks attached to plutonium and some consensus has been reached on the notion that breeders should not be exported "prematurely." But, given the depressed state of the world nuclear market, the question of "premature" exports of breeder reactors has become somewhat academic.

By contrast, when looking at the events of the past four years, it becomes clear that the Europeans have been quite successful in bringing about a gradual change in the original Carter policy. Interestingly enough, most of the changes in the original U.S. policy were obtained in the very early stages of the controversy, when the Europeans reacted as a "bloc" to Carter's speech and the NNPA. However, as soon as the United States started to shift (essentially to the advantage of France), the situation became deadlocked again, as France and Germany were now split, and as the controversy was deliberately frozen in the INFCE "truce" as well as in bilateral consultations. Although this is not readily acknowledged by U.S. officials (or ex-officials of the Carter administration), the United States gradually moved from a position where breeders and reprocessing were ruled out to one where the United States recognized the "special needs" of the developed nations (Europe and Japan), and merely asked in 1978 "those who bet on breeders" to behave responsibly in marketing these reactors.[24]

---

[24] Americans, of course, and especially those who were closely associated with the Carter policy, argue that the administration's original policy was never meant to threaten European interests and that, therefore, it did not have to change in this respect. (See Joseph Nye's article in this volume.) To Europeans, however, this explanation is highly debatable. U.S. policy as announced in April 1977 and the U.S. attitude as evidenced in the INFCE nearly three years later are considerably different. Indeed Mr. Nye implicitly recognizes this change when he refers to the "pragmatist" line and the "evolutionary" concept which characterized U.S. policy beginning in mid-1978.

The point is that this change was forced upon the United States by the resistance of European and other foreign countries and was not just the product of bureaucratic factors inside the Carter administration.

Confirming this gradual evolution towards the recognition of the breeder, the Carter administration went so far as to launch a 1.5 billion dollar R&D breeder program in August 1978. In essence, by 1978–79 when efforts were also being made by INFCE to restore some consensus between Europe and the United States on the post–INFCE nuclear regime, the Carter policy had shifted from an original universal "no" to the plutonium economy to a more subtle question on "where the line should be drawn between those states which can have breeders and reprocessing plants and those which cannot."

The irony, of course, is that by moving from this plain "no," which was unacceptable to all of the Europeans, to this more subtle question, the United States triggered a major quarrel among the Europeans themselves. For the question "where do you draw the line" really raised the old problem of discrimination against Germany and Japan.

So far, no answer has been found to this question, although as noted earlier, the question alone has caused many tensions between Germany and France, as well as between Germany and the United States. In a sense, the battle has ended in a "draw" because most nuclear programs remain frozen. Given the present state of nuclear depression throughout the world, the answer to this question will in fact depend less on a possible political settlement among the major parties involved than on the duration of this cycle of nuclear depression. The latter is in turn a function of a series of societal, economic, and technical parameters—many of which are beyond the control of any government. In this connection, the case of Germany is extremely enlightening: after fighting for four years against the United States and France in order to assert its right to own a large scale reprocessing plant, Bonn has had to cancel its plans for the Gorleben facility, as a result of domestic pressures from local environmentalist groups. Thus, ironically, what the United States could not enforce upon Germany by coercion (NNPA) or persuasion (INFCE) was achieved by the Germans themselves.

What may we conclude?

This analysis points to the somewhat academic and unrealistic character of this four-year controversy. In essence, the United States has been fighting to prevent a spread of breeder and reprocessing plants which in fact never took place. Meanwhile, the Europeans have been struggling to assert their rights to own such facilities, while most of these countries have been unable to keep their domestic programs active when confronted with increasing societal and economic pressures.

The distressing aspect of this otherwise ironic situation is that while Europeans and Americans were busily quarreling over the future of the plutonium economy—which, in any case, they alone are technically and economically able to develop—clandestine proliferation by Third World countries using small scale facilities has managed to proceed unhindered.

A further distressing fact is that while a few of the proliferation objectives have been obtained, the plutonium controversy has greatly damaged the overall climate of European-American relations at a particularly inappropriate time, given the gravity of the current East-West crisis, and the fragility of transatlantic relations in the present period.

If one lesson should be learned from the experience of the past seven years, it is that nonproliferation policy is too complex an issue to be derived from only a series of abstract principles that can be written and rewritten according to the dominant fears of a given period.

In the future, the principal effort should be concentrated on the tailoring of nonproliferation policy to the actual development of nuclear energy throughout the world. Had this been done four years ago, Europe and America would have been saved from fighting a largely irrelevant battle on the "plutonium economy" and could have instead worked jointly towards managing the most pressing proliferation issues in the Third World—which have very little to do with the "plutonium economy" and breeder reactors.

4

The Actual Growth and Probable
Future of the Worldwide Nuclear Industry

Irvin C. Bupp

At the end of the 1970s nuclear power plants were being built in France and in the USSR more or less in accordance with plans developed several years earlier. Nearly everywhere else nuclear power was in deep trouble.

Well before the accident at Three Mile Island, American electric utility companies had all but stopped ordering atomic-powered generating equipment. They purchased less than half a dozen reactors between 1975 and 1980. In the same period there were about fifty cancellations of previous orders, and more than twice as many deferrals for periods ranging from five to ten years. [1]

In mid-1979 there were about 240 operational nuclear power plants in the world. These plants represented an aggregate generating capacity of about 130 gigawatts (GW). About 40 percent of the world's operational nuclear capacity was in the United States. The rest was widely dispersed among twenty-one other countries of which only two, Japan and the USSR, accounted for more than 10 percent each. See Table 1 for a summary of worldwide nuclear generating capacity in mid-1979.

The world's mid-1979 total of 131 GW of operational nuclear capacity represented slightly less than one-third of the approximately 420 GW that had been ordered since the first power producing reactors were purchased in the early 1950s in England. But, during the late 1970s there were numerous cancellations or indefinite deferrals of reactor orders outside the United States as well in, for example, Australia, Austria, China, Denmark, Iran, New Zealand, and Norway. Moreover, de facto moratoria on new orders took

[1] *New York Times,* 16 March 1980, Section 3, p. 1.

Table 1: Worldwide operational nuclear generating capacity

Country	Number of power reactors operational	Operational capacity (GW)	Percent of world-wide operational capacity
1. Argentina	1	0.3	< 1
2. Belgium	3	1.6	1
3. Bulgaria	2	0.8	< 1
4. Canada	10	5	4
5. Czechoslovakia	2	0.5	< 1
6. German Democratic Republic	6	2	2
7. Finland	3	1.5	1
8. France	16	8	6
9. India	3	0.6	< 1
10. Italy	4	1.4	1
11. Japan	22	0.5	11
12. Netherlands	2	14.5	< 1
13. Pakistan	1	0.1	< 1
14. S. Korea	1	0.6	< 1
15. Spain	3	1	< 1
16. Sweden	6	4	3
17. Swtizerland	4	2.	2
18. Taiwan	2	1	< 1
19. UK	33	7	5
20. USSR	30	14	11
21. Federal Republic of Germany	13	9	7
Total non-U.S.	167	76	41
22. United States	74	54	41
Worldwide total	241	131	100

Source: Kidder, Peabody, & Co., "Electric Utility Generating Equipment: Status Report on Worldwide Nuclear Reactors," (October 1979).

shape in several other countries: the Federal Republic of Germany, the Netherlands, Italy, Sweden, and Ireland.

What will the 1980s bring? Will the approximately 300 reactors under construction at the beginning of the decade be completed on schedule or even completed at all? Only for the partially built reactors in France and the USSR is the answer almost a certain "yes."

Elsewhere, this question is only one of the many questions about the future of nuclear power that remain very much open. Another open question concerns the moratoria on new orders. Will they end, so that nuclear generating capacity in the 1990s will grow beyond the 420 GW worldwide limit that will be reached if all remaining orders are filled? Or will there be new waves of cancellations, perhaps many of plants that in 1979 were already or would soon be substantially completed? Will many plants that were operating at the beginning of the 1980s be prematurely shut down before the end of the decade?

None of these questions is easy to answer even for a single country, much less for the whole world. In order, though, to get a rough sense of what the decade ahead promises, it is useful to consider two groups of countries. The

Table 2: Countries with realistically good prospects for nuclear generating capacity greater than 5 GW at the end of the 1980s

Country	Probable Capacity
	(GW)
1. US	50–150
2. France	45–60
3. USSR	30–40
4. Fed. Rep. Germany	30–40
5. Japan	25–35
6. UK	10–15
7. Canada	10–15
8. Sweden	10
9. German Dem. Rep.	5–10
10. Spain	5–10
11. Taiwan	5–7
12. S. Korea	4–8
13. Switzerland	4–7
14. Belgium	4–6
15. Brazil	3–6

first is made up of some fifteen, each with a realistically good possibility of having operational nuclear capacity greater than 5 GW at the end of the 1980s. These countries are listed in Table 2, together with my own guess about the rough lower and upper limits of their probable respective operational nuclear capacities at that time.[2]

The second group of countries is made up of thirty-four in which there is some realistic possibility for operational nuclear capacity in the approximate range of 0.5 to 5 GW by the end of the 1980s. These countries are listed in Table 3.

Table 3 is not a prediction that twenty-eight countries will acquire nuclear generating capability in the coming decade. It is only an informed guess about the probable outer boundaries of the geographic dispersion of relatively small scale nuclear power programs by the end of the 1980s. The important point is, in fact, the small individual scale of each of these possible programs. For nearly all of the countries listed in Table 3 the only realistic prospect is for one or two nuclear power plants to be built in the 1980s.

Even with very good information about the political and economic conditions of these countries, it would obviously be impossible to make certain predictions about the future of small reactor construction programs that today

---

[2] I would like to emphasize the noun "guess." Table 2 is not the output of a model, nor is it a "scenario." It is informed speculation based on wide familiarity with the literature on the worldwide nuclear industry and innumerable conversations and meetings with other scholars, public officials, and business executives in the United States and abroad. For comparison I suggest seeing Chase Manhattan Bank, Division of Energy Economics, "World Economic and Energy Outlook to 1990," (New York, March 1980).

Table 3: Countries with a realistic possibility for operational nuclear capacity of 0.5 to 5 GW by the end of the 1980s (asterisks indicate some operational capacity in 1979)

1. Luxembourg	14. Bulgaria*	27. Iraq
2. Austria	15. Romania	28. Egypt
3. Portugal	16. China	29. Libya
4. Denmark	17. Italy*	30. South Africa
5. Finland*	18. Mexico	31. Australia
6. Ireland	19. Argentina*	32. New Zealand
7. Netherlands*	20. Indonesia	33. Venezuela
8. Yugoslavia	21. Philippines	34. North Korea
9. Greece	22. Thailand	
10. Turkey	23. India*	
11. Poland	24. Pakistan*	
12. Czechoslovakia*	25. Israel	
13. Hungary	26. Iran	

may be in prospect, in serious contemplation, or in abeyance. Today's or tomorrow's decisions are all too clearly subject to reversal the day after tomorrow. Moreover, even in the dozen or so countries where somewhat larger programs (say 3–5 reactors) are a realistic possibility, or where there is already some indigenous capability, the future is not much less uncertain. The recently modified prospects for nuclear power in Iran hardly need emphasis here.

With political and economic turmoil the probable rule, rather than the exception, among the less developed countries, it seems foolish to speculate much beyond the rough guesses in Table 3 about the future shape of the reactor market in that part of the world. A related point does, however, deserve emphasis. It has become indisputable that building and operating nuclear generating equipment is an expensive, complex, and demanding job. It calls for very high orders of specialized technical and managerial skills and robust financial resources. It seems to me that one of the nuclear critics' most telling points has been that the fit between these needs and the corresponding assets of the developing countries is not good. On the whole, the plain trend of logic as well as evidence is in the direction of skepticism and conservatism regarding the near-term growth of reactor markets in the less developed countries.

Because of fundamental political and economic uncertainties, developments beyond the early 1990s are simply speculation for most countries. But in the spirit of providing some very rough calibration for what the longer-term future of nuclear power might plausibly be, I will suggest three final groups. The first are additional countries which might very well have nuclear generating capacities on the order of 10 GW by the early years of the next century. The second are countries which might join the 0.5–5 GW category by that time. And, finally, there is a handful of countries that might complete on the order of 30 GW of nuclear capacity during the coming twenty-five years or so. All three groups are listed in Table 4.

Table 4: Possible countries with additional GW capacities by the early twenty-first century

Additional countries with the possibility of 10 GW by the early 21st century	*Additional countries with a possible 0.5-5 GW by the early 21st century*	*Countries which might complete 30 GW of capacity by the early 21st century*
1. Belgium	1. Malaysia	1. Canada
2. Finland	2. Hong Kong	2. Spain
3. Italy	3. Zimbabwe	3. Italy
4. Switzerland	4. Puerto Rico	4. UK
5. Poland	5. Peru	5. German Dem. Rep.
6. China	6. Cuba	
7. Brazil	7. Colombia	
8. Mexico	8. Chile	
9. S. Korea	9. Kuwait	
10. Taiwan		
11. India		

Tables 1–4 imply something both fundamental and significant: for the rest of this century the combined markets of the developed and the developing countries will, very probably, provide reactor manufacturing of the noncommunist world with less than 25 percent of the work for which it was equipped in 1979, and, almost certainly with no more than 50 percent.[3]

Reviewing Tables 1–4, some would contend that while the uncertainties are clear enough—they cut two ways. Is it not also plausible that we may soon see the end of the pattern of cancellations and deferrals of the late 1970s in both the developed and the developing countries? An affirmative answer is clearly the grounds for many recent projections about the future of nuclear power.

Thus, the authors of one study note that "the nuclear option is seriously at issue," and that "we simply do not have a good historical precedent to permit us to judge whether the present political difficulties of nuclear power will severely constrain this energy source for the indefinite future, or will turn out to be merely a transitory phenomenon."[4]

They then, however, proceed to "assume [that] national and international political impediments to the deployment of nuclear power will gradually disappear over the next few years."[5] With much the same logic, the prestigious International Fuel Cycle Evaluation, published in February 1980, contains

[3] This proposition is the chief conclusion of an original and provocative recent report, Mans Lonnroth and William Walker, *The Viability of the Civil Nuclear Industry* (New York & London, 1980) by the International Consultative Group on Nuclear Energy; jointly sponsored by the Rockefeller Foundation and the Royal Institute of International Affairs.

[4] Thomas J. Connolly, et al., *World Nuclear Energy Paths,* International Consultative Group on Nuclear Energy (New York and London: the Rockefeller Foundation and the Royal Institute of International Affairs, 1979).

[5] Ibid., p. 2.

projections of worldwide nuclear power growth in the coming twenty to forty years which exceed in aggregate installed capacity the estimates in Tables 1–4 by factors of two to three or more.[6]

"Systematic confusion of expectation with fact, of hope with reality, has been the most characteristic feature of the entire thirty-year effort to develop nuclear power."[7] That sentence was written in 1976. Four years later it remains only too true. Mistaking aspirations with likely accomplishments is an important characteristic of INFCE, and of many other official studies or reports.

Several things appear to cause this confusion. The first is adherence to an image of opposition to nuclear power that one might call a "Four Seasons Metaphor." Like the icy sludge of a Boston winter, nuclear opposition is destined to melt away in the warm sunshine of spring. Only slightly more sophisticated, and equally at odds with the available evidence, is the belief that opposition to nuclear power is the temporary concern of a poorly informed fraction of the population who have been misled by a band of antinuclear zealots. Except for the zealots, public opposition will disappear as soon as the "true economic and technical facts" are known. In fact, research in the United States and Western Europe has repeatedly pointed out that more information or educational efforts mobilize latent fears about perceived nuclear hazards, rather than deepening a consensus in support of nuclear growth.[8]

A more subtle motivation behind many optimistic official projections about the nuclear future is conscious or unconscious reluctance to give ammunition to the enemy. In part such reluctance may be based on a realistic anxiety about making self-fulfilling prophecies. There is probably some merit to the private admissions of many nuclear industry executives and supportive public officials that full candor about a difficult problem can only make it more difficult. Hence, there is no alternative to an optimistic public posture.

This seems short-sighted. By nearly universal consensus, credibility is one of the nuclear advocates' principal problems. Projections of nuclear growth which, even taken at face value, would be implausible to anyone who can read and can count may be worse than useless. Not only do they further undermine the credibility of their authors and/or sponsors, they confirm the fears of some less extreme critics that support for any nuclear program carries with it commitment to programs far larger than they might be prepared to accept under any circumstances.

Finally, there is the matter of simple ignorance, particularly regarding the actual technical, economic, or political status of nuclear programs in foreign

---

[6] IAEA, *The International Nuclear Fuel Cycle Evaluation,* 8 vols. (February 1980).

[7] Irvin C. Bupp and Jean-Claude Derian, *Light Water: How the Nuclear Dream Dissolved,* (New York: Basic Books, 1978), p. 188.

[8] Roger E. Kasperson, "Institutional and Social Uncertainties in the Timely Management of Radioactive Wastes," testimony prepared for the California Energy Commission re Nuclear Regulatory Commission Rulemaking Procedure for Confidence in Radioactive Waste Management, May 1980.

countries. All too often, public officials and business executives in one country repeat without independent confirmation someone else's inaccurate, out-of-date, or self-serving claims about circumstances abroad. A good example is the apparent widespread lack of knowledge among even relatively well-informed American nuclear interests about many aspects of the French program.[9] Furthermore, within a given country important information is often poorly diffused among different sectors of business, government, and academia. For example, there is little visible appreciation in the U.S. Department of Energy of the serious financial difficulties of the investor-owned electric utility industry. If it persists, such ignorance would allow department officials to endorse predictions of new nuclear power plant purchases by utility companies in the early or mid-1980s that are implausible on financial grounds alone.[10]

As recently as 1978 Sir Brian Flowers seemed to reflect the opinion of most of the world's government and business leaders in declaring: "Nuclear power is the only energy source we can rely upon for massive contributions to our energy needs up to the end of the century, and if necessary beyond."[11] At the time, this confidence struck only some of us as misplaced. Two years later, it is no longer open to serious question that the nuclear dream of the 1960s and 1970s has, indeed, dissolved. Any further growth of nuclear power during the 1980s will be extremely modest measured against earlier expectations.

What happened to the nuclear dream? How did the energy source from which so much was expected, by so many, and so recently get into such trouble? There are no simple answers to these questions. And the debate over the relative merits of alternative answers seems certain to continue for some time. In the limited space available here, it is possible to highlight only a few of the most important structural and institutional causes of the diminished, if not vanishing, prospects for nuclear growth.

Electricity-demand growth

For approximately twenty-five years, from the late 1940s to the early 1970s, there was rapid and steady growth in the demand for electricity in all industrialized countries. This growth averaged about 7 percent per year. Since 1974 the situation has changed dramatically. Highly erratic, but generally slow growth and even periods of decline have everywhere replaced the rapid and

---

[9] Jean-Claude Derian and Irvin C. Bupp, "Running Water: Nuclear Power on the Move in France," prepared for a meeting of the Keystone Radioactive Waste Management Discussion Group, Keystone Center for Continuing Education, Keystone, Colorado, September 1979.

[10] Irvin C. Bupp, et al., "Some Background Information on the Financial Condition of Certain Investor-Owned Electric Utility Companies," prepared for a conference on "Conservation and the Electric Utilities," Keystone Center for Continuing Education, Keystone, Colorado, March 1980.

[11] Sir Brian Flowers, "Nuclear Power: A Perspective on the Risks, Benefits, and Options," *Bulletin of the Atomic Scientists* 34, 3 (March 1977): 21ff.

steady pattern of the 1950s and 1960s. Between 1975 and 1980, projections of future growth rates were successively scaled back. In early 1980 few experts anywhere were predicting a return to steady 7 percent growth. Most foresaw half that or less.[12]

One reason for the downward revisions of projected electricity growth during the rest of the century is pessimism about the prospects for economic growth in many countries. But the most important is heightened awareness of price elasticities. It is evident that electricity consumers in the developed countries have responded to the steeply rising prices of the 1970s with substantial efforts to conserve. In the United States this response has been particularly evident in the industrial sector. But, recent studies have identified significant, as yet untapped, conservation potential in the residential and commercial sectors.[13] It is also evident that major improvements are both technically feasible and cost effective in the energy use efficiency of a number of technologies: household appliances, industrial motors, and new or reapplied methods of space conditioning.

Consumer response to rising electricity prices is, however, only one of several factors that have brought radical change to the electric generating business. During the 1950s and 1960s this business operated in a highly congenial environment. Not only was there rapid and reliable growth in the demand for its product, there were also easily achievable economies-of-scale in production and distribution systems, steady or even declining fuel prices, and, perhaps most important, little need to worry about social costs external to a narrowly conceived manufacturing and delivery process. The effect operated in a carefree "virtuous circle" of declining real product costs, and, hence, prices, high returns on invested capital, and readily accessible finance.

These happy circumstances nearly all changed for the worse during the 1970s. The internalization of many of the social costs of central station, steam-electricity production and distribution caused plant construction costs to begin to rise early in the decade. Fuel costs, too, began to rise. Inflation took its toll in accelerating the costs of money. In a word, manufacturing costs started to rise rather than fall over time. The result was the transformation of a virtuous circle into a vicious one: paying for new equipment meant raising the price of electricity. But this dampened demand growth below the forecast level on which the need for the new equipment had been predicated. This in turn

[12] David Bodansky, "Electricity Generation Choices for the Near Term," *Science*. 207 (15 February 1980): 721–27. See also: National Research Council, *Energy in Transition: 1985-2010*, Final Report of the Committee on Nuclear and Alternative Energy System (Washington, D.C.: National Academy of Sciences 1979); Hans H. Landsberg, et al., *Energy: The Next Twenty Years;* Report of a Study Group sponsored by the Ford Foundation and administered by Resources for the Future (Cambridge, Mass: Ballinger, 1979), Ch. 2.

[13] See for example, J. Roger Beers, et al., "Choosing an Electric Energy Future for the Pacific Northwest: An Alternative Scenario" (San Francisco: Natural Resources Defense Council, May 1980). See also, Roger W. Sant, "The Least-Cost Energy Strategy" (Arlington, Va.: Energy Productivity Center of the Carnegie-Mellon Institute 1979; Gerald Leach, et al., "A Low Energy Strategy for the UK" (London: International Institute for Environment and Development, 1979).

caused a shortfall in revenues requiring higher prices to cover fixed charges. This further depressed demand and so on. These were novel circumstances for most electric utility company executives. Unfortunately those who produced electricity responded to changing economic circumstances more slowly than those who consumed it. Part of the industry's lethargic response was understandable. Because of the very long lead-times involved in planning and building generating equipment many electric power producers in the United States and elsewhere had no financially realistic alternative to proceeding with construction programs that were well underway before the magnitude and probable permanence of the drop in demand growth become unambiguously apparent.

Lead-time problems do not, however, fully exonerate the recent behavior of many electric utility industry executives. It has been apparent for at least a decade that the fundamental cost structure of the industry has changed. Rising, not falling, marginal costs of production have become a basic economic characteristic of the business.

The marginal cost of electricity is based on the capital and operating costs of new power plants and on the operating costs of the most expensive, least efficient plants in a system whose operation could be curtailed by the availability of new capacity. It will, therefore, vary across generating systems, depending on fuel mix and on the age and efficiency of installed capacity. For any given system, estimating the marginal cost of electricity over long periods of time requires a forecast of the future price of fuel that could be displaced as well as a forecast of the cost of new plant construction and operation. It is certain, however, that for all U.S. electric power companies the marginal cost of electricity rose steadily throughout the 1970s. One study estimates that for the companies in the state of California, the minimum value of the marginal cost of generating electricity was about 4 cents per kilowatt-hour (kwh) in early 1980 and would rise in real terms to a range of 5–8 cents per kwh by 1985 and to more than 10 cents per kwh by the early 1990s.[14]

A decade of rising marginal costs and the prospect for more of the same means something very important for a business whose prices are set by public authorities on the basis of average, not marginal costs: at any given time the price of the industry's product-electricity will be less than the cost of producing it. This carries with it a host of strategic implications for capacity planning and management. During a period of falling marginal costs (and hence prices higher than costs), it is highly desirable to prefer the risk of excess capacity to the risk of insufficient capacity. From a business point of view, this is not nearly so clear when marginal costs are rising. Such circumstances call for very tight capacity management; for a strategy of adding capacity in relatively small increments whose lead-times are as short as possible.

---

[14] California Energy Commission, "Estimating Utilities' Prices for Power Purchases from Alternative Energy Sources," Staff report (March 1980), pp. 500–80.

Executives in the U.S. electric power industry were slow to respond to this challenge during the latter half of the 1970s. An important consequence is that the 1980s will be a period of considerable over-capacity in the country's generating system as a whole.

In the United States, peak load growth slowed dramatically after the 1973 Arab oil embargo. Between 1973 and 1979 the reserve margin of the country's electrical generating system rose from about 20 percent to about 35 percent, compared with a desired level of 20–25 percent. The reserve margin would have been even higher in 1979 if nuclear capacity ready to enter service had been licensed on schedule, instead of being delayed by the aftermath of the Three Mile Island accident. In mid-1980, scheduled capacity additions averaged about 25 GW for the decade ahead, more than double the 1973–1979 average annual increases in peak demand. If the capacity additions scheduled in 1980 actually materialize, and if peak load growth averages 3 percent per year, the U.S. generating industry's reserve margin will be nearly 55 percent by the end of the decade. (At 2 percent peak load growth it would be nearly 70 percent.)

More strikingly, even if there were no further nuclear capacity additions beyond that which was on-line in 1979, the industry's capacity reserve margin would be about 35 percent at the end of the decade.[15]

Outside the United States, particularly in Western Europe and Japan, a significant countervailing force emerges in government policy to encourage electrification. In some countries, this could push electricity demand growth back toward historic rates and hence provide a potential market for new power stations. For several years the governments of France, the Federal Republic of Germany, and Sweden, for example, have encouraged the expanded use of electricity for space heating.

These policies are usually justified by the presumed consequent reduction in demand for and/or dependence on imported oil. The technical merits of this argument are, however, much flimsier than many public officials and business executives appear to understand. The nuclear critics are right that it is a misleading oversimplification to view the oil dependence problem as merely a question of how to supply substitute energy—of any kind, at any price—to replace oil. Demand for energy is not homogeneous; the real challenge is to

---

[15] Charles A. Benore, "Electric Utility Industry Investment Outlook" (New York: Paine Webber Mitchell Hutchins Inc., May 1980), pp. 6–7.

It is important to note that the excess capacity of the U.S. electric power industry is by no means evenly spread across the country. Actual supply shortages could even materialize in many parts of the midwest, in California, and in southern Florida. Moreover, the apparent excess capacity would, of course, be reduced sharply if significant amounts of oil-fired equipment became unusable.

My colleague at the Harvard Business School Robert A. Leone has developed a considerable body of instructional material on the challenge of capacity management in rising cost industries, for the automobile, steel, and forest products industries, as well as electric power. Much of this material is taught in a course called "Manufacturing Policy" as part of the Harvard MBA curriculum.

replace oil with the type of energy that is best suited to a particular end use. There is considerable merit in Amory Lovin's quip that using electricity for space heating is like "using a chain saw to slice butter."

On the other hand, it is also true that in many countries, particularly in Western Europe and Japan, official promotion of centrally generated, steam-electricity is based on several considerations. Among them, cost-effectiveness may by no means be the most important. Many officials in other countries see in the promotion of nuclear power a means to such diverse ends as currency protection, industrial development, competition for high technology export markets, and national security. This perception may turn out to be mistaken, but it is not completely irrational.

Political obstacles to nuclear growth

Adverse macroeconomic conditions—some directly attributable to oil price increases—have hurt nuclear power. But it is also evident that political opposition to the technology has played an important independent role. In fact, in no country can politics and economics be easily separated. It has, for example, become popular for nuclear critics to maintain that "nuclear power has failed the test of the marketplace."[16] This seems disingenuous.

The worldwide controversy that the nuclear critics have themselves pro-duced has obviously had an adverse effect on the absolute costs of nuclear power. And, even with the longer lead times in plant licensing and con-struction, and the increased environmental and safety regulation imposed on reactors, their costs relative to coal plants remain more competitive than many nuclear critics contend.[17]

The opposition to nuclear power is by no means a homogeneous political movement either across countries or within a given country. In Europe and Asia, as in the United States, some nuclear critics oppose the technology in ab-solute terms and want existing facilities dismantled as soon as possible. Others appear prepared to accept plants that are either operating or under con-struction, but oppose new commitments. Still others are worried about specific issues—reactor safety, nuclear weapons proliferation, waste disposal—but claim a willingness to accept nuclear power in principle. Finally, some persons, who seem to be more numerous or at least more visible outside the United States, oppose nuclear power as a symbol of an entire social structure which they reject.[18]

---

[16] Amory Lovins, et al., "Nuclear Power and Nuclear Bombs" *Foreign Affairs* (July 1980).

[17] Hans H. Landsberg, et al., *Energy: The Next Twenty Years,* op. cit., ch. 12; see also, Bupp and Derian, *Light Water,* op. cit., ch. 9.

[18] Dorothy Nelkin and Michael Pollock, "Ideology as Strategy: The Discourse of the Anti-Nuclear Movement in France and Germany," *Science, Technology and Human Values,* 5, 30 (Winter 1980); See also Sadruddin Aga Khan, "The Nuclear Power Debate in Western Europe," *Bulletin of the Atomic Scientists* (September 1979).

Although there are wide variations across countries in the forms that opposition to nuclear power has taken, it is evident that there are certain conditions under which this opposition can influence nuclear growth and others that, at least in the short term, effectively preclude it from doing so.

For example, reactor siting decisions are subject to local or provincial government approval in the United States, the Federal Republic of Germany, Canada, Japan, and Sweden, but not in the United Kingdom or France. In general, local or provincial government involvement seems to work to the advantage of the nuclear critics. Licensing decisions can be challenged in the courts in the United States and the Federal Republic of Germany, but not in Canada, France, Japan, Sweden, or the United Kingdom. Again, the former rules generally help the nuclear critics.

In Sweden, the United Kingdom, and France, authority to certify the "need" for a new reactor rests unambiguously with the national government. In the Federal Republic of Germany and Canada it rests with regional governments, as it also does to a growing degree in the United States. In this area, too, regional governmental control is an asset for nuclear critics.

On the whole, the evidence of the 1970s strongly suggests that in the developed countries nuclear power is vulnerable to criticism where political authority is fragmented by federalism and/or where judicial authorities exercise broad mandates to challenge administrative agencies. Conversely, nuclear development benefits from centralization of government and narrow limits on rights of judicial review. Only in France and the USSR have nuclear advocates been able, for the time being at least, to prevent their opponents from tying reactor licensing and other aspects of nuclear decision making in a tangle of procedural knots that will take time and political power to undo.

Many American nuclear advocates, however, often speak and act as if they do not understand that the explanation for the striking success of the French nuclear program is not their "greater rationality," but rather is deeply set in the electoral, administrative, and legal structures of the country itself. Licensing reform is not merely administrative rationalization. It is modification of the basic rights of political participation.

During the 1960s and early 1970s, generally the major political parties in Western Europe were favorable or indifferent to nuclear power. Although conservative parties remain largely pronuclear, some new patterns began to emerge in 1978 and 1979. Minority "center" parties in Scandinavia became decidedly antinuclear, while liberal parties in the Federal Republic of Germany and the United Kingdom split on the issue. This was an important development, since many of these parties held the balance of power in coalition governments.

The large social democratic parties of central and northern Europe—in Austria, Switzerland, Denmark, the Federal Republic of Germany, Norway, Sweden—were all deeply divided over the nuclear issue and, as a consequence often lost significant political power. The powerful communist parties of southern Europe—in France, Italy, and Spain—remained strong nuclear advocates, although they typically demanded nationalization of various sectors of the industry. Across western Europe, an antinuclear alliance of farmers and urban intellectuals faced an equally odd pronuclear coalition of urban workers and members of the industrial establishment.[19]

Appreciation of the predicament of nuclear power in the United States at the beginning of the 1980s is especially important for speculation about what is likely to happen in much of the rest of the world, particularly in the other representative democracies. Developments in the United States are much more likely to decisively influence the future of nuclear power abroad than vice-versa.

I want to emphasize that this is a judgement about politics, not about technology. It is based on the hypothesis that if the United States is perceived or can be portrayed by nuclear critics as having "abandoned the nuclear option," then sooner or later elected public officials in all of the representative democracies will come under pressure to do likewise. Such pressure seems likely to develop most rapidly and to be the least resistible in Scandinavia and the Federal Republic of Germany. But, in time, even French officials are likely to feel it. Obviously, the consequences anywhere are difficult to predict. But what is crucial is the direction of the causal linkage: movement from a U.S. nuclear collapse to similar developments abroad seems to me, on political grounds, to be far more likely than movement from nuclear success abroad to a revival of the U.S. program. Stated differently, salvaging the U.S. nuclear program will have to be done domestically or it will not be done at all.

Nuclear power's bleak future in the United States

In 1980, the investor-owned electric power companies in the United States were in very deep financial trouble. Many were all but technically bankrupt, dangerously illiquid, and hamstrung for capital by the need to maintain simultaneously high common stock dividend payments and costly power plant construction programs.[20] Continuing escalation of nuclear power plant capital costs combined with near paralysis of the federal government's licensing apparatus threatened as many as two dozen companies with financial collapse.

At the time of the April 1979 accident at Three Mile Island about ninety nuclear plants were under construction in the United States. These ninety or so were then scheduled to begin operation at the approximate rate of eight to ten

---

[19] The observation on the relative nuclear positions of the European political parties arise from conversations with my colleagues Jean-Claude Derian and Mans Lonnroth in early 1980.

[20] E. Kahn, "Bankruptcy Risk in the Utility Industry: Policy Issues," working draft, Lawrence Laboratory, Berkeley, June 1980; See also, Irvin C. Bupp, et al., "Some Background Information on the Financial Condition of Certain Investor-Owned Electric Power Companies," prepared for a conference:"Conservation and the Electric Utilities," Keystone Center for Continuing Education, Keystone, Colorado, 28–30 March 1980.

per year during the 1980s. By the end of 1979, some forty-five electric utility companies had already spent on the order of $40 billion on these projects.

The accident at Harrisburg began a period of great uncertainty for these companies, captured by a remark made a few days later by an executive of one of them: "We've spent $400 million on a $1 billion new nuclear plant. The fate of that investment now appears to depend on the outcome of a semihysterical process."

In fact, the Nuclear Regulatory Commission did, for a time, formally suspend the granting of new licenses. This suspension was, in principle, lifted late in 1979. In practice, however, the effect was minimal. Two new reactors were given limited authority to load fuel and to conduct certain tests. But the timing of full resumption of "normal" licensing activities remained highly uncertain in mid-1980. In June 1980, the U.S. Congress passed legislation by a nearly unanimous vote of both Houses that, among other things, required the NRC to withhold new reactor operating licenses pending its approval of "emergency response plans" for each new plant. This requirement alone is certain to mean additional delays of problematic length for most reactors nearing completion.

In late 1979, the NRC, under Federal Court order, announced a "rule-making" proceeding to review its confidence that radioactive waste can be disposed. Several of the most effective antinuclear organizations, joined by the governments of several states—California, New York, Wisconsin—have mounted a major effort to challenge the credibility of the federal government's waste disposal program. The "waste confidence" proceeding that began in late summer of 1979 will, at best, be an extremely difficult undertaking for the Nuclear Regulatory Commission. A number of outcomes are possible, but it is a good bet that in 1980 or 1981 progress on waste disposal will be linked in some fashion to new reactor licenses. [21]

The NRC has also said it would review its basic siting standards for nuclear power plants. Again, various things might happen, but it is all but certain in 1980 or 1981 that the NRC will issue relatively restrictive new criteria governing the location of reactors. Some members of the Commission have stated that any modification of siting standards for new reactors would oblige the agency then to consider the very difficult question of whether to allow older plants that do not meet the new standards to continue or to begin operation. It is, of course, only reasonable to suppose that any or all NRC decisions on these matters will provoke legal challenges by the aggrieved parties.

These circumstances nearly guarantee many additional months if not years of chaos, delay, and unpredictability in reactor licensing policy and practice. But even they are only part of the story. It is critical to bear in mind that the NRC by no means retains the old Atomic Energy Commission's effective

---

[21] For an excellent summary of the issues in this important proceeding see "Statement of Position of the California Energy Commission in the Matter of Proposed Rulemaking on the Storage and Disposal of Nuclear Wastes," available from the Office of Commissioner E. E. Varanini, Jr., 1111 Howe Avenue, Sacramento, California, July 1980.

monopoly over nuclear regulatory policy. Instead, at least a dozen independent agencies and bureaus in the Executive Branch claim jurisdiction over various aspects of nuclear power plant licensing and operation. Differences on both strategy and objective exist among these organizations. In certain cases many are proceeding at direct cross-purposes.

In the U.S. Congress, the 1960s monopoly of legislative authority held by the Joint Committee on Atomic Energy has been replaced by competition among as many as two dozen separate committees and subcommittees, again, often moving at cross-purposes or in direct conflict. No locus of potential central power or authority exists.

Institutional decentralization, if not fragmentation, is, of course, a typical and not a unique characteristic of the American political system. It does not necessarily mean programmatic stalemate or policy immobilization. But it is a characteristic that presents special problems for the resolution of conflict with highly polarized and deeply entrenched minority positions. In the American political system, real compromise—the ubiquitous "deal"—is usually required in order to move ahead. But a deal, in turn, requires that each party is willing to concede something of value in the interest of settlement. The stalemate over nuclear power is the fully predictable result of one or more parties to a dispute holding out for total victory in a system which provides others with numerous opportunities to prevent that outcome.[22]

The central fact about the political environment in which the Three Mile meltdown occurred is that the nuclear advocates and the nuclear critics both in and outside the federal government can in large measure block each other's goals, frustrate each other's policies, and hence prevent the development of any coherent strategy in reactor licensing.

This breakdown raises very serious questions about the future of the approximately seventy nuclear plants that were operating at the time the meltdown at Three Mile Island occurred. It also represents a clear and present danger to the operation of the ninety plants that were being built and the forty that were on order. Most obvious of all, though, it makes the question of new orders—an end to the four-year-old purchasing moratorium—moot for at least several years.

Reviewing the results of earlier research, a French government official said: "What you have told is the story of the abuse of a technology." The phrase has stuck in my mind. In the United States more than thirty years of such abuse—by nuclear advocates as well as nuclear critics—has deeply, prob-

---

[22] For nearly three years, I have been Executive Director of the Keystone Radioactive Waste Management Discussion Group. During that period some 120 different persons met about a dozen times. They included nuclear industry executives, antinuclear activists, government officials, and academics, representing a wide variety of opinions over the acceptability of nuclear power.

From these meetings it is my personal opinion that currently, in the United States, the chief obstacle to a "deal" on nuclear power is the intransigence of the pronuclear interests. Far too many influential nuclear advocates refuse to abandon or at least defer reprocessing and breeder reactors. In effect they still want the whole cake. I view such behavior as suicidal.

ably mortally, wounded nuclear power. A worldwide diagnosis, with the probable exceptions of France and the USSR, is not qualitatively different.

A mortally wounded technology

In 1980 most of the world's political and economic leaders still probably strongly agree with the proposition that "nuclear power has an important role to play." For the rest of this century and for the early decades of the next century nuclear power will be the only feasible alternative to coal for the generation of base-load electricity.

Is such an alternative needed? The answer, naturally, varies from country to country. But for all countries it is very difficult to be certain, in part, because no one can do much more than guess about how much new base-load electrical generating capacity will be needed in the decades ahead. There are even bigger uncertainties about the health, safety, and environmental impacts of coal. The best bet from what is already known, however, is that the news about coal is going to be very discouraging. Hence, it does seem likely that energy policymakers in most countries will continue to want a nonoil or a non-gas alternative to coal for base-load electric power production.

There are probably two necessary conditions to keeping the nuclear option to coal open in most countries. The first is unassailable validation of the operational safety of light water reactors. The second is equally unassailable validation of the environmental safety of radioactive waste disposal.

My own guess is that the second of these is, politically and institutionally, by far the more difficult.

The American radioactive waste disposal program has a long way to go in an especially complex and hostile political environment. Many local and state officials—including the governors of certain key states—seem determined to prevent even the storage of spent fuel, to say nothing of the ultimate disposal of waste material, within their jurisdictions. This pattern is likely to be repeated in other countries.

In spite of official rhetoric about "indefinite deferrals" and in spite of the nuclear industry's fervent desires, reprocessing of spent reactor fuel is a dead letter in the United States. There is simply no chance of it happening on any commercially significant scale in this century. The French will surely press ahead at La Hague in the face of very high costs, very real technical uncertainties, and unresolved occupational health and safety issues. Their probability of unambiguous success in the 1980s is, most likely, on the order of 50–50. The future of the English and Japanese reprocessing programs is simply indeterminant.

On balance, it is highly probable that no commercially significant reprocessing—i.e., on the order of a few hundred tons or more of spent fuel per year—will occur anywhere, with the possible exception of La Hague, until at least the 1990s. Even then, reduced demand for light water reactors seems nearly certain to hold worldwide average uranium prices well below the $100 per pound range where reprocessing, by optimistic estimate, may be economically attractive.

This means that essentially all of the spent fuel that will be discharged from nuclear power plants around the world will be stored in water pools for considerable periods of time, perhaps several decades. Moreover since transportation systems are essentially nonexistent, most of this storage will probably be at power plant sites. This is almost certainly the case in the United States where on-site spent fuel inventories will threaten the widespread shutdown of many operating reactors as early as the mid-1980s.

Finally, a small handful of breeder reactor research and development programs will remain highly visible, politically diversionary, and commercially inconsequential symbols of the vanished dreams of the older generation of the world's nuclear advocates.

These prospects combine to make an arresting and a disturbing picture. Are we headed toward a "worst of all possible" outcomes, in which a mortally wounded technology makes only marginal, temporary, and expensive contributions to legitimate energy supply and energy security needs, while at the same time it effectively removes one of the most important technical and economic barriers to quite widespread nuclear weapons proliferation?

At this point it will be no surprise that my own answer is a gloomy "yes."[23]

General appreciation of this highly probable outcome is obscured by the rhetoric of those on both sides of the battle over the technology's future. Advocates persist in confusing aspiration with accomplishment. This enhances the anxieties of many nuclear critics, who often react by lamenting some of the very circumstances—skyrocketing construction costs, stagnation in responsible spent fuel management and waste disposal—that they themselves have helped bring about.

Advocates and critics alike have demonstrated considerable ingenuity in substituting unsubstantiated dogma for pragmatic confrontation of some really tough issues. Take, for example, the standard argument of nuclear advocates that further increases in oil prices will automatically ratify the economic attractiveness of nuclear power. The truth of this proposition is far from self-evident. One predictable consequence of continued oil price rises is general economic inflation. Another is recession. It is doubtful that such macro-economic conditions are congenial to the rapid growth of a highly capital intensive technology with pay-off lead-times of a decade or more. Indeed the most obvious general economic consequences of continued oil price increases seem at least as likely to deter additional investments in nuclear

[23] I find support for this opinion in Pierre Lellouche, "Breaking the Rules Without Stopping the Bomb," in this issue of *International Organization*.

power as to promote them. For one thing an inflationary economy that may also be in recession is hardly a congenial climate in which to try to pass on investment costs to present consumers. But in the United States, and perhaps elsewhere, it is increasingly likely that consumers as well as equity investors will have to bear a greater share of the capital cost burden of nuclear power plant construction.

Among many economists there is growing speculation that there may be a causal link, rather than a mere correlation, between the increasing oil prices of 1973–1980 and the sluggish performance of the world's industrialized economies during the same period.[24] The magnitude of this link, if it exists, is likely to remain both speculative and controversial for some time. For the purposes of this review of the prospects for nuclear power, it is only possible to table the strong suggestion that rising oil prices may not have the automatically salutary effects for the world's nuclear industry that have been conventionally assumed.

Moreover, the chief threat to the nuclear investments of even the state-owned utilities outside the United States is probably macro-economic constraints on public expenditures. Such constraints have already slowed down nuclear power growth in Canada, where the Ontario provincial government has sharply restricted Ontario Hydro's capital budget.

One can even imagine circumstances in France where the combination of inflation and recession would oblige the government to retard the pace of EDF's nuclear investment.

On the other side of the battle, most nuclear critics have not come to grips with the implications of the tens-of-billions of dollars that have been invested in assets that are not close to the end (in the majority of cases have not even begun) their productive lives. Abandoning these assets before they have returned their enormous original investment cost would be a national economic trauma everywhere nuclear programs exist. Even if mistakes have been made in the pace and scope of nuclear development, it is simply an illusion to suppose that their costs can be limited to the individuals or organizations who made them.

The unpleasant truth is that neither killing off nor resuscitating the world's mortally wounded nuclear technology is going to be easy if it is done responsibly. All of the automatic outcomes of the current situation are also bad outcomes. Yet the time remaining to avoid them is terribly short. A conservative guess would be less than five years.

---

[24] This was a topic of considerable discussion at the 1980 Annual Meeting of the International Association of Energy Economists, held at Cambridge University, England, 23–25 June 1980.

5

Multinational Alternatives and Nuclear Nonproliferation

Lawrence Scheinman

The application of multinational institutional arrangements to sensitive nuclear fuel cycle facilities has attracted the attention of nonproliferation policymakers since the outset of the nuclear age. The Baruch Plan was the earliest and most far reaching formulation of this approach. It proposed that, rather than leaving potentially dangerous nuclear activities to national development, subject only to inspection to assure nondiversion of technology for military purposes, such activities should be placed under international ownership and control.

Institutional arrangements in the Atoms-for-Peace era conversely emphasized political commitments and verification safeguards, rather than organizational strategies designed to curtail the spread of national fuel cycle facilities, and, indeed, expected the spread of such facilities as fuel cycle development progressed. In the past decade, especially since 1974, there has been a resurgence of interest in institutional arrangement more comprehensive than international safeguards, and considerable attention is again being given to multinational alternatives. In this chapter we will examine the rationale for multinational institutions, and then review some of the multinational experience in the nuclear sector. We will consider why multinational approaches have drawn renewed attention in the years since the 1974 Indian detonation.

The author, currently Professor of Government at Cornell University, was Senior Advisor to the Undersecretary and Deputy to the Deputy Undersecretary of State for Security Assistance, Science and Technology during the first two years of the Carter administration. As one of the artisans of U.S. nonproliferation policy he was an advocate of multinational strategies and his contribution to this volume should be read with this involvement in mind.

We will also assess the political feasibility of multinational approaches to fuel cycle problems, and evaluate the potential policy consequences for non-proliferation.

The rationale for multinational institutional arrangements

The rationale for multinational institutional arrangements for the nuclear fuel cycle is relatively straightforward. The dispersion of nationally controlled sensitive facilities now threatens to transform weapons proliferation; the adequacy of international verification safeguards for preventing this is at issue, while bilateral controls are becoming less feasible and less effective, and the international community is not ready for more comprehensive international solutions.

The objective of nonproliferation policy is to maintain a separation between peaceful and nonpeaceful uses of nuclear energy, and to ensure that access to the peaceful benefits of nuclear technology does not increase the risk of weapons spread. International cooperation in peaceful nuclear energy has thus far been premised on political commitments to use nuclear transfers exclusively for peaceful purposes, combined with an acceptance of international safeguards to verify compliance with such commitments.

No nuclear fuel cycle is entirely free of some proliferation risk, but the level of nuclear activity in virtually all the nonnuclear weapon states was generally regarded, until the early 1970s, as fitting within the capabilities of IAEA safeguards. The dissemination of materials and facilities which could pose a serious proliferation risk (plutonium, highly enriched uranium, reprocessing facilities, enrichment plants) was very limited. International nuclear commerce was conducted on the basis of the political commitments referred to above, reinforced by the NPT, which extended safeguards undertakings for participating nonnuclear weapon states to all peaceful nuclear activities, regardless of whether they were based on imported or indigenously developed materials. And there was high confidence in the system of international safeguards to verify compliance with those commitments. Coincidentally, this was an era in which the United States exerted predominant influence over the shape, structure, and conditions of international nuclear development and commerce.[1]

As discussed by Joseph Nye in this issue, an erosion of confidence in the international nuclear regime set in with the diminishing of U.S. predominance,

---

[1] For a general overview of the evolution of nonproliferation policy and the strategy of the Carter administration see Joseph S. Nye, "Nonproliferation: The Long-Term Strategy," *Foreign Affairs* (April 1978): 601–23; and Lawrence Scheinman, "Towards a New Nonproliferation Regime," *Nuclear Materials Management* VII, 1 (Spring 1978): 25–29. See also Bertrand Goldschmidt, "A Historical Survey of Nonproliferation Policies," *International Security* II, 1 (Summer 1977): 69–87.

and the increasing dispersion of sensitive technologies for which verification safeguards were not fully adequate. This was accompanied in 1974 by the graphic illustration of the Indian test, showing the ultrafine line between peaceful and nonpeaceful uses of nuclear technology, and also suggesting a limited effectiveness of international safeguards alone for sustaining a nonproliferation regime. The transition to a new and more complex level of nuclear development, leading states into a position to possess directly weapons-usable materials, put a fundamentally different cast on the definition of regime effectiveness.

The central problem for nonproliferation policy after 1974, then, was how to cope with this challenge to regime effectiveness. In principle the problem could be approached technically (seeking to modify materials or facilities to neutralize their proliferation threat, identifying alternative fuel cycles which might avoid or limit access to sensitive materials), institutionally (establishing rules and arrangements to reduce the risks associated with deployment of sensitive technologies, such as limiting the character, location and operation of sensitive facilities, and placing conditions on the use of the material they produce), or through a combination of mutually reinforcing technical and institutional measures.

In fact both technical and institutional strategies were devised for dealing with the problem of sensitive materials. Explicitly technical approaches lie outside the purpose of this essay. Nevertheless, it is important to note that extensive technical analyses of fuel cycles (and particularly their components) were undertaken at the national and international levels. These assessments suggested various technical ways of increasing fuel cycle proliferation-resistance, but they also underscored the economic, technical, and timeliness limitations inherent in many of them. The International Nuclear Fuel Cycle Evaluation (INFCE), for example, found several potential technical improvements which were more promising for dealing with subnational seizure threats than national proliferation risks, either because the technical improvement could be reversed, or because a determined state could build a clandestine facility to carry out the illicit activity. As one analyst has pointed out, "one of the clearest messages to emerge from these studies (INFCE, NASAP) is that, in general, the impact of (technical) measures on the full range of proliferation risks is limited"[2]—i.e., they do not, of themselves, compensate for the identified deficiencies of verification safeguards for sensitive materials and facilities, since they do not come to grips with the issue of prevention of misuse. This does not foreclose deployment of existing, or as yet unidentified, technical approaches to improving the proliferation resistance of the nuclear fuel cycle, but it does place them in a less prominent context than some might have anticipated.

---

[2] Edward Wonder, "INFCE and International Institutions," in *Next Steps After INFCE: U.S. International Nuclear and Nonproliferation,* Rodney W. Jones, ed. (Washington, D.C.: Georgetown University, March 1980).

Institutional responses have both near- and long-term dimensions. They also address a different level of the problem—control over misappropriation of nuclear material and technology, rather than the detection of such misappropriation, which is the central thrust of international safeguards today. In the near-term, the American-initiated supplier state discussions (in what came to be known as the London Group) sought to achieve some consensus on export policy—to avoid the risk that commercial competition would undermine international safeguards objectives. Following its own intended export policy practice, the United States also sought agreement for a moratorium on further transfers of sensitive technology, or at least a mandatory supplier state involvement wherever any future transfer might be made. The eventual supplier guideline dealing with this matter only recommends, but does not require, such involvement;[3] but the principal supplier states capable of making such transfers have indicated their intention not to make any such further transfers in the foreseeable future.

Seeking to impose a moratorium on transfers of sensitive technology might be an appropriate initial response to gain time while more far-reaching and effective international arrangements are devised, but technology denial itself cannot be a viable long-term nonproliferation strategy. Some structurally-intermediate arrangement to deal with the problem over the longer term has to be found, if nonproliferation is to remain effective—since national forbearance in seeking access to advanced higher-risk technologies cannot last indefinitely, and Baruch-type solutions remain inconsistent with political realities.

In such circumstances, a number of alternatives can be identified, including: (1) supplier-state commitments to fully-reliable assurance of supply, together with multilateral and/or international fall-back provisions in the event of supplier breach of obligation, such as an internationally negotiated nuclear fuel safety net, or an international nuclear fuel bank; (2) the conducting of sensitive activities on a national basis, under carefully defined and significantly augmented international controls, particularly over resulting sensitive nuclear materials; and (3) joint arrangements for technological activity, such as multinational sensitive fuel cycle ventures.

All of these approaches deal in some measure with the problem of control, although the extent to which they do so depends heavily on the commitments to which the participants agree. The first approach really amounts to a consumer dependence on enhanced supplier integrity, coupled with international mechanisms in the event of a breach of commitment. While potentially attractive to many, this approach, as suggested in the analysis undertaken in the INFCE Working Group III, may not be satisfactory where countries want reduced external dependence or a direct equity stake in the sup-

[3] International Atomic Energy Agency, "Communications Received from Certain Member States Regarding Guidelines for the Export of Nuclear Material, Equipment, and Technology," INFCIRC/254 (Vienna: IAEA, February 1978).

ply system upon which they must rely.[4] The second approach essentially endorses national development and deployment of sensitive fuel cycle facilities, although under substantially upgraded controls and restraints.[5] Whereas the first alternative appears weighted toward nonproliferation interests, by implicitly curtailing the spread of sensitive activities, and thus may not adequately meet all energy security concerns, the second alternative very likely would be found deficient on nonproliferation criteria.

The third approach, that of multinational arrangements, is tantamount to denationalizing sensitive fuel cycle activities by placing decisions on the operation of nuclear facilities, as well as on the disposition of their product, in the hands of the collectivity rather than the individual states. On its face it appears to meet energy security concerns by providing participants with a legal and economic stake in the supply system, and to meet nonproliferation concerns by limiting the spread of sensitive facilities, localizing and complicating the risk of proliferation, and going beyond conventional verification safeguards. It also, however, involves the development of new organizational arrangements of a potentially complex political, economic, and managerial nature, and importantly requires states' agreement forsaking exclusively national control over energy technology.

In the remainder of this article we will explore the various aspects of multinational institutional arrangements as they relate to nonproliferation. Any evaluation must take three factors into account. (1) There is no single, generic multinational formula that would be satisfactory for all technologies and all partners. While all such ventures will have to meet certain basic requirements, successful implementation of multinationalism will depend on the flexibility of its application. One of the apparent virtues of the multinational concept is that it is capable of being developed in a variety of ways, as such ventures as EURODIF, URENCO and EUROCHEMIC illustrate. (2) Multinational arrangements are not stand-alone nonproliferation options. Arranging multinational ownership, management, or operation does not offer any significant nonproliferation benefit by itself, and even could have the counterproductive effect of stimulating an unnecessary early deployment of high-risk technology. Multinational arrangements must be part of an integrated regime which covers not only the facility itself, but the material produced—although different organizations could have different responsibilities under an umbrella regime. In the case of multinational reprocessing, for example, it would contribute little to nonproliferation if participating members were free to remove the separated plutonium from the reprocessing

---

[4] IAEA, "Assurances of Long-Term Supply of Technology, Fuel, Heavy Water and Services in the Interest of National Needs Consistent with Nonproliferation," INFCE/PC/2/3 (Vienna: IAEA, January 1980).

[5] This approach is examined and endorsed in Myron B. Kratzer, *Multinational Institutions and Nonproliferation: A New Look,* Occasional Paper No. 20 (Muscatine, IA.: The Stanley Foundation, 1979).

plant to use as they saw fit, subject only to international safeguards. To be effective in nonproliferation terms, a multinational arrangement would have to ensure not only that the facility and its technology could not be abused, but also that its product would be subject to appropriate international or multinational controls over its storage, release, use, and disposition. For maximum effectiveness, the control arrangements would have to be established in a framework of understandings and commitments incorporating all of the principal elements of sensitive fuel cycle activity. (3) An institutional arrangement can only be as strong as the foundation upon which it is built. Multinationalism, or any other institutional approach, cannot substitute for consensus; it can only reflect and reinforce that consensus. To be viable, institutions must be politically acceptable, thus requiring a consensus on the nature, purpose, and limits of the nuclear fuel cycle, and on how nonproliferation and energy security goals relate to one another.

Multinationalism in historic perspective

The term multinational has been used to describe a broad array of institutional arrangements, from joint ownership and management of facilities at one end of the spectrum, to market-sharing arrangements between nationally owned and operated facilities at the other.[6] While this demonstrates flexibility, it also entails a lack of precision that reduces the analytic utility of the concept. We will use multinational in the broad sense when discussing different specific ventures; but in later evaluating multinationalism for nonproliferation objectives, we will define it as an arrangement in which three or more governments agree to the establishment of an entity involving joint ownership, and where national decisions regarding the entity are subordinate to group determination. Joint ownership may or may not extend to joint operation. The essential point is that control and decision making are not defined or carried out on a purely national basis.

Some generic observations

A number of multinational ventures in sensitive nuclear fuel cycle activities have been established in the past. Almost without exception they have involved the West European countries which were technologically advanced and shared common interests. They have been largely focused on the development and initial deployment of emerging nuclear technologies, and they have

---

[6] For a useful discussion of multinational nuclear arrangements see Horst Mendershausen, "The Multinationalization of Reprocessing and Enrichment: How and Where?" a Paper Presented to the International Conference on Reconciling Energy Needs and Nonproliferation, Bad-Godesburg (May 1979). See also Abram Chayes and W. B. Lewis, eds., *International Arrangements for Nuclear Fuel Reprocessing* (Cambridge, Mass.: Ballinger Press, 1977).

been primarily motivated by economic, technical, commercial, or resource considerations, rather than by nonproliferation concerns. This does not mean that nonproliferation factors were entirely lacking in the shaping of the arrangements, or that nonproliferation did not benefit from their establishment. But it does underscore the factors which have been most important in prompting states to accept some limitation on national decision making and authority. Each of the four principal nuclear ventures normally regarded as multinational—URENCO and EURODIF (uranium enrichment consortia), and EUROCHEMIC and United Reprocessors Group (URG) (spent fuel reprocessing and plutonium separation consortia)—placed restrictions on the transfer of technology to parties outside the arrangement, but principally for commercial reasons. In the case of EURODIF no provision was made for sharing the most sensitive (barrier) technology even among consortia members—the technology being reserved exclusively to the host state. On the other hand, in no instance was membership in the venture conditioned on national renunciation of efforts to develop the technology covered by the agreement, or alternative technologies which could provide sensitive material. This is, of course, precisely the kind of consideration that arises when nonproliferation objectives are taken into account. It is clear from this example, however, that nonproliferation and economic considerations can coincide and be mutually reinforcing, and that state acceptance of restraints in order to achieve a technical or resource benefit can work to the advantage of nonproliferation.

Efforts to sustain multinational arrangements over time have been somewhat less successful in reprocessing than similar efforts in the field of uranium enrichment. In part this is because reprocessing technology is much more widely known, and uses more conventional industrial techniques than enrichment, which until recently was based exclusively on a very sophisticated, industrially-complex and highly classified gaseous diffusion technology. Even the newer and presumably simpler centrifuge enrichment technology is still in an emergent state, and subject to the kind of uncertainties which made joint ventures involving cost- and risk-sharing more appealing.

It might also be explained by the fact that reprocessing is essential to the use of breeder reactors. Such breeders have generally been regarded as the ultimate rationale for making a large-scale nuclear commitment in the first place. For countries committed to deployment of breeders, economy-of-scale arguments for multinational facilities would not be very persuasive, since national plants in this area would rival multinational facilities in size. As national facilities, moreover, they would not be burdened by the inevitable problems of joint management and operation.

For countries with smaller programs, the attractions of large multinational reprocessing facilities could be significant, if they brought state-of-the-art technology and economies of scale to bear in support of their own more modest requirements. However, even these countries might find smaller national plants preferable, for the same operational and management reasons as countries with larger programs, and might not even find economy-of-scale arguments so persuasive, in view of the relatively modest cost (several percent) attributable to reprocessing, as compared with the total cost of nuclear power generation.

Specific historic cases

EUROCHEMIC, the first multinational nuclear venture, was created in the 1950s under the auspices of the European Nuclear Energy Agency (ENEA) of the Organization for European Economic Cooperation (OEEC).[7] Its termination in 1974, in the face of competition from larger national installations in member countries, has frequently been offered as proof of the weakness and improbability of effective multinational arrangements. This, of course, quite misses the point. EUROCHEMIC was established to serve as a training center in which reprocessing technologies could be acquired, various fuel types and techniques could be explored, and industrial experience could be developed. It was *not* designed as a means of averting the spread of reprocessing technology, or as an alternative to national development, even though some of its members (particularly the smaller states) might have hoped for the eventual emergence of a single European reprocessing consortium which would provide a partnership of a magnitude beyond their purely national capabilities. In terms of its mandate, EUROCHEMIC was a success. It facilitated and launched the basis for industrial capability in a new technological field. If it did not evolve into Europe's commercial industrial reprocessing enterprise, this must be measured against its mandate.

In view of its avowed technology transfer purpose, and the absence of any ban on parallel national technological development, EUROCHEMIC would not be a particularly good model for nonproliferation-oriented multi-nationalism. On the other hand, ten years of such multinational training and development activity in a high technology area represents an experience and institutional dynamic which can provide important lessons for future ventures—lessons with respect to the appropriate breadth or limitation of mission, organizational arrangements, allocation of ownership shares and interest, financial obligation, and degree of restraint imposed on participants regarding parallel activity. Indeed, its provision for an external control organ of participating state governments to deal with problems of common concern while avoiding interference in operational activities has been taken into account by subsequent multinational nuclear industrial ventures.

URG is a successor multinational reprocessing venture to EURO-

---

[7] EUROCHEMIC's experience is discussed in Bertrand Goldschmidt, *Le Complexe Atomique* (Paris: Fayard, 1980) and more extensively in International Energy Associates Ltd (IEAL), "Institutional Arrangements for the Reduction of Proliferation Risks," Report to the Department of Energy, December 1979.

CHEMIC in only the broadest sense of that term. It was created in the early 1970s by the three principal partners in EUROCHEMIC—Great Britain, France, and the Federal Republic of Germany—basically in anticipation of an overcapacity of reprocessing services and a desire to avoid the risk of destructive competition among European industries.[8] It was intended to rationalize the use of existing capacity, to coordinate planning, construction, and deployment of new plants, and to facilitate the exchange of technical information. One of its first acts, in retrospect of no mean significance, was to successfully encourage deferral of German plans to build a commercial reprocessing plant. Deferral ultimately pushed construction of that plant at Gorleben into a rather changed domestic and international context, with environmental and antinuclear forces at home contesting continued nuclear development in West Germany, and with American nonproliferation policy encouraging continued deferral of commercial reprocessing plant construction, until economically justified in the framework of a firmly established breeder reactor development program.

When reprocessing came to be seen as a problem of undercapacity in the mid-1970s, as a result of changes in U.S. nuclear planning, and a slowdown in both Great Britain and France for technical reasons, URG still played a market-planning role in the allocation of existing and planned capacity, although more emphasis was given to technical exchanges than to commercial coordination. URG neither owns nor operates reprocessing plants; while the transfer of URG country technology to non-URG countries requires the unanimous consent of the three shareholders, and apparently their governments as well (unless laboratory scale transfers are involved, which would be a significant transfer in nonproliferation terms, though not in a commercial or industrial sense), the organization is an international collaborative arrangement rather than a multinational venture.

The two uranium enrichment consortia, URENCO and EURODIF, are institutional expressions of the movement towards a European enrichment capability which first appeared in the early days of EURATOM, but was largely deflected by U.S. policies that undercut the economic appeal of a European enrichment program.[9] Today, despite strain, they represent two different economic and industrial models of multinational ownership and operation, neither of which was established for explicitly nonproliferation purposes, but both of which contribute to that end.

URENCO is the more complex of the two organizations, embracing enrichment facilities in three countries—Great Britain, West Germany and the Netherlands. Based on the Treaty of Almelo, URENCO owns and operates

---

[8] On URG see C. Allday, "Some Experiences in Formation and Operation of Multinational Uranium-Enrichment and Fuel Reprocessing Organizations," in Chayes and Lewis, op. cit., pp. 177–88.
[9] This early episode is treated in Lawrence Scheinman, *Atomic Energy Policy in France Under the Fourth Republic* (Princeton: Princeton University Press, 1965), pp. 177–80.

gas centrifuge enrichment facilities in the three participating states, helps to coordinate research and development (which, since 1974, is the responsibility of each of the shareholders individually, rather than a collective responsibility), assures equal access to developments in centrifuge technology by any of the members, and executes contracts for the sale of services to third countries, based on the unanimous agreement of the participants.[10]

Industrial-operational and political responsibilities are kept separate. An intergovernmental Joint Committee, on which each of the participating governments has equal representation and voting rights, and which operates on the principle of unanimity, deals with all political aspects of URENCO activities. This includes such issues as membership, supervision, and control of the dissemination of centrifuge technology, and safeguards and nonproliferation conditions associated with contracts for enrichment services. URENCO provides a good example of the potential nonproliferation value of multinational arrangements, as well as the viability and utility of separating political and other decision-making authority. In 1975, the Federal Republic of Germany contracted to sell URENCO enriched uranium to Brazil. Although the agreement provided for the application of international safeguards to the material, it did not place any restrictions on the extraction and storage of plutonium produced in burning the URENCO-supplied fuel. This was regarded as insufficient by the Dutch government, as a result of which West Germany ultimately had to negotiate a revised agreement with the government of Brazil, including a requirement that any plutonium derived from URENCO-supplied fuel would be placed under an acceptable international plutonium storage regime. Multinationalism, in this case, helped to reinforce a nonproliferation objective, and, because of the division of political and managerial authority, did so without disrupting the industrial and operational responsibilities of the organization.

EURODIF involves five participating countries—France, Italy, Spain, Belgium and Iran—but only one enrichment facility.[11] Unlike URENCO, which has an external market orientation, EURODIF is intended to serve the domestic fuel requirements of its members. The level of investment of each member corresponds to its percentage share of the product, and sensitive barrier technology is provided and held by only one member, France. Other nonsensitive technology is shared, and nonsensitive equipment procurement is allocated among the members. Thus, while excluding the transfer or sharing of sensitive technology, EURODIF does provide participants with security of

---

[10] On URENCO, see Report of the Atlantic Council's Nuclear Fuels Policy Working Group, "Nuclear Power and Nuclear Weapons Proliferation," vol. II (June, 1978); IEAL, "Institutional Arrangements for the Reduction of Proliferation Risks," op. cit.; and C. Allday, op. cit.

[11] There is relatively little information available on EURODIF. A useful if incomplete description is to be found in M. Pecquer, J. H. Coates and M. Mezin, "Uranium Enrichment: One of Today's Industrial Realities," *Revue de l'Energie* 25, 265 (Aug.–Sept. 1974): 199–214.

supply, an equity share in a production enterprise utilizing proven advanced technology, and industrial spin-off benefits in all but the directly sensitive technology sector. Because EURODIF is not a manufacturing entity as is URENCO, this places limitations on the scope of spin-off benefits; but it does offer an added inducement, beyond that of access on a preferred basis to a secure supply of enriched uranium. EURODIF partners also have access to the data and information necessary to reach informed judgments on decisions in which all the participants share.

EURODIF is simple and straightforward in comparison with URENCO, since management, operations, and technology remain under the national control of the host state, and its potential contribution as a model for nonproliferation is proportionately greater. On the other hand, precisely because of the managerial, operational, and technological limitations this approach imposes on all but the host nation, its appeal may be limited to states which have little interest in the opportunity to participate in management-related activities or to have access to advanced technology, but are content to have assured access to fuel supply on a timely, predictable, and economically attractive basis.

Neither of the two enrichment consortia have been trouble free. URENCO has faced difficulties both in terms of technology and investment. It was originally intended that URENCO would develop a single centrifuge technology that would be exploited on a centralized basis. All of the participants, however, already had made heavy investments in technology development at the time URENCO was established, and they proved unwilling to forego this investment in favor of a common technological approach. As a result, it was decided in 1974 to permit each of the shareholders to continue developing its own technology and to determine which technology it will use in building new facilities. Insofar as investment was concerned, URENCO plants were to be built with equal ownership and investment by the three partners, regardless of location. By the mid-1970s that formula was revised in favor of a two-thirds national, one-third partners investment arrangement, in response to differences among the shareholders regarding the timeliness of constructing new facilities and the appropriate marketing philosophy.[12] At the present time, the formula has been revised to reflect a 90 percent national ownership in URENCO facilities. This change also has affected the management distribution, making each of the plants far less multinational than originally intended. All facilities, however, operate under the provisions and constraints of the Treaty of Almelo, and no shareholder has the ability to take any significant action without the approval of the other two partners.

EURODIF's problems have been of a somewhat different nature. Changes in the pace of national nuclear development has affected the timing

---

[12] See Allday, op. cit.

of requirements for enriched uranium, particularly in Italy which took a 23 percent share in EURODIF production at the time the organization was created. Unable to absorb its share of EURODIF production, yet required to take and pay for it, Italy has sought to alter its relationship to the consortium.[13] Some Italian political leaders have gone so far as to urge withdrawal entirely, but the dominant view has been to negotiate a reduction in Italy's share in EURODIF. This was accomplished in the summer of 1980 when the French partner, Cogema, agreed in principle to purchase more than one-half of Italy's interest, reducing the latter from 23 percent to 16 percent of EURODIF and, correspondingly, increasing Cogema's share of EURODIF from 42 percent to 51 percent, giving it majority control of the organization and further reducing its multinational character. This and the URENCO experience point up economic sensitivities of multinational arrangements which may serve as a lesson for other nations contemplating similar ventures. While not precluding continued interest in such arrangements, this experience could make economic justification and rationale even more salient than before in decisions to follow a multinational fuel cycle strategy.

As two U.S. initiatives which failed to materialize demonstrate, not all efforts to establish multinational nuclear consortia have been successful.[14] In 1971, in the context of growing European sentiment favoring an increased independence of supply and a development of a European-based enrichment enterprise (already reflected in the URENCO agreement and French initiatives to establish what became EURODIF), the United States offered to transfer enrichment technology under specified conditions. Those conditions included an acceptance of international safeguards and controls over plant and product, an opportunity for American industry to compete in supplying components and services, an avoidance of direct competition with U.S. enrichment production activities and, most importantly, an establishment of a multinational consortium to receive the transferred technology and to construct and operate a plant. Classified information, including information relevant to making an informed economic and technical judgment regarding the offer, was to be withheld until a commitment to construct a plant was made by the multinational consortium. This meant that the consortium would not know what it was getting until agreement was reached, an arrangement often referred to as "buying a pig in a poke." In addition, only diffusion technology would be shared with the multinational group, while centrifuge technology, in which European interest was growing, would be accessible only to American

[13] *Nuclear News,* June 1980, p. 38.
[14] The following discussion draws principally on Edward Wonder, *Nuclear Fuel and American Foreign Policy* (Boulder, Co.: Westview Press, 1977) and Bertrand Goldschmidt, *Le Complexe Atomique,* op. cit. See also Lawrence Scheinman, "Security and a Transnational System: The Case of Nuclear Energy," in *Transnational Relations and World Politics*, Robert O. Keohane and Joseph S. Nye, Jr., eds. (Cambridge, Mass.: Harvard University Press, 1972), pp. 276–300.

domestic firms, whom the U.S. government (in particular, the AEC) was seeking to interest in assuming responsibility for future enrichment activity, on the ground that enrichment had reached commercial status. This offer was rejected by the industrial states to which it was directed. The technology transfer conditions were regarded as unacceptable, not because of the multinational requirement, but because of the insistence that commitment to the project precede access to information and technology. The latter requirement was perceived by the Europeans as signifying lack of serious U.S. intent, and as a ploy to head off movement toward increased independence in nuclear fuel supply—in other words, as a political and commercial strategy to preserve U.S. nuclear influence and to avert the emergence of a strong and independent competitive enrichment industry. Suspicions about U.S. commercial motivations made later nonproliferation-motivated U.S. proposals suspect.

A second initiative was taken in 1974 at the Washington Energy Conference, against the background of the oil crisis and its emphasis on increased cooperation among the industrial states in developing alternative sources of energy supply. Nuclear energy was one of the centerpieces of efforts to diversify the energy resource base, and Secretary of State Kissinger stressed American readiness to explore the sharing of enrichment technologies, and the establishment of multinational arrangements to that end. Departing from its earlier offer, the United States now indicated interest in cooperative arrangements in centrifuge as well as diffusion technology—a proposition which (had it been made in 1971) would have found a responsive audience in Europe, where the lower capital and operating costs of centrifuges were appealing. The offer also avoided the offensive preconditions that characterized the 1971 approach.

Despite the greater openness and flexibility of this American initiative, there was little serious interest on the part of others. To some extent this might have reflected continued uncertainty about U.S. motives and objectives. More probably, it reflected the fact that URENCO had gotten underway between 1971 and 1974 and was in the process of shaking out some of the problems associated with multinationalization, while EURODIF was just beginning as a multinational entity; both were concerned to avoid any unnecessary complicating side-excursions which might have unsettling effects on such new ventures. These concerns, of course, relate back in part to uncertainty about ultimate American intentions. Additionally, the negotiating of a multinational arrangement, and the launching of a multinational enterprise, had moved from hypothesis to experience; this made many of the prospective partners for a joint activity extremely cautious about moving into further international institutional arrangements.

In any event, the 1974 initiative did not result in the launching of a new multinational enterprise; but it also did not lead to a termination of U.S.

interest in exploring the possibilities for applying multinational formulas to sensitive fuel cycle activities.

Some interim conclusions

Before turning to the more recent and more explicitly nonproliferation-inspired interest in multinationalism, it would be useful to draw some conclusions from the historic experience just discussed. Four points in particular would seem to bear emphasis.

Most significant, perhaps, states have in a number of instances voluntarily entered into arrangements which place constraints on their capacity to act independently in response to purely national dictates and interests. In none of the cases, of course, did participation in a multinational venture preclude national pursuit of a research and development program in that technology;[15] and in some cases (e.g., EUROCHEMIC), acquisition of technology and experience motivated participation in the first place. It is not to be excluded, however, that a satisfactory experience in a multinational venture, in securing reliable and adequate supplies of fuels or services without a sense of undue dependence on an external source of supply, could lead states to conclude that this way of meeting their nuclear requirements is preferable to more independent, but possibly more costly and technologically less sophisticated, alternatives.

Not all states would share this view—for some, technological parity, independence, or other considerations would preclude participation in such ventures, unless doing so did not impair concurrent or future ability to choose a national alternative strategy. But this does not void the general point that multinational institutional arrangements have been successfully implemented in sensitive high technology areas and could become an important component of a future international nuclear regime. Political acceptability cannot be a priori ruled out.

Certainly none of these ventures would have been initiated or would have survived if they did not meet important economic criteria, and this is our second point: multinational arrangements must demonstrate economic, financial, and commercial viability. Whether, as some would argue, they must in all respects surpass alternative national performance is a more debatable point, but they cannot impose substantial excess costs and expect to survive. Costly high technologies which can benefit from economies of scale are attractive possibilities for joint ventures, especially for countries whose programs are not sufficiently large to justify the level of technical, financial, and manpower investment that would be required to put a viable system into place. Where, as in

---

[15] While one could view the URENCO provision for rotation of enrichment contract allocations as an effort to delay as long as possible the construction of an enrichment plant in the FRG, and URENCO itself as a way to divert any autonomous enrichment activity in Germany, it still remains true that the FRG was completely free to develop enrichment technology.

the case of EUROCHEMIC, the economic rationale fails to be sustained, the venture terminates. But even in the face of some economic uncertainty, it is not a foregone conclusion that the arrangement will collapse if participants are persuaded either of the long-term logic of the enterprise (e.g., URENCO), or of the even more substantial costs of seeking purely national alternatives.

For example, a reprocessing enterprise whose economics are dubious, but which, nevertheless, resolves a waste problem which might not be easily resolved on a national basis, may be preferred despite its economic uncertainty, especially if waste management arrangements are a precondition for licensing reactor operations in the participating countries. The key point is that a multinational venture must make basic economic sense to be considered, and to survive, in the absence of some compelling other reasons to establish and operate it in the first place.

A third point relates to structure and organization. Several of the nuclear ventures, and some other high-technology multinational consortia such as INTELSAT, have adopted two-tiered governing structures which serve to separate normal management decision making from questions which are essentially of a political nature.[16] One formidable argument against multinational arrangements is that they are not only complex in operational, financial, and economic terms, but also sensitive to political differences which could have severe negative effects on their normal operations. The development of a multitiered structure to separate nonoperational from operational activities, and political from commercial-managerial considerations, does not completely eliminate the risk, but it does reduce the threat of unnecessary complications, and the probability that separable decisions will interfere with each other.

This ties in with the earlier observation about organizational flexibility. Each of the multinational arrangements discussed had different attributes, affecting either the degree of technology sharing (full sharing in URENCO, URG, and EUROCHEMIC; no sharing in EURODIF); or the financing formulas and claims on the product (proportionate shares and claims in EURODIF, equal investment requirements in URENCO at least at the outset); or the scope of activity (production and marketing in the case of URENCO; fuel production only in the case of EURODIF; technology development and training in EUROCHEMIC). This suggests a continuing plausibility for multinational ventures, consistent with the participants' objectives in securing supplies of services and fuels, the general requirements of economic and commercial attractiveness, and the broader international concern about reinforcing international safeguards and nonproliferation.

Perhaps the greatest uncertainty arises in transferring the experiences of primarily technologically advanced industrial societies to a broader group of states with a much more heterogeneous set of objectives and priorities, and a

---

[16] On INTELSAT, see Eugene Skolnikoff, "Relevance of INTELSAT Experience for Organizational Structure of Multinational Nuclear Fuel Cycle Facilities," in Chayes and Lewis, op. cit., pp. 223–30.

rather different perspective on such concepts as equity, nondiscrimination, and fair play. If multinationalism means, as it would, fewer facilities (which may be important for economic reasons) then locational issues could become very important. A continued siting of most such facilities in advanced industrial states because of practical considerations could be rejected by developing countries as an untenable perpetuation of the technology gap. Difficulties would also arise because of asymmetries in what advanced and developing countries could bring to the common enterprise, and the consequent asymmetries in the allocation of responsibility and decision-making authority. A major question then remains on whether, and under what conditions, our past experience is transferable to future arrangements; to what degree will alternative institutional arrangements be acceptable on economic, technological, political, and nonproliferation grounds to the different potential participants. As noted earlier, generic solutions are not likely to be identifiable, and each arrangement will have to be tailored to the project, technology, and participants involved.

Multinationalism and nonproliferation

Interest in multinational fuel cycle arrangements took on a sense of urgency with the expansion of peaceful nuclear programs. Control of nuclear technology had largely been based on political commitments that were monitored and verified by international safeguards, designed to detect any illicit effort to divert material from the peaceful nuclear fuel cycle. The nuclear universe to which those safeguards applied consisted largely of power and some research reactors which, with a few exceptions, did not give access to directly weapons-usable material. Sensitive technologies and facilities capable of producing directly weapons-usable materials were confined to a relatively small number of states.

The Indian nuclear test of 1974, and the spread of sensitive nuclear facilities to countries whose programs were only in a rudimentary stage of development and lacking any serious rationale for advanced sensitive technologies, raised fundamental questions about the adequacy of international safeguards by themselves to prevent proliferation. As explained in the Nye chapter, a reactive policy based only on denial would ultimately fail, and would bring resentment and even greater international instability in its wake. Longer-range attention focused, therefore, on identifying the appropriate additive protective measures to deal with the inevitable spread of nuclear energy and technology. The ultimate goal was development of a regime embodying agreed rules, norms, institutions, and proliferation-resistant technologies to reduce the proliferation risk to manageable proportions. Institutional arrangements, particularly multinational schemes, figured prominently among alternative means of reinforcing nonproliferation, and security considerations thus came to occupy a place alongside political and commercial considerations in judging the feasibility of the multinational alternative to purely national fuel cycle facilities.[17]

Public support for, and promotion of, multinational concepts for explicitly nonproliferation considerations was first articulated by the United States when its representative to the 1974 General Conference of the International Atomic Energy Agency spoke in support of "the establishment of internationally approved facilities to handle all the spent fuel arising from power reactors"[18] as an alternative to individual countries developing their own technology for this purpose. Subsequently, the United States strongly supported a provision in the final declaration of the 1975 NPT Review Conference that "regional or multinational nuclear fuel cycle centers may be an advantageous way to satisfy, safely and economically, the needs of many states . . . while, at the same time facilitating physical protection and the application of safeguards."[19] Multinationalism was also strongly advocated by Secretary of State Kissinger in a speech before the UN General Assembly in September 1975, where he stated that "the greatest single danger of unrestrained nuclear proliferation resides in the spread under national control of reprocessing facilities. . . . The United States, therefore, proposes, as a major step to reinforce all other measures, the establishment of multinational regional nuclear fuel cycle centers."[20] One immediate result of this was American endorsement of an IAEA study of regional nuclear fuel cycle centers.[21]

Emphasis on multinational strategies was not confined to the executive branch. H. Con. Res. 371 (Zablocki) reinforced endorsement of multinational centers, as an alternative to national development of sensitive portions of the fuel cycle.[22] Subsequently Senate Resolution 221 (Pastore-Mondale) expressed concern over the "proliferation threat posed by the possibility of development of a large number of independent enrichment and reprocessing facilities,"[23] and argued in support of U.S. initiatives for the development of regional, multinational centers.

American policy during the past several years has, for a number of reasons, been ambivalent toward early development of multinational reprocessing arrangements. One consequence has been an international uncertainty about real U.S. objectives and intent in the peaceful nuclear fuel cycle. Three factors deserve emphasis in this regard.

First, assessments of the justification and timeliness of plutonium separa-

[17] See references cited in footnote 1 on these points.
[18] IAEA, GC(XVIII)/OR. 169(23), (Sept. 1974).
[19] U.S. Arms Control and Disarmament Agency, *Documents on Disarmament, 1975*, pp. 146–58, esp. p. 151.
[20] Ibid., p. 476.
[21] See IAEA, *Regional Nuclear Fuel Cycle Centers* (Vienna: IAEA, 1977), two volumes.
[22] House Concurrent Resolution 371, *Congressional Record*, 30 July 1975, p. 25918.
[23] Senate Resolution 221, *Congressional Record*, 12 December 1975, p. 521961.

tion evolved considerably. The conventional nuclear wisdom which prevailed into the mid-1970s had been that the recycling of plutonium in mixed oxide fuels in light water reactors was technically logical and economically appropriate. This view changed amid rising uncertainties regarding the economics of recycle, and the absence of any compelling resource-scarcity reason to deploy plutonium in light water reactors. Also important was the sharply increased sensitivity to the weapons risk in widespread dissemination of reprocessing facilities and separated plutonium.

Second, it became increasingly clear in the late 1970s that disposal of spent fuel in unprocessed form was feasible as a waste management option, and that, contrary to conventional thinking, the waste disposal problem was not alleviated by reprocessing, but rather was of the same order with or without reprocessing. This revised view was essentially endorsed in the INFCE study.

Third, perhaps most important in view of the diminished economic or technical urgency of reprocessing and the U.S. preference to link plutonium separation to economically-justifiable breeder reactor development, the United States sought to avoid a situation in which the existence of added institutional arrangements would be used as a pretext for premature commitments to sensitive nuclear activity. In other words, multinational alternatives were to be encouraged when the activity in question was economically justified, but were not themselves to become an excuse for undertaking an activity for which no compelling reason existed.

This underlying philosophy is largely reflected in the provision in the 1978 Nuclear Nonproliferation Act that a necessary condition for reprocessing or other sensitive fuel cycle activities involving U.S. origin fuels is that they take place under "effective international auspices," and in the provision which requires the President to seek agreement on policies which include a "prohibition against reprocessing," except in a facility under "effective international auspices and inspection."[24] While not explicitly requiring a multinational arrangement, this language, especially in the context of recent nonproliferation policy, reflects continued U.S. interest in multinational arrangements as a component of a long-range nonproliferation strategy.

Two questions remain to be considered: why should states acquiesce in the political limitations that multinationalism entails, and, even if they do, how effective a role can multinational arrangements play in achieving nonproliferation goals.

The political acceptability of multinationalism

We noted earlier that institutional arrangements can reinforce a consensus, but cannot create one where it does not exist. In dealing with the

[24] The Nuclear Nonproliferation Act of 1978 (P.L. 95-242), 92 Stat. 210 (1978), 42 U.S.C. s. 2153b (b) (1) and (2).

problem of acceptability, we will make several assumptions regarding consensus, in particular: (1) that there exists widespread support for finding ways to meet energy requirements while minimizing the risks of nuclear weapons proliferation; (2) that sensitive materials and the facilities which produce them create special problems for which safeguards alone may not be adequate to achieve nonproliferation; and (3) that additional measures reaching beyond traditional bilateral or multilateral arrangements may therefore be necessary, including mutual agreement to limit use of nuclear technology and materials.

The first two assumptions seem to have won widespread support in the recently concluded International Nuclear Fuel Cycle Evaluation.[25] The third also enjoys broad, but more guarded and qualified, support in the international community. For example, the dangers of plutonium and reprocessing are recognized, along with the possibility of minimizing those dangers if reprocessing were limited to a few large-scale facilities. But support for taking steps in this direction remains in abeyance, in the absence of general agreement about who will have access to what, and when, and with what degree of certainty. In short, the relinquishing of national control can only be contemplated in the context of a regime which satisfies such political and economic requirements as participating states regard as essential. And, even in these circumstances, it is probable that participating states will hold relinquishment hostage to continued satisfaction with the multinational arrangement.

Some states will strongly resist a derogation of national sovereignty under virtually any conditions. The reasons for this might range from an unshakeable conviction that maintaining a nuclear weapons option is essential to long-term national security (e.g., Israel or South Africa), to vaguer notions about the prestige value of full national control over advanced technologies (e.g., Brazil or Argentina), or about the principle of absolute equality of all states (e.g., India), to more concrete economic concerns about security of energy supply, amid uncertainty that this requirement can be met on a reliable basis through reliance on external sources of supply.

Some of these states are unlikely to be persuaded to reconsider their position in the absence of significant changes in the international political and security environment, or unless they make a very fundamental reassessment of their own political and security interests. By the same token, however, their position should not dictate the objectives to be sought, the shape and character of the regime to be developed, or the level of effort to be expended in pursuit of those goals.

States which do not a priori reject the idea of some limitation on national authority and conduct, and who see genuine security advantages in a system involving self-restraint (i.e., the vast majority of industrial states and a significant number of developing countries) will nevertheless condition giving support for multinational arrangements on an acceptable balance of benefits

---

[25] See, Statement of Ambassador-at-Large Gerard Smith, U.S. Representative to the INFCE, Final Plenary Conference, 25 February 1980.

and costs. Nonproliferation may be a valued objective, and even a priority concern, but the price of securing it will be carefully weighed, in terms not only of the effectiveness of the measures proposed to achieve nonproliferation, but also of the costs which may be incurred in energy security, economics, equity, and discrimination. There are no inherent reasons why multinational ventures cannot satisfy that concern.

In terms of energy security, participation in a multinational arrangement could remove concern about excessive external dependence. While not entirely free of risk, and theoretically subject to the integrity of the host state, equity and/or managerial participation could enhance the credibility of fuel supply, by contrast with reliance on independent external suppliers. The same argument that works against a host-state's abrogation of its nonproliferation commitments, discussed earlier, works in favor of enhanced consumer-partner security; a much higher political threshold must be crossed, before acting contrary to international commitments, than where the facility is under single-state control. If the economic terms and conditions are attractive, and the political undertakings convergent, the multinational alternative may well be regarded as an effective way to achieve higher levels of mutual dependence among participating members, thus securing energy supply and reinforcing market predictability.

These considerations are applicable equally to enrichment and reprocessing. The technology of enrichment is still the preserve of a relatively few states. Costs and the demands of technological sophistication, along with close supplier state control of the technology, serve as deterrents to its dissemination. Dependence will thus remain characteristic of the enrichment marketplace for some time to come. The uncertainties which have beset supply during the past several years, as suppliers have sought tighter guarantees against weapons proliferation, could lead consumer states to seek equity shares in enrichment facilities, even if the technological know-how remained (at least for the near-term) the preserve of the host state. An equity stake in production, and a voice in policy management, would provide the basic rationale. The interest of the supplier would be largely nonproliferation, but he also would benefit in that new excess production capacity would not emerge to threaten market stability.

Reprocessing is accessible to a larger number of states, so that the same deterrents which apply for enrichment are not to be found here. On the other hand, far from resolving the waste management problem, reprocessing compounds it; it generates dangerous high-level wastes, posing significant intermediate storage problems, with permanent disposal technologies remaining to be demonstrated. New reactor licensing is dependent on defining waste disposal plans in an increasing number of states, and the lack of a solution has impeded nuclear development in several cases. The possibility of avoiding such problems could be a powerful incentive for a state to join in a multinational arrangement, even if participation entailed concurrent renunciation of national reprocessing activity.

Insofar as equity and discrimination are concerned, multinational arrangements can play an important ameliorative role. One widespread argument in favor of national reprocessing and enrichment activity is that such operations are now carried out in weapons states and in a few advanced industrial countries. Pleas regarding the weapons proliferation risk remain unconvincing, as long as these states continue to assert a right to develop these technologies under exclusive national control; attempts to foreclose further development elsewhere under these conditions will likely be seen as nothing more than blatant discrimination, contradicting the provisions of Article IV of the Nonproliferation Treaty, which ensured full and complete access to the peaceful benefits of nuclear energy.

However, multinational arrangements, with the most advanced nuclear states placing their own sensitive facilities under multinational auspices, could significantly weaken the argument about discrimination in the peaceful nuclear sector, and could go far toward achieving a degree of equity acceptable to most of those states which were ever willing to consider an alternative to purely national arrangements. Even if not all existing facilities in the advanced nuclear states were multinationalized, with multinational agreement only reached for all new facilities, a substantial inroad on the claim of discrimination would be made, and one important barrier to the acceptability of the multinational approach to nonproliferation would be overcome.

The efficacy of the multinational approach

Two arguments have been raised against the efficacy of multinational arrangements: limited effectiveness (inability to prevent eventual dispersion), and potential counterproductiveness (technology transfer and the legitimation of proliferation-prone activities). A third argument, inefficiency (administrative-operational complexity) is not proliferation-related, and is not treated here.

The argument of limited effectiveness is based on the presumption that not all potential developers of technology will join the arrangement, and that entry into a multinational venture does not foreclose future development of national facilities. In addition there is a problem in the siting of sensitive fuel cycle facilities. If they are placed in nonnuclear-weapon states they could constitute a proliferation risk; if efforts to limit that risk rest on confining facilities to so-called safe and stable environments, which essentially mean western industrial states, then the problem of discrimination arises once again vis-à-vis aspiring and sensitive Third World countries. Finally, some analysts would argue that research reactors and facilities (which produce, or require the use of weapons-usable materials in significant quantities) are more of a pro-liferation risk than production facilities (certainly more widespread), and that the focus on peaceful fuel cycle production facilities is thus misguided.

The argument about potential counterproductiveness contends that the greatest risk is that multinationalism will accelerate deployment of sensitive facilities which otherwise might have evolved more slowly, because project managers will be able to argue that the risks associated with such activities are now under effective nonproliferation constraints. If the main argument against dispersion of sensitive facilities was that international safeguards could not alone ensure against misuse, and multinational institutions are then advanced to meet this problem, pressures will then inevitably mount to relax technological constraints, on the ground that the proliferation risk has now been resolved.

A second counterproductiveness argument is that multinational owner-ship and operation would accelerate technology transfer. Demands for physical transfer of technology might dominate the politics of the institution, and the information and experience derived could later be used in a clandestine national plant, to circumvent the very risks that multinational institutions were designed to control. In view of this risk, multinationalism might be less desirable as a nonproliferation measure than would be reliance on a small number of large national plants sited in a limited number of stable (read "privileged few") locations.

These are formidable arguments and cannot be dismissed out of hand. Yet national control under international safeguards alone is untenable in non-proliferation terms, while monopolizing fuel cycle technologies in the name of nonproliferation would not be acceptable to nonnuclear weapon states, and would lead to a more profound crisis of confidence than exists even today.[26] If the objective of nonproliferation is not to foreclose the legitimate development of sensitive nuclear technologies, but rather to reduce the risks of abuse or misappropriation, which increase in a situation of purely national control, then alternatives to national control become relevant; multinational ventures thus appear to be a potentially constructive way to bridge considerations of nonproliferation, energy security, and equity.

With respect to limited effectiveness, two points need to be made. First, the very existence of multinational facilities removes some of the conventional justifications for building national plants, such as lack of alternatives, waste management problems, resource requirements, technology development, and experience, and the unacceptability of total dependence on external sources of supply. Participation in multinational ventures could moreover be predicated on states' acceptance of commitments not to engage in parallel national ac-

---

[26] On erosion of confidence, see Bertrand Goldschmidt and Myron B. Kratzer, *Peaceful Nuclear Relations: A Study of the Creation and Erosion of Confidence,* (New York and London: Rockefeller Foundation and Royal Institute of International Affairs, November 1978).

tivity, as long as those ventures provide reliable, economically competitive services on a timely basis.

Second, as we noted in discussing acceptability, if advanced states participated in such multinational arrangements (perhaps submitting all, or even some, of their facilities to such a regime) this could go very far toward neutralizing equity and discrimination arguments, and could significantly increase the political threshold for any state's move into a purely nationally owned and operated facility. It is significant that French President Giscard d'Estaing, in a February 1979 press conference, explicitly endorsed the notion of multinational reprocessing for the future, including consideration of placing future French facilities under multinational auspices.[27] The basic point is that the more that can be done to remove economic or technical arguments for national facilities, the more service is done for nonproliferation. With the presence of multinational alternatives, the justifications for a national program become far less persuasive than if no alternatives existed; the degree of ambiguity surrounding a national decision to develop sensitive facilities diminishes, and the international community becomes correspondingly more alert to the possible nuclear intentions of the state in question. The importance of this point cannot be stressed too much.

On the issue of potential counterproductiveness, while critics rightly note that pressures may mount to accelerate and legitimate high-risk activities, they also overlook two significant factors. One is that the collectivity of states that would have to share losses as well as profits in multinational ventures would take an even harder look at development strategy and timing than would an individual state which would more likely be swayed by political or prestige factors; this in itself has the effect of restraint. More importantly, multinational arrangements, at least as articulated by the United States, have not been viewed as an isolated nonproliferation measure, but rather as one component of a more comprehensive regime. Such a regime has been defined as needing to cover institutional arrangements for technology dissemination, but also such questions as the legitimate uses of technology and material, the appropriate timing for their production and distribution, and the conditions for their use, storage, transfer, and ultimate disposition.[28]

With respect to technology-sharing problems, a distinction should be made between reprocessing and enrichment. The basic technology necessary to build a small reprocessing plant dedicated to deriving modest amounts of material for explosive purposes is already well known. Technology denial will in no way change that situation. Hands-on experience in a large commercial facility could speed up acquisition of the information and expertise to handle a

---

[27] Press Conference by Valery Giscard d'Estaing, 15 February 1979, Press and Information Division 79/25, French Embassy.

[28] See Nye and Scheinman articles, op. cit., and Thomas Pickering, address before the Atomic Industrial Forum, Altanta, Georgia, 12 March 1979 (mimeo).

comparable large-scale plant; but this risk might be better handled by securing political commitments to preclude replication of any facility unless it is a part of, and explicitly endorsed by, the multinational regime. There are strong commercial reasons why this type of agreement might be sought, quite aside from nonproliferation concerns. Agreements also might be negotiated to establish a phased access to certain aspects of technology, based on the evolution of the participating state's nuclear program, and the economic need for expanding plant capacity.

Enrichment presents a different problem, because far less scientific and technological information has been disseminated. As we have already seen, however, both EURODIF and URENCO appear to have successfully come to grips with this issue. The service-equity EURODIF arrangement, which has the stronger nonproliferation value, may not be regarded as satisfactory in the future, although satisfaction ultimately depends on the partners, their interests, and the overall characteristics of the arrangement. It is worth noting, however, that (from an energy-security point of view) technology access was a less important issue in the INFCE working-group discussions on assured supply than was the existence of a competitive and transparent market with several independent sources of supply, as free as possible from political intervention in the absence of violation of nonproliferation undertakings.[29]

If multinational arrangements are part of a broader protective regime, it would appear then that they can play an important nonproliferation role and contribute to the reinforcement of acceptable international nuclear cooperation. Whatever limitations they may have, it is reasonably certain that a phased sharing and dissemination of high-risk technologies under a comprehensive regime would be preferable to (and ultimately more supportive of nonproliferation than) alternatives which encouraged or facilitated national nuclear autonomy.

Some conclusions

In the final analysis, the most compelling argument for or against multinational institutional arrangements for sensitive fuel cycle activities may emerge from the future shape and character of supplier state (particularly U.S.) nuclear policy. If some form of extranational control over these activities, above and beyond international safeguards and nonproliferation commitments, becomes the price for stability of supplier state behavior, and for the renewed constructive international cooperation which is so essential to all states, then the multinational approach may come to be regarded as a politically acceptable alternative to national ownership and control. It is not the

---

[29] See INFCE Working Group III, cited in footnote 3.

only alternative that one could visualize, but it does hold middle ground, between those alternatives based so much on safeguards that they are more façades than genuine protective measures, and those which, because of their extensive reliance on formal international organizations, would place too heavy a demand on national sovereignty. The performance of such complex activities as enrichment and reprocessing at a multinational level among largely homogeneous states would be difficult enough.

The key question is what the supplier states (especially the United States which remains so central to any international nuclear regime) are prepared to offer in return. Most countries are concerned primarily with reaping the benefits of peaceful nuclear energy. Energy security, including access to nuclear power on a timely, predictable, and economically attractive basis is (as we discussed earlier) their principal objective. Such states seek supplies of fuel and necessary services, assured against arbitrary and capricious supplier state behavior. They also seek guarantees that any new nonproliferation conditions that might later be found to be necessary (in the context of changing technological or international political conditions) will not be unilaterally or arbitrarily imposed on dependent states, but will be dealt with on a basis of equality and mutual understanding. This has not really been characteristic of nuclear cooperation during the past several years, as key suppliers, recognizing defects in the regime, sometimes took very quick and dramatic action in an effort to redress the situation.

Finally, such states want a voice in the shaping of the regime, and in the determination of the rules of the game in which they have become involved. For the most part they recognize the risks of widely dispersed weapons-usable materials, and understand the need for restraint. But they do not accept the notion that some states are more equal than others in the peaceful nuclear sector, and they consequently reject the establishment of principles which codify discrimination. Forbearance in the development of national sensitive fuel cycle facilities, because the economics of it are unattractive, or the technology too complex, is one thing. Forbearance on the grounds that it is not healthy for too many states to engage in sensitive activities, or to stockpile sensitive material, is quite another.

Pragmatic and judicious use of multinational institutional arrangements may bridge these different interests, and may thus be effective in promoting the cause of nonproliferation, while meeting energy security concerns, and ameliorating the sense of discrimination which so widely pervades the nuclear arena. The concept appears basically sound; the challenge lies in fashioning institutional arrangements so as to meet the political, economic, operational, and management concerns that inevitably will enter into any consideration of multinational activity, and so as to insure that multinationalism does not become a pretext or a subterfuge for activities which could undermine the stability of the international nuclear regime.

It would be good to remember how much the nuclear question is really sui generis, because of the unique attributes of the problem of proliferation, so that some of the conventional wisdom from other fields of endeavor, scoffing at multinational formulae, may not (and indeed should not) apply here. Multinational institutional arrangements, to repeat, are not the whole of a grand design, or a comprehensive solution to proliferation problems, or even the most appropriate strategy for all situations. Proliferation is, after all, fundamentally a political problem; its solution, if one exists, must be found in the political arena. Everything else is only prologue.

Yet, for many states, multinational arrangements may provide an opportunity to share in a more sophisticated industrial activity than would be the case on a purely national basis; for some others, such arrangements may simply have to be regarded as a nonproliferation cost, to be borne in order to maintain a viable international nuclear system. And that is a common stake.

6

The Tlatelolco Regime and Nonproliferation in Latin America

John R. Redick

Considerable progress towards nonproliferation in Latin America has been achieved. The most notable contribution is the Latin American Nuclear-Weapon-Free Zone established by the Treaty of Tlatelolco (Treaty for the Prohibition of Nuclear Weapons in Latin America) in 1969.[1] This paper discusses the current status of Tlatelolco, the circumstances which permitted the creation of the nuclear-weapon-free zone, and its international relevance. Particular attention is given to the current and projected nuclear programs and Tlatelolco postures of Latin America's three leading countries: Mexico, Argentina, and Brazil. Finally two dynamic regional trends are identified as having particular importance to nonproliferation prospects in Latin America: (1) horizontal transfer of nuclear technology and (2) Argentine-Brazilian nuclear convergence following their agreement of May 1980.

The Tlatelolco regime confronts a number of unpredictable obstacles, yet its importance extends beyond its obvious benefits to the Latin American region. It is integrated with, and supportive of, the international nonproliferation regime which has at its core International Atomic Energy Agency (IAEA) safeguards. Tlatelolco's success will favorably impact on the political vitality of the nonproliferation regime. Alternatively Tlatelolco's failure could not help but weaken international confidence in the global regime.

Views expressed in this paper are those of the author and do not necessarily reflect the views of The Stanley Foundation.
[1] The Treaty of Tlatelolco's negotiating process was completed in 1967 and the nuclear-weapon-free zone came into force in 1969 when the requisite number of nations completed ratification.

Latin America and the nonproliferation regime in the 1980s

At the outset of the 1980s the nonproliferation regime, centered primarily upon the Nonproliferation Treaty (NPT) and the IAEA safeguards system, appears threatened. Serious differences of view persist between the United States, Western European nations, and Japan regarding a variety of nuclear issues—particularly the terms and procedures for the transfer of nuclear materials and equipment. Equally serious issues divide the United States (along with certain other nations such as Canada) from many developing countries with growing nuclear programs. The latter group of countries raise legitimate questions regarding assurance of supply and sanctity of contracts. Of deep importance is the rupture of superpower détente and vital efforts at vertical disarmament with the consequential deemphasis on cooperative nonproliferation endeavors (despite shared U.S.-Soviet concern).

Under these less-than-optimum circumstances a number of multilateral nonproliferation efforts are being undertaken early in the decade. The International Nuclear Fuel Cycle Evaluation (INFCE) has completed its work with the final plenary session in Vienna in February 1980. The two-year technical exchange of information on the nuclear fuel cycle involved sixty-six nations and five international organizations. While INFCE provided no dramatic breakthroughs, it did permit a period of reduced tensions, dialogue, and produced a body of organized and useful information.[2]

Latin American participation in INFCE was limited to four nations: Argentina, Brazil, Mexico, and Venezuela. Only one nation, Argentina, was actively involved, serving as co-chair of one of INFCE's eight working groups on spent fuel management. Argentine officials remained mildly skeptical of the INFCE exercise as an exchange among the most advanced nuclear countries with only limited relevance to developing countries with growing nuclear programs. One Latin American regional organization, the Agency for the Prohibition of Nuclear Weapons in Latin America (OPANAL), was asked and ultimately did submit a formal position paper to INFCE's final plenary.[3]

There appears to be general consensus that despite INFCE's ambiguous conclusions, follow-up steps, involving most, if not all, of the key suppliers and consumer countries which participated in INFCE, are essential. To retreat to the pre-INFCE pattern of a separate suppliers group vis-à-vis consumer nations could shatter remaining support for the nonproliferation regime. Thus some sort of post-INFCE consultative mechanism should, and most probably will, be created. One proposal which appears to enjoy the support of some Latin American and other developing nations is that important multilateral

---

[2] *Report of the Technical Coordinating Committee* (TCC), INFCE, January 1980.

[3] The author explores INFCE results with particular relevance to institutional development of the nuclear fuel cycle in Latin America in "Latin America: Policy Options Following INFCE," in *Next Steps After INFCE, U.S. International Nuclear and Nonproliferation Policy,* Rodney Jones, ed. (Washington, D.C.: Center for Strategic and International Studies, March 1980).

discussions on outstanding nuclear issues should be held under the auspices of the IAEA (specifically that the Board of Governors might create a Committee of the Whole).[4] This forum has particular appeal to Latin American nations which comprise six of the thirty-four members of the Board of Governors (a body in which Argentina and Brazil have traditionally exercised important influence). However, the United States has resisted this initiative without fully opposing the idea of some sort of low level consultative mechanism.[5]

In addition to the necessity for creating a consultative mechanism following INFCE, considerable emphasis is being given to the second NPT Review Conference scheduled for August 1980. The Review Conference will be the second held under the procedures of Article 8 of the NPT (which now totals 111 parties). However, unlike INFCE and the proposed IAEA committee, two of Latin America's most advanced countries, Argentina and Brazil, will not be represented. Moreover, several other less advanced Latin American countries will also not be part of the NPT Review process: Chile, Colombia, and Cuba.

Four Latin American countries—Mexico, Peru, Venezuela, and Ecuador—participated in the work of the Preparatory Committee of the Review Conference. Only Mexico can be said to have a significant nuclear program under way. Moreover, even Latin American supporters of the NPT such as Mexico are growing increasingly critical of certain aspects of the agreement—notably the perceived failure of implementation of Article 4 (sharing of the peaceful benefits of nuclear energy) and Article 6 (calling for significant disarmament efforts by all nations). This increasing disenchantment by NPT supporters from developing countries has particular relevance in Latin America as it could conceivably spark a movement to withdraw support of NPT in favor of Tlatelolco. While by most interpretations Tlatelolco parties have obligations at least equal if not more complete than the NPT, any Latin American withdrawal could do grievous injury to the latter agreement.

A final probable forum for discussion of nuclear issues is the proposed international conference on the peaceful uses of nuclear energy. Latin American countries supported the decision of the 34th UN General Assembly to convene, no later than 1983, "an international conference for promotion of international cooperation in the peaceful uses of nuclear energy under the auspices of the UN system, with IAEA fulfilling its appropriate role." The conference being promoted by Yugoslavia would be limited to key supplier and consumer nations. As a sort of "political INFCE" it would attempt to resolve vital issues

---

[4] The rationale for this idea is discussed in greater depth in a Stanley Foundation Conference report, *Conference on Nonproliferation: 1980s,* 29 January–3 February 1980, Vienna, Austria.

[5] The United States remains unenthused over the IAEA as a principal forum for post-INFCE discussions as it would confront considerable criticism over its supply policy. Moreover the United States could not expect to dictate to the Board of Governors the terms of reference for a committee of whole. Instead the U.S. has supported an alternative approach of a group of experts to advise the Director General.

left unresolved by INFCE, within IAEA forums, or other consultative mechanisms which might be developed in the interim.

As the above suggests, while the early 1980s will not lack multilateral forums for discussion of key nuclear issues, the degree of Latin American participation will vary. The two threshold countries, Argentina and Brazil, remain in a largely self-induced state of divorce from most nonproliferation endeavors with the exception of membership in the IAEA and a degree of support for the Tlatelolco regime.

Tlatelolco regime

Current status

The Tlatelolco Treaty is currently in complete force for twenty-two Latin American countries including Mexico, Venezuela, Colombia, and Peru. Under the terms of the Treaty parties are fully pledged to keep their territories entirely free of nuclear weapons; to neither develop, test, nor import such weapons, nor to permit foreign nuclear bases to be established (not prohibited by the NPT). Four significant Latin American countries—Argentina, Brazil, Chile, and Cuba—are not full parties to the agreement.

The Treaty includes two accompanying Protocols designed to assure strong international support for the agreement. Additional Protocol I is designed for states having territorial interests in the Americas whereby such countries agree to keep their possessions free of nuclear weapons as defined under the appropriate articles of the Treaty. Additional Protocol II applies to the nuclear weapons states which pledge ''not to use or threaten to use nuclear weapons'' against the full parties to the Treaty. International (non-Latin American) support for Tlatelolco as represented in Protocol ratification is high with the Treaty being adhered to by all three major nuclear weapon states: the United States, the Soviet Union, and China. These along with Great Britain and France have ratified Protocol II. Protocol I has been ratified by the Netherlands and Great Britian whereas the United States and France have signed but not yet completed ratification.

With respect to the four significant Latin American nonparties, Brazil and Chile have technically ratified the agreement, Argentina has signed and announced its intent to ratify, and Cuba has neither signed nor ratified. Under the complex ratification arrangements devised by negotiating parties (Article 28), Brazil's and Chile's ratification is conditional. That is, it will not come into force for their territories until all appropriate Latin American states have ratified, and the relevant Protocols ratified by all states having territorial interests in the Americas or nuclear weapon states. However, Tlatelolco is now virtually complete and in practical terms the remaining obstacles are: Argentina's final ratification, Cuba's signing and ratification, and ratification by the

United States and France of Protocol I. Assuming these goals are reached, all Latin American countries would become full parties to Taltelolco. This has particular significance since several countries not party to the NPT (Argentina, Brazil, Chile, and Cuba) would be for the first time in a legal nonproliferation status.

A further significance of Tlatelolco is that three current full parties are not NPT parties: Colombia, Barbados, and Trinidad and Tobago. Also a number of Tlatelolco parties are not parties to the Partial Test Ban Treaty prohibiting underground nuclear testing: Colombia, Grenada, Haiti, Jamaica, Paraguay, and Surinam.[6]

The probability of Cuban ratification is influenced greatly by the status of U.S.-Cuban relations. Soviet ratification of Protocol II has enhanced the likelihood that Cuba will adhere in the future, and recent Cuban statements at the UN have indicated a certain softening of view toward the Treaty. Cuba is not a party to the NPT but Soviet officials have indicated that the 440-MWe unit under construction and all future units will be subject to IAEA safeguards. (Cuba is an IAEA member.) It is likely that the Soviet Union will require return of spent fuel as it does for Eastern European nations.[7] Cuba will also complete with Soviet assistance in 1980 a zero-power research reactor incapable of producing significant quantities of plutonium. It is significant that if Cuba ratifies Tlatelolco, OPANAL (and therefore representatives from other Latin American countries forming part of OPANAL's Council) will have the right to carry out special inspections in Cuba on the request of any party suspecting an illegal activity (Article 16).

Failure by the United States to ratify Protocol I has permitted Cuba one viable excuse to cushion it from pressure of other Latin American countries, primarily Mexico. There continue to be contracts between Mexico and Cuban authorities regarding Tlatelolco and there have been discussions with U.S. officials on the topic as well. Cuba has apparently conveyed the view to U.S. officials that other events should be completed first as regards to the Tlatelolco ratification procedure before Cuba would act (if at all), whereas the United States has stressed that it is not a bilateral issue between the two countries.[8]

French ratification of Protocol I is not yet complete but it is hoped that it will be forthcoming following a May 1980 visit by President Portillo to France. However U.S. ratification, announced by President Carter in April 1977, has been delayed due to unfortunate circumstances. In August 1978 the U.S. Senate Foreign Relations Committee discussed ratification of Protocol I and

---

[6] *Treaty of Tlatelolco,* Hearings before the Committee on Foreign Relations, U.S. Senate, 15 August 1978, Testimony of Charles van Doren, ACDA, p. 23.

[7] For a thorough review and analysis see Jorge F. Perez-Lopez, "The Cuban Nuclear Power Program," *Cuban Studies* (January 1979). It is of note that in May 1980 the Soviet Union and Cuba signed a new agreement for nuclear cooperation in several areas.

[8] Testimony of John Bushnell, Department of State, *Treaty of Tlatelolco,* op. cit., pp. 27–28.

questions were raised by several Senators regarding a memo sent over National Security Advisor Brzezinski's signature to the Joint Chiefs of Staff "requesting" their support for Protocol I ratification. Committee members demanded access to the memo, which was refused on executive privilege, yielding an interpretation by some that undue pressure was being put on the Joint Chiefs of Staff by the Carter administration regarding Protocol I. The fact that there is no evidence to suggest DOD views on Tlatelolco have ever failed to be fully taken into consideration did not prevent the issue from further complicating the ratification procedure.[9]

A more significant issue raised by some U.S. Senators was the interpretation accompanying the Soviet ratification of Protocol II (May 1978), that "permission for transit rights of nuclear weapons in any form would contradict the goals of the Treaty—and would be incompatible with the non-nuclear status of the contracting parties, etc." The view of the U.S. State Department is that the negotiating history of the Treaty clearly suggests the current full parties to the agreement definitely intended that each Latin American nation, in the free exercise of its sovereignty, would maintain the right to permit foreign countries to temporarily convey nuclear weapons through their national territory. This position was clearly asserted with U.S. ratification of Protocol II and in practice a number of Tlatelolco parties have granted such privileges to the United States since the Treaty went into effect in 1969. U.S. military aircraft carrying nuclear weapons have frequently over-flown and landed in national territories and naval vessels have visited ports and passed through territorial waters. Rather than failing to ratify Protocol I due to the Soviet's interpretation, ACDA officials argue that the U.S. position on this point can best be asserted by restating its correct interpretation along with formal U.S. ratification of the protocol.[10]

The failure of the United States to carry through its ratification of Protocol I has had the unfortunate impact of slowing Tlatelolco's momentum. It has clearly impacted on Cuba's failure to take action and on Argentina's reluctance to follow through on its announced intent to ratify. It has also led to considerable unhappiness on the part of Tlatelolco supporters in Latin America and raised questions regarding the sincerity of the U.S. commitment to nonproliferation in the region. This view is perhaps most aptly summarized

---

[9] The charge of pressure on the Joint Chiefs of Staff was groundless as published testimony, from earlier Protocol II hearings and the more recent Protocol I hearings, amply illustrated that DOD preferences were taken into full account in the U.S. interpretation. It is a point of fact the U.S. interpretation accompanying our earlier Protocol II ratification was largely drafted (with DOD's assistance) to meet DOD concerns. The Department of State's recommended declaration (to be made as part of the U.S. ratification of Protocol I) included a statement that "understandings and declarations attached by the U.S. to its ratification of Additional Protocol II would apply also to its ratification of Protocol I." *Additional Protocol I to the Treaty for the Prohibition of Nuclear Weapons in Latin America,* Message from the President, 24 May 1978.

[10] *Treaty of Tlatelolco,* op. cit., Testimony of van Doren, p. 35.

in a terse note to the U.S. State Department from OPANAL Secretary-General Gros Espiell in February 1980, which said in part:

> The failure of the U.S. to ratify Additional Protocol I, almost three years after its signature, deeply preoccupies the Latin American parties to the Tlatelolco Treaty. This lack of ratification appears to demonstrate little interest in the question of the military denuclearization of Latin America. Such an action by the U.S.—clearly incompatible with the repeated declarations of President Carter and Secretary of State Vance of full and total support for the Tlatelolco Treaty—[affects] negatively the negotiations to obtain the signatures and ratifications of those which are still not full parties to the Tlatelolco Treaty (Cuba, Guyana, Argentina, Brazil, and Chile).
>
> All the credibility of the U.S. policies on the matter relating to nuclear proliferation in Latin America will be compromised, in actuality, if it does not proceed quickly with ratification of Additional Protocol I.[11]

Preconditions

Are there particular circumstances unique to Latin America which have generated significant progress toward creation of a complete nuclear-weapon-free zone in the region? Are nuclear-weapon-free zones likely to be established in the Latin American pattern elsewhere in the world? These questions can best be addressed by briefly identifying the special preconditions which made the establishment of the Tlatelolco Treaty possible.

1. The Latin American nuclear-weapon-free zone represented a fortunate establishment of a legal instrument in advance of military/technological momentum. In the early 1960s nuclear technology was not yet well advanced in Latin America and consequently interest groups which might be expected to oppose such an effort were not a major inhibiting factor. With the exception of Mexico, those Latin American countries with the most advanced nuclear programs (Argentina, Brazil, Chile) were those which, up to this point, have still not fully adhered to the agreement.

2. The Latin American nuclear-weapon-free zone is a rare example of the value of human leadership and tenacity. It was the effort of a very small group of individuals led by the then Mexican Under-Secretary García Robles which initiated the proposals and fought for their acceptance and implementation by other Latin American nations and even their own governments.

3. The Latin American nuclear-weapon-free zone received a strong external stimulus from the Cuban Missile Crisis of October 1962. This factor is in-

[11] Memorandum by OPANAL Secretary General Gros Espiell to the U.S. Department of State, 7 February 1980.

escapable not only because of the numerous references which may be found among speeches by Latin American diplomats at the time, but also in the proximity of the proposals for a nuclear-weapon-free zone to the Missile Crisis. The initial proposal for the Latin American nuclear-weapon-free zone was introduced during the height of the Crisis in October. Subsequently this was followed with a four-power UN proposal in November and a joint declaration of five Latin American presidents five months later in April 1963. The genuine apprehension experienced in most Latin American capitals regarding the Missile Crisis was engendered by dint of their position as helpless onlookers while nuclear war threatened to break out in their own area. The Latin American region, it appeared, had become an expendable pawn to the great powers. The abrupt withdrawal of missiles from Cuba by the Soviets, disdainful of Castro's wishes, in a sense underscored this feeling of helplessness. What had been attempted in Cuba, it was concluded, could be attempted elsewhere in other Latin American nations by other nuclear weapons states including the United States. Beyond any other factor, the Crisis underscored to the Latin American nations that the existence of nuclear weapons within the area could make them the possible target of a nuclear attack.

4. The nuclear-weapon-free zone received an early stimulus from the strong support of democratic governments which existed at that time in Latin America. It is a nearly forgotten fact that the first apparent reference to the possibility of creation of a nuclear-weapon-free zone in Latin America was made in 1958 by Costa Rica in a draft resolution presented to the Council of the OAS. In October 1962 the Brazilian representative formally introduced the concept to the First Committee of the UN General Assembly (Brazil at that time having a civilian government). In November Brazil was joined by three other countries having democratic governments, Bolivia, Chile, and Ecuador, in the introduction of a draft resolution in the First Committee of the UN calling for a nuclear-weapon-free zone. And in March of 1963 Mexican President Lopez Mateos proposed to the democratically elected presidents of Bolivia, Brazil, Chile, and Ecuador that the five nations join in a common effort to achieve the denuclearization of Latin America. While there is logic in the view that Mexico would naturally seek the cooperation of those countries which had demonstrated the most interest in the creation of a nuclear-weapon-free zone in the region,[12] another interpretation has been advanced by two respected Mexican political scientists. The choice of the particular four governments, it was stated, was due to the fact that at that time each had a "popular" character and each had demonstrated in practice a foreign policy independent of the United States.[13]

[12] Alfonso García Robles, "Las Relaciones Diplomaticas Entre Mexico y el Brazil," *Foro Internacional* IV (1963–1964): 371.

[13] Ruy Mauro Marini, Olga Pellicer de Brody, "Militarismo y Desnuclearizacion en America Latina. El Caso de Brazil," *Foro Internacional* VIII (July–September 1967): 1.

5. Latin America may have been particularly receptive to the creation of a nuclear-weapon-free zone because of certain shared cultural and legal traditions as well as commonly held perceptions as to a regional identity. The lack of severe armed conflict relative to other regions is also a contributing factor (although Latin America is not as free of such conflicts as some might argue). Certainly a common denominator element among Latin American countries is the desirability to prevent disruptive non-Latin American interference and involvement in the hemisphere. This prevailing view yields a sort of defensive character to the nuclear-weapon-free zone effort. A corollary to this is the relative lack of superpower pressure on, and involvement in, the region. The Cuban Missile Crisis was a major exception and it, in part, precipitated a reaction leading to the zone's creation. Appreciation of this fact leads to the conclusion that a greater level of superpower competition in the region or the development of additional security relationships of Latin American countries with a superpower would complicate and inevitably weaken future prospects for the Tlatelolco regime.

International relevance

In 1979 the 34th UN General Assembly adopted a total of thirty-nine disarmament resolutions, four of which involved nuclear-weapon-free zones.[14] In addition to Latin America, resolutions were adopted calling for creation of nuclear-weapon-free zones in the Middle East, South Asia, and Africa. At other forums serious proposals have been advanced for nuclear-weapon-free zones in Scandinavia, the South Pacific, and Central Europe, as well as other regions.[15] None of the proposals have advanced much beyond the talking stage. The Latin American zone stands as a solitary example of a functioning nuclear-weapon-free zone agreement.

It is tempting to argue that the Latin American situation is unique and that the particular set of circumstances which have permitted progress to be achieved there are unlikely to be duplicated. Yet, while it is beyond the scope of this paper to explore the receptivity of other regions to nuclear-weapon-free zone proposals, the symbolic and substantive example of a successful Latin American arrangement has international relevance. The Tlatelolco lessons of personal leadership, careful and lengthy preparation and negotiations (via a preparatory committee), a flexible ratification process, carefully defined machinery, linkage of the regional control systems to the IAEA, etc., all have

[14] U.N. Centre for Disarmament, Fact Sheet 11, *General Assembly Resolutions on Disarmament—1979 Session.*
[15] See, for example: William Epstein, "A Nuclear-Weapon-Free Zone in Africa," and Roderic Alley, "Nuclear-Weapon-Free Zones: The South Pacific Proposal" (Muscatine, IA.: The Stanley Foundation, 1975); also *Nuclear-Weapon-Free Zones,* Vantage Conference Report (Muscatine, IA.: The Stanley Foundation, 1975).

been noted and have achieved important precedents. Other regions may indeed reach a point of relaxation of tensions among countries within a prospective zone, and reduced pressure from external countries, so as to permit negotiations toward a nuclear-weapon-free zone. Under such circumstances the process by which Tlatelolco was achieved will have relevance as well as the substance of the final agreement itself. However, in the current international climate the outlook for additional nuclear-weapon-free zones is not favorable due to reduced likelihood of the necessary superpower cooperation and support.

A related issue is whether the Latin American region may be changing in ways likely to make it a less suitable environment for a nuclear-weapon-free zone. It is clear that Latin American nations are moving into an increased level of international involvement ("a new internationalism") which represents a definite change in the pattern of interrelationships between Latin America and the rest of the world.[16] There is a clear acceleration of international activism on the part of Latin American nations, including an increased level of involvement with Western European countries and Spain, accompanied by a gradual lessening of U.S. presence and influence in the region. Such events were predictable as Western European nations recovered from World War II and emerged as strong economic competitors to the United States (for example in nuclear technology) and as Spain achieved a new degree of acceptability. Yet to a considerable degree it can be argued this represents more of a return to a pre-World War II pattern than an entirely new model of relationships.[17] There is little evidence to suggest that Latin American countries are losing their regional identity as relations with non-Latin American countries are enriched and deepened. Enhanced international involvement of Latin American countries in a variety of areas need not, and most probably will not, be a negative factor for the future nonproliferation status of the region and the vitality of the nuclear-weapon-free zone. A caveat to this is that the principal nuclear supplier countries affecting the Latin American region (the United States, Canada, France, and the Federal Republic of Germany) must better coordinate their policies regarding transfer of nuclear equipment and materials and in support of the Tlatelolco regime.

A final concern is whether Latin America may be becoming a more troubled region—subject to higher levels of competition and pressure from the superpowers. Such a trend, if established, would complicate and exacerbate divisions among Latin American countries thereby undercutting the

[16] See, for example: Roger W. Fontaine, James D. Theberge, eds., *Latin America's New Internationalism* (New York: Praeger, 1976) and Abraham F. Lowenthal and Albert Fishlow, *Latin America's Emergence* (New York: Foreign Policy Association, February 1979).

[17] The new energy linkages between Latin American and energy producing countries (i.e., Brazil and Iraq) have a potential to create an entirely new quality of relationships. However Latin American nations are seeking to develop coordinated approaches to energy problems through OLADE.

cooperative environment necessary for the nuclear-weapon-free zone. However, despite an enduring Soviet-Cuban tie, indications of some external involvement in Central America, and some limited Soviet cooperation with Peru and Argentina, there is little evidence of a significant increase in U.S.-Soviet rivalry in the region. Tacit Soviet and U.S. acquiescence on the continued desirability of a nonproliferation status for Latin America, and support for the Tlatelolco regime, should continue to be feasible.

Nuclear momentum and regional nonproliferation support

While the growth of nuclear power appears to be slowing throughout the non-Communist world in the early 1980s, Latin America is relatively less affected than other regions. A U.S. trade publication has recently identified Latin America as "the largest export market for reactor vendors in the next twenty years" and estimates that there will be 20–30 operating power reactors and 30–40 under construction by the year 2000.[18] While such predictions appear to be somewhat optimistic, a diversity of factors continue to impel Latin American countries toward nuclear development. For Brazil the heavy burden of imported oil and prestige enhances nuclear power's attraction, whereas oil producing countries such as Mexico and Venezuela view nuclear power more as a step toward diversification of energy sources. For Argentina the national security/prestige factor is important, but nuclear power is already making a small but important contribution to energy needs. The important point is that Latin American interest in nuclear power continues to be high and national investments are likely to show a marked increase in the early 1980s.

The focus here is on Latin America's three most advanced countries in terms of nuclear energy development: Argentina, Brazil, and Mexico. Others such as Chile, Peru, and Cuba, followed more distantly by Colombia and Venezuela, are demonstrating varying degrees of interest and involvement. However, nuclear development in Latin America has been spearheaded by Mexico, Argentina, and Brazil and these countries have each experienced disputes with more advanced supplier countries. Moreover it is these three countries which are (or will be) nearing a technical capability to develop a nuclear explosive device in the 1980s.

Accelerating momentum of nuclear technology is impacting on the degree of support among Latin American countries for the nuclear-weapon-free zone.

---

[18] "Latin America: Emerging Nuclear Market," *Nuclear News,* September 1979. For equally optimistic assessments by Latin Americans see M. B. A. Crespi: "La Energia Nuclear en America Latina: Necesidades y Possibilidades," *Interciencia* 4, 1 (January–Feburary 1979); Marcelo Alonso, "Inter-American Cooperation in Nuclear Energy"; Juan Barreda Delgado, "Nuclear Power in America—General Scope" (both the latter papers were presented to the American Nuclear Society's Executive Conference, Pan-American Nuclear Technology Exchange, Miami, April 1979).

Of particular importance is the Tlatelolco posture of the three most advanced Latin American countries due to the military potential of their programs and their influence on the positions of other countries in the region.

Mexico

The Portillo administration, which completes its term in 1982, has undertaken a cautious approach to nuclear development. Primary emphasis has been given to management of the extensive hydrocarbon reserves in a nation which, until 1974, was net importer of oil. Natural gas is being emphasized for internal industrial use, thus permitting more oil for export or use in the nation's growing petrochemical industry. The 1980 budget of $74 billion reflects an increase in spending of nearly 30 percent over 1979 with 25 percent of the total being slated for the oil industry alone.[19] Oil and gas production in the first quarter of 1980 was at approximately 2 million barrels a day with a maximum of 2.5 million set for 1980. Approximately 70 percent of Mexico's total oil exports go to the United States (850,000 barrels a day), although Mexico is seeking to reduce this percentage to 60 percent.

In this overall context the government approach to nuclear energy, as outlined in the Programa Nacional de Energia Nuclear in 1979, is one component of an energy diversification program.[20] That is Mexican policymakers are seeking to diversify their energy options and to structure their nuclear industry so as to minimize dependence on foreign, particularly U.S., technology.

In mid-1980 Mexico's first nuclear power plant, 654-MWe U.S.-supplied unit, was 35 percent complete with start-up set for May 1982. An identical unit was 21 percent complete with start-up scheduled for one year later.[21] When the two units are complete they will supply nearly 10 percent of the nation's total electric power needs.

The construction of the U.S.-supplied reactors has resulted in considerable friction between the United States and Mexico. Mexican resentment has been intense regarding perceived efforts to interfere with their nuclear program due to the Nuclear Nonproliferation Act in 1978. It is of note that the decision to purchase U.S. units did not imply to the Mexicans that enriched uranium would also be purchased from the United States. Rather Mexico applied to the IAEA for enriched uranium, the first such request in history to that body for fuel for a power reactor. The IAEA offered the Mexican enrichment contract to various suppliers and ultimately it was decided that the United States would supply the enriched uranium. The core for the first unit will be French-supplied uranium enriched by the United States (with which Mexico has two ten-year enrichment contracts to cover the two units). Reloads

[19] The *New York Times,* 9 December 1979, 24 April, 5 May 1980.
[20] *Hispano* (Mexico City), 21 January 1980 (special issue on Mexican nuclear energy program).
[21] *Nuclear News,* February 1980.

and uranium for future Mexican power units will come from domestic supplies.[22] The important point, in the view of Mexican policymakers, was to emphasize the auspices of the IAEA as opposed to a strictly bilateral relationship on nuclear matters with the United States.

The first unit was originally scheduled to be completed in 1977, but construction problems and ultimately obstacles engendered by the U.S. Nuclear Nonproliferation Act of 1978 led to a long delay in issuing an export license (for ultimate delivery of the enriched uranium) until February 1979. This resulted in distinct resentment by Mexican officials who strongly believed such restrictions should be unnecessary due to the IAEA involvement in the arrangement, the fact that the entire Mexican program is under full scope safeguards, and Mexico's leadership position in nuclear nonproliferation matters.[23] This latter point was a source of particular annoyance as Mexico, under the leadership of former Foreign Minister Alfonso García Robles, was in the forefront of negotiations resulting in the Tlatelolco Treaty.[24] In the words of an official of the Mexican energy commission:

> It is logical that in a country that has taken such a strong antinuclear weapons stand, measures imposed by developed countries to obstruct transfer of technology promote resentment.[25]

Mexico possesses significant uranium reserves with proven amounts now estimated at over 11,000 tons, and estimated reserves as high as 600,000 tons (exact figures vary but it does appear that reserves exist that are more than adequate for national needs for the indefinite future).

Mexico is actively exploring with several foreign suppliers the next steps in its nuclear program. Canada, France, and Sweden are all carrying out technical studies and it is likely a decision will be made within two years or less to purchase another power unit from one of these countries. A recent program for cooperation with Spain has also been negotiated. In a country which

---

[22] *Nucleonics Week*, 24 January 1980.

[23] For example: Dalmau Costa, Director General, Mexican Institute for Nuclear Research, "Transfer of Technology and the Fuel Cycle," paper prepared for the American Nuclear Society's Executive Conference, Pan-American Technical Exchange, April 1979, Miami, Florida; and Antonio Gonzalez de Leon, "Las Relaciones Mexico-Estados Unidos: el Caso de la Energia Nuclear," *Foro Internacional* 19, 2 (October–December, 1978).

[24] For a recent description of the Tlatelolco Treaty see Alfonso García Robles, *The Latin American Nuclear-Weapon-Free Zone,* Stanley Foundation Occasional Paper 21, May 1979.

[25] Juan Eivenschutz, "Energy Situation and the Outlook for Nuclear Power in Mexico," paper prepared for the American Nuclear Society's Executive Conference, Pan-American Technical Exchange, April 1979, Miami, Florida.

several years ago boasted of having no formal bilateral programs of nuclear cooperation with any country, this amount of foreign involvement is significant. Mexican authorities are also looking to the possibility of receiving future supplies of enriched uranium from multinational organizations (EURODIF, COREDIF), as well as investing in multinational arrangements.

While a decision on the next power unit may come prior to the end of the Portillo administration in 1982, it is probable that major decisions regarding the future Mexican program will be left to the next administration. It would seem likely that Mexico will avoid becoming linked to one supplier, as Brazil has, and will put great emphasis on the domestic production of uranium, and full mastery of the nuclear fuel cycle, ultimately moving toward the manufacture of heavy components.[26] Mexico's interest in a trade of oil for advanced nuclear technology is quite evident.

In contrast to Argentina and Brazil, Mexico's dedication to the peaceful uses of nuclear energy is clear and unambiguous. This is evident in an amendment to Article 27 of the Constitution which passed on the urging of former President Echeverria. However, nuclear energy has become a highly nationalistic issue, with particular concerns expressed by some in the labor movement and congress regarding U.S. influence in the nuclear industry. Legislation was passed in 1978 restricting the exportation of uranium and private investment (domestic or foreign) in the uranium industry (despite the objections of some officials in the Mexican nuclear industry). Support within the Foreign Ministry for the overall goal of nonproliferation continues, although there is increasing disenchantment with the NPT (the perceived failure of the superpowers to live up to their obligations under the agreement, especially Articles 4 and 6).

Mexico's commitment to Tlatelolco remains firm. There is considerable (and justifiable) pride in the leadership of Alfonso García Robles, the current Ambassador to the Committee on Disarmament (CD) and the author of the Treaty. OPANAL is headquartered in Mexico City and Mexican diplomats including the President continue to seek international and Latin American support for Tlatelolco.

Whether Mexico's commitment to Tlatelolco will retain its intensity in the future is arguable. Among some younger Mexican foreign ministry officials there may be growing cynicism regarding the nation's traditional emphasis on nuclear disarmament, and this could translate into a reduced focus on Tlatelolco. The Foreign Ministry and the growing nuclear establishment have been especially irritated by the perceived total lack of recognition of their nonproliferation leadership, evident in the application of U.S. nonproliferation policy. The military influence may also be slowly increasing as that body's percentage of the national budget steadily increases (it has exceeded that spent on education for a number of years) and its leadership cultivates more international contacts.

If there is a shift in intensity in Mexico's support for Tlatelolco it will best be understood in the context of that nation edging towards a more assertive and less legalistically defined foreign policy style with the confidence of its new-found oil power.[27] Mexico's original commitment to Tlatelolco had a variety of motivations but it was principally a manifestation of a defensive foreign policy style. Analogous to Finland, Mexico existed within the shadow of the superpower from which it had suffered much in the past and with which it needed to maintain good relations. The support for the nuclear-weapon-free zone was an effort to maintain its independence by, in effect, avoiding becoming intertwined in cold war conflicts between the great powers. Such confrontations, it was held, posed security dangers and forced Mexico into taking a clear stance with the United States on cold war issues, often a very unpalatable position in terms of domestic politics. The energy crisis and oil have provided Mexico with leverage for dealing with the United States on a range of bilateral issues and a greater ability to assert more independent foreign policy positions. While support for Tlatelolco and nonproliferation will no doubt continue to be reflected in Mexican foreign policy, its leadership in this area may lessen in the years ahead.

Argentina

Argentina continues to be the nuclear leader among Latin American nations with a program progressing steadily and with clearly defined goals. At the present time it is the only Latin American nation with an operating power reactor, fuel fabrication facility, and a small heavy water production facility. A small reprocessing facility has also operated in the past.

Argentina's energy situation is relatively favorable in contrast with that of its northern neighbor, Brazil. Oil output has increased at a steady rate and the national oil utility (YPF) estimates that the nation will reach self-sufficiency by 1982. At the present time nuclear accounts for 4 percent of the total national electric production and by 1995 it is estimated that it will contribute 10 percent.[28] The nation is also well endowed with uranium, with estimated deposits of 27,000 tons of high quality and another 31,000 tons available at higher cost, more than enough to meet its own projected needs through 1990. Uranium exploration has been under way for over two decades and uranium production is well advanced.[29]

Argentina also has a small operating fuel-fabrication facility with plans for an industrial scale plant to be operating in the early 1980s. Having learned from West Germany (from which it has imported zirconium tubes for a

---

[26] *Nucleonics Week,* 24 January 1980.

[27] Mexico oil leverage on the U.S. and related issues are discussed in The Stanley Foundation, *Conference on International Issues: Mexico and the U.S.,* Vantage Conference Report, June 1980.

[28] *Electrical Week,* 18 July 1979. Another source provides a different picture for 1979: thermal 59.9 percent, hydro 26.5 percent, nuclear 8.1 percent (*Latin American Weekly Report,* 15 February 1980).

[29] *Nuclear Fuel,* 12 November 1979. Yellowcake production of 1000 metric tons is set for 1984.

number of years) Argentina has recently initiated a pilot facility to produce zirconium at its Constituyentes Atomic Facility near Buenos Aires, to be followed by an industrial scale unit at its Ezeiza facility.[30] Moreover under an agreement implemented in early 1980, the Soviet Union is supplying the technology (including on-site technical experts) for the zirconium production facility. It is expected that Argentina will ultimately supply zircaloy to Brazil from this facility as part of the two nations' bilateral program for nuclear cooperation.[31]

Argentina has benefited from operational experience in reprocessing technology, having previously constructed a laboratory-size facility which separated small amounts of plutonium and was subsequently shut down in the early 1970s. Argentine officials, aware of the leverage which reprocessing provides, have been deliberately ambiguous in their statements about future reprocessing plans but have indicated that an enlarged pilot facility may be operational in the early 1980s at Ezeiza.[32] It is estimated that Argentina's one power reactor has produced the equivalent of several hundred kilograms of plutonium. At the present time, however, spent fuel is being stored in proximity to the power reactor for possible future reprocessing. Argentina also possesses a small pilot heavy water production facility, in close proximity to its power reactor, which currently produces approximately three tons per year. This will be augmented by a Swiss supplied industrial scale facility capable of producing 250 tons per year.

In addition to the nation's first power reactor (370-MWe) obtained from West Germany and operating since 1974, a second Canadian supplied natural uranium unit is scheduled for completion in May 1981. A third German supplied 750-MWe is scheduled for completion in the late 1980s. The decision of a supplier for the country's third reactor was a protracted affair which was decided on 1 October 1979 when Argentina announced the awarding of the reactor contract to West Germany and an accompanying contract to a Swiss company to build a turnkey heavy water production plant.[33] Various factors contributed to the German success in competition with Canada including the

[30] *La Nacion* (Buenos Aires), 6 October 1978; *Nuclear News,* September 1979.

[31] Foreign Broadcast Information Service, *FBIS,* Worldwide Report, *Nuclear Development and Proliferation,* 28 March 1980, p. 36.

[32] The ambiguity of Argentine statements is revealed in statements by CNEA President Castro Madero: "We are de facto full scope safeguards—when we in the future build a reprocessing plant that will also be under safeguards from the very moment fuel from either the research reactors or Atucha comes in, because all fuel elements are under safeguards and they carry safeguards along with them" (*Washington Post,* 16 October 1978). And Castro Madero: "Pilot reprocessing facility [is] under IAEA safeguards *when reprocessing safeguarded fissionable materials."* (Letter from Admiral Carlos Castro Madero, 17 September 1979—emphasis added. An inference which can be drawn from the choice of words is that Argentina would not consider its reprocessing facility as being under safeguards if it were reprocessing unsafeguarded fuel.

[33] The circumstances surrounding the Argentine decision to purchase the German unit are explored in greater detail in the author's "U.S. and Latin America: Policy Options Following INFCE," op. cit.

good operational experience of the German supplied Atucha I and the economic and related difficulties surrounding the construction of the nation's second unit supplied by Canada. However, it is widely acknowledged that the critical factor which encouraged Argentine authorities to opt for the somewhat more expensive German unit was the Canadian insistence on full scope safeguards. There is considerable evidence to suggest that in order to land the contract German officials may have misled the Canadians into believing they too would demand full scope safeguards. In the meantime an arrangement was developed with Switzerland and word was permitted to reach the Argentines, who correctly read the signals and split their order (thus avoiding full scope safeguards from either supplier).

U.S. officials have acknowledged the heavy water contract falls somewhere in a "grey" area regarding the London supplier guidelines, but nonetheless have attempted to pressure both Switzerland and Germany to require very tight de facto safeguards. Other levers utilized by the United States were threatened holdup in approval of a reactor vessel subcontract which must be obtained by the German supplier from a U.S. manufacturer, and raising the possibility of a cutoff of U.S. supplies of low enriched uranium for Argen- -tina's research reactors (and also for Argentine retransfer to other Latin American countries). These and other actions could be interpreted as mandated by the U.S. Nonproliferation Act of 1978. However in June 1980 the Carter administration did approve, with NRC support, shipment of a small order (3.6 kilograms) of low enriched uranium to Argentina, despite the fact that the 10 March 1980 deadline mandated by the 1978 nonproliferation legislation had passed. In addition, after securing the order for the third reactor, the Germans in the spring of 1980 temporarily refused to grant an export license to the German company in an effort to appease the United States and possibly obtain an Argentine commitment to full scope safeguards. Argentina reacted to U.S. and German pressure through ploys of its own: by sending a delegation to the Soviet Union to explore the possibility of Soviet supply of components for nuclear plants and low enriched uranium for research reactors, and by initiating renewed discussions with Canada regarding the next four Argentine power reactors (which Germany was considered to have the inside track on, following the most recent Argentine purchase).

It is also notable, however, that as a part of the German contract Argentina has apparently reconfirmed its commitment to ratify the Tlatelolco Treaty. Until the late 1970s German policymakers had given scant attention to Tlatelolco (and indeed were generally ignorant of its provisions). However, largely due to an educational effort undertaken by U.S. State Department and ACDA, Tlatelolco became, to the Germans, an object of interest and greater attention. Argentina's reaction to, initially, U.S. and, subsequently, German emphasis of Tlatelolco in nuclear negotiations is significant and best understood in the context of the overall Argentine posture regarding the Latin American nuclear-weapon-free zone.

In contrast to Brazil's early involvement (1962) in the Tlatelolco effort, Argentina joined the original Treaty negotiations only after they were well underway. The fact that Argentina was initially ignored by the democratic Latin American countries in the original invitation for an organizing session was not lost on the Argentines and this impacted on their position when later they did join the negotiations. Argentina was already laboring under a certain degree of resentment at not having been invited to join Brazil and Mexico as delegates to the new expanded Geneva Disarmament Talks in the early 1960s (a fact which in part may explain why Brazil has adhered to the Partial Test Ban Treaty, whereas Argentina has not). When Argentina joined the Tlatelolco negotiations in Mexico City it immediately allied itself with Brazil (whose position changed significantly following the 1964 military coup) and worked to stiffen a number of the provisions of the Treaty (including the ratification procedure).

Ultimately Argentina did sign Tlatelolco in September 1967, but thus far is the only holdout among Latin American nations which had taken part in the actual negotiations. Brazil and Chile have taken the technical step of ratifying the Treaty without taking advantage of paragraph 2 of Article 28 which allows them to waive certain requirements and permits the Treaty to come into full force for their national territory (an action taken by Mexico and the other 21 current parties to the agreement). While Argentina has announced its intent to ratify, it has not done so and thus its position is distinct from that of Chile and Brazil. The distinction is more than symbolic as Chile and Brazil have by their actions indicated they will take no measures contrary to the spirit of the Treaty.

The Argentine announcement of intent to ratify Tlatelolco (and thus put itself in a position similar to Brazil and Chile) followed a September 1977 meeting between Presidents Carter and Videla. It was specifically outlined in a 21 November 1977 Joint Communique, following a visit by Secretary of State Vance. In the same Joint Communique the United States gave recognition to Argentine interest in heavy water and in becoming a significant nuclear supplier country—an important linkage to the Argentines and one underestimated by U.S. officials. Subsequent problems regarding the interpretation of the Joint Communique and the linkage of the heavy water issue to Tlatelolco ratification, may well have complicated the Argentine ratification process. Even CNEA President Castro Madero, a strong Tlatelolco supporter (over the criticism of some in the Argentine government) began to raise questions regarding Tlatelolco.[34] These doubts and concerns grew as Tlatelolco ratification became involved in competition for the nation's third reactor and heavy water unit in 1979.

In 1980 Argentine officials still maintain their intent to ultimately ratify Tlatelolco. However, they have raised a number of complex issues which in

[34] Carlos Castro Madero, "Argentina. Situacion Nuclear Actual," *Esrategia* (March–April 1978).

turn have promoted renewed questioning by some as to Argentina's real motivations. These issues, representing a mixture of previous Argentine positions raised during the negotiating process and some new variations, deserve careful study. Three interrelated issues are of particular import: protocol "interpretations," the completeness of required IAEA safeguards, and PNEs.

From the Argentine point of view one of the more critical weaknesses of Tlatelolco is the flexibility of the process whereby nuclear weapon states adhere to the Treaty through Additional Protocol II. Under the terms of the Treaty no reservations are permitted to nuclear weapon states in the ratification process. However during the Tlatelolco Treaty negotiations, in order to gain U.S. support (and the support of other nuclear weapon states) García Robles negotiated an arrangement whereby "interpretive declarations" would be permitted which "lack the juridical character of a reservation" and do not affect the fundamental obligations assumed by Latin American nations.[35] In the view of Argentina this ratification process opened a gigantic loophole in that in ratifying Tlatelolco the United States, Soviet Union, and Great Britain have included "interpretations" which, if accepted, have the result of modifying the rights of the Latin American parties to the Treaty.[36]

The complications raised by the "interpretation" issue are perhaps best illustrated by the second issue stated above: the legality of PNEs under the Treaty. The United States and the Soviet Union have each included very specific interpretive statements in their Protocol II ratifications that PNEs are not permitted under the terms of the Treaty. Most Tlatelolco parties including Mexico also share the U.S. view that PNEs are not, under present circumstances, permitted under the Treaty (essentially the Mexicans argue that Article 18 is subsumed under Article 5 and that technology does not now exist to distinguish a "peaceful" nuclear explosion). The Argentine position on PNEs is that Tlatelolco's Article 18:

> recognizes the right of the Contracting Parties by their own means or in association with Third Parties to carry out explosions for peaceful purposes including explosions which may call for the use of instruments similar to those used in atomic weapons.[37]

Argentine officials also argued during the Tlatelolco negotiations for a very subjective interpretation of the key factor which distinguished a PNE from a weapon: the "intent" of the user.[38] This Argentine position has not been altered up to the current time but the nation is described as voluntarily abstaining from the use of PNEs while leaving open a possibility for their

[35] COPREDAL/AR/46 and 47, 11 and 12 Feburary 1967 (working documents of the Tlatelolco Treaty Preparatory Committee).
[36] This is argued forcefully in Juan E. Gugliamelli, "Argentina Ratifica el Tratado de Tlatelolco, Mientras las Superpotencias Condicionan su Adhesion al Segundo Protocolo Adicional," *Estrategia* (May–August 1978).
[37] U.N. Document A/C.1/PV15, 10 October 1967.
[38] COPREDAL/AR/41, 8 February 1967.

development (for peace or defense) should a national security need arise.[39] Both the United States and West Germany have attempted to gain Argentine acceptance of a PNE ban in recent discussions without success. Argentine officials cite the PNE issue as a prime example of a modification of the rights of Tlatelolco parties by nuclear weapon states. They assert U.S.-Soviet Protocol statements (as well as the U.S. position on the issue of the transit or transportation of nuclear weapons through the zone) amount to a clear reservation rather than an interpretation. The U.S. position is that conflicting interpretations (between nuclear weapon states and some parties to Tlatelolco or between the nuclear weapon states themselves) do not necessarily serve to make the Treaty inoperative or have the effect of rupturing the overall objective of the Treaty. Rather, the interpretation provides an essential element of flexibility which permits overall progress toward creation of the full nuclear-weapon-free zone.[40]

A third and also interrelated issue is whether Article 13 of the Tlatelolco Treaty actually requires parties to negotiate full scope IAEA safeguards. The exact wording of the relevant portion of Article 13 of the Treaty is:

> Each Contracting Party shall negotiate multilateral or bilateral agreements with the International Atomic Energy Agency for the application of safeguards to its nuclear activities.

The United States in its interpretive statements accompanying ratification of Protocol II (and suggested for Protocol I) has clearly viewed the agreement as requiring full scope IAEA safeguards.[41] Moreover a review of Tlatelolco negotiating documents clearly sustains the view that full scope safeguards were the explicit intent. Disagreement during the negotiations was between those favoring a multilateral OPANAL-IAEA system of common safeguards or individual safeguards to be negotiated by each party with the IAEA. Brazil and Argentina argued for the bilateral relationship and Mexico and others favored the multilateral with both options being mentioned in Article 13. However, the comprehensive and full scope nature of IAEA safeguards was not an issue and was never challenged by Argentina and Brazil.

The safeguards issue has current relevance as Argentine officials are involved in negotiations with the IAEA over what CNEA officials claim could be the first true "Tlatelolco safeguard agreement." The Argentine position here is carefully defined in a self-serving manner since until recently all agreements negotiated under Article 13 of the Tlatelolco Treaty were also related to the NPT (which Argentina rejects). Argentine officials suggest that its safeguard agreement as negotiated with the IAEA could be the true

---

[39] Gugliamelli, op. cit., footnote 36. Gugliamelli's position on this is disputed by some in the Argentine CNEA as not necessarily representative. However over the years, Gugliamelli has often reflected a persuasive strain of Argentine thinking on nuclear issues.

[40] *Treaty of Tlatelolco,* op. cit., Testimony of van Doren, p. 21.

[41] *Treaty of Tlatelolco,* op. cit., Testimony of van Doren, p. 23.

precedent for a Tlatelolco agreement since Argentina is not a party to the NPT (as have been all previous Latin American nations which have negotiated agreements with the IAEA under Article 13). However, in July 1979 Colombia, a party to Tlatelolco but not NPT, signed a full scope safeguard agreement with the IAEA as specified by Article 13. This has raised problems for the Argentines as U.S. officials have suggested that Argentina should clearly adhere to the Colombian model in its safeguard agreement. Argentina has responded by what is generally perceived as delaying tactics in its negotiations with the IAEA, in an effort to precisely define safeguard requirements, and with the objective of avoiding any legal commitment to de jure full scope safeguards.

The Argentine positions on Tlatelolco assume greater significance with growing prospects for cooperation with Brazil on nuclear issues. Such cooperation can indeed have beneficial results in reducing tensions and uncertainties between the two countries. However it can also take a negative character if it should become an effort to cooperate on frustrating the goals of the Tlatelolco Treaty. It is quite conceivable that Argentine officials may seek to alter the relatively more favorable Brazilian position on Tlatelolco.

Brazil

In 1980 the Brazilian commitment to nuclear energy has been affected by two interrelated factors: (1) enhanced concern regarding the safety and environmental aspects of nuclear power and (2) shifting views regarding the nation's energy goals as impacted by both rising costs of imported fuel and growing problems and expense of the German supplied nuclear power units. The cost of imported energy is having a devastating impact on Brazil. In 1979 the Brazilian government estimated the nation produced about 15 percent of the oil it consumed and imported one million barrels per day at a yearly cost of between 6.5 and 7.5 billion dollars.[42] The impact of this on the nation's balance-of-payments and overall economic health has prompted the government to undertake ambitious programs for alternative fuels, including alcohol, and to further emphasize hydroelectric programs. The nation's Third National Development Program, announced in late 1979, put heavy emphasis on hydroelectric development somewhat at the expense of the nuclear component. Under "Plan 95" of the National Electrical Utility, ELECTROBRAS, 69,000-MWe of hydroelectric facilities would be added by 1990 (in addition to the existing 22,000-MWe), whereas by the year 2000 it was estimated that nuclear would provide, at most, no more than 10,000-MWe, accounting for slightly more than 3 percent of the nation's electricity.[43]

[42] *Latin American Economic Report,* 20 July 1979.
[43] *BOLSA Review,* November 1979, p. 666; *Latin American Regional Report* (Brazil), 9 November 1979.

Testing was done in 1980 on the nation's first Angra I 626-MWe U.S.-supplied light water reactor with a start-up time set for September 1980. Work on Angra II, the 1,245-MWe light water unit supplied by the Federal Republic of Germany, was postponed to mid-1980 due to structural/seismic problems with the completion date optimistically set for August 1986. A new site for the second German unit, Angra III, was selected in mid-1980, with 1988 completion date targeted but unlikely. Sites for the third and fourth German units (units 4 and 5) have not been selected and completion dates are set for the mid-1990s.[44]

The cost estimates for the entire German contract have risen dramatically (now above 30 billion) and this, along with rising environmental consciousness, is weighing against nuclear development and in favor of tapping the vast amounts of as yet unexploited hydroelectric resources. By mid-1980 there had been three major Congressional investigations of the nuclear program with additional challenges being mounted on a regular basis in the nation's media. Whether internal opposition to the scope and direction of the nuclear program will lead to a partial curtailment of the original German contract remains an object of ongoing debate in Brazil.

Construction began in early 1979 on a demonstration nozzle enrichment plant with a scheduled completion date for late 1983 or early 1984. A small pilot facility is already installed in Belo Horizonte.[45] A full commercial scale nozzle enrichment plant should be operational by 1987 with the goal of meeting the nation's own enrichment requirements and developing an eventual export market for enriched uranium in the Latin American region.[46] Plans, financing, and site location for a pilot reprocessing unit were completed in 1979 but actual construction has been postponed and the original startup date of 1984 seems unlikely. Brazilian officials have deemphasized the need for a commercial scale reprocessing facility to far into the future.

Growing signs in late 1979 of a partial curtailment of the German order by the newly installed government of President Figueiredo led to a German threat not to transfer enrichment and reprocessing equipment. Further strains in Brazilian-German nuclear cooperation occurred with disputes involving joint companies established in Brazil as part of the original 1975 contract. Despite vain government attempts to suppress publication it was reported in the Brazilian press that a hitherto secret arrangement existed giving the German exporting company practical control over the so-called joint company (NUCLEN) which oversees the transfer of nuclear information (as well as nuclear power plant design and engineering) from Germany to Brazil. The

[44] Interview with NUCLEBRAS President Nogueira Batista, 1 March 1980 (*FBIS,* op. cit., 15 April 1980, no. 38); *Nuclear News,* February 1980.
[45] *Latin American Energy Report,* 13 March 1980.
[46] Interview with Nogueira Batista, 1 March 1980 (*FBIS,* op. cit., 28 March 1980, no. 36).

storm of criticism provided renewed impetus to ongoing Congressional investigations and a general assumption that the scope and actual transfer of technology is being restricted by the Germans.

With the reaffirmation by the Brazilian government in the spring of 1980 of plans to proceed with nuclear units 4 and 5, one-half of the original German contract for 8 units seems secure. Brazilian officials continue to emphasize their intent to proceed with the full 8 unit order, although completion time has been extended five additional years until 1995. The Brazilian German equipment company, NUCLEP, which had been idle, began in 1980 to fashion components for the second and third units. Future prospects for NUCLEP include the possibility of producing equipment for Argentina as part of that nation's arrangement with Germany.

However, despite optimistic projections, the Brazilian nuclear program faces serious problems. Brazil's contract with URENCO (from which it is to receive enriched uranium for all the German power units) will now have to be renegotiated. This is due to the construction delays for the German supplied power units in Brazil which have caused the demand for enrichment services to be much less than the quantities contracted with URENCO. However, an added factor is the inability of Brazil to produce sufficient uranium from its current mining facilities to be enriched by URENCO despite the fact that it is now generally acknowledged that Brazilian uranium reserves are quite high. The nuclear programs budget for 1980 was slashed to $140 million, in part as a result of the pressure of ELECTROBRAS and of the powerful Planning Minister Antonio Delfim Netto.

Brazilian-U.S. relations, which suffered considerably as a result of disagreements following the 1975 contract, have taken a turn for the better with the advent of the new Brazilian government in 1979 and a greater appreciation of the limits and costs of certain actions by the Carter administration. A March 1979 visit by Vice President Mondale for discussions with the new Brazilian government set the tone for the current U.S. posture of reducing tensions and emphasizing the desirability of Brazil continuing to retain its current de facto full scope safeguard status. At the present time all nuclear facilities including the nearly completed Angra I unit are under IAEA safeguards and the German contract also carries with it a very comprehensive agreement. The URENCO agreement also includes an arrangement for a storage facility for Brazilian produced plutonium.

Brazil continues to be more favorably inclined toward Tlatelolco than Argentina. It has signed and ratified the agreement (although, as stated earlier, the Treaty is not yet in force for that nation). Moreover Brazilian ratification represents an important expression of support with political significance. This was made explicit in a formal government statement on nuclear policy, *The Brazilian Nuclear Program*, issued in 1977. In the statement Brazil declared that:

Furthermore the Treaty of Tlatelolco contains, in its Additional Protocol II, a provision committing nuclear powers not to utilize nuclear weapons in Latin American countries, or threaten these countries with such utilization. Full enforcement of the Treaty of Tlatelolco depends at the moment upon the acceptance of this commitment by those powers. Having signed the Treaty, Brazil has committed itself according to the canons of international law not to perform any act which defeats the objectives of the Treaty to which there corresponds the guarantee that the other signatories will do likewise.

On subsequent occasions Brazilian officials have continued to maintain the significance of their country's ratification of the Tlatelolco Treaty. In statements to the First Committee of the UN General Assembly in 1979 the Brazilian delegate drew a sharp distinction between the Latin American nuclear-weapon-free zone and zones proposed for other portions of the world. A key difference it has stressed is that Tlatelolco enjoys the firm support of the nuclear weapon states.[47] This point together with Brazil's strong statement that it will take no actions contrary to the objectives of the Treaty stands in some contrast to the position of Argentina.

It is clear that Brazil shares the Argentine position on PNEs and their legality under the Treaty. Yet thus far Brazilian officials have not been predisposed to raise issues, as have the Argentines, regarding the protocol ratification procedure of the nuclear weapon states, transit rights claimed by the United States, etc. Whether the differences are of style or substance remains to be seen.

Regional trends

A number of dynamic factors can be identified as impacting on nonproliferation prospects in Latin America for the early 1980s. These include a reduced U.S. influence on Latin American programs and a concurrent rise of European (particularly German) involvement, a continued trend by the more advanced Latin American nations toward full mastery of the nuclear fuel cycle, and a growing disenchantment with the NPT. However, most Latin American policymakers continue to oppose the presence of nuclear weapons in the region and to support the goals of the Tlatelolco Treaty (although, as pointed out earlier, there are clear differences of view regarding certain aspects of the Treaty). The fact that at present every publicly known nuclear facility in the region is under IAEA safeguards (or under negotiation pursuant to their implementation) stands in significant contrast to other more troubled areas of the world.

Barring unanticipated meddling by the nuclear weapon states, two trends can be identified as having particular future significance for nonproliferation

[47] U.N. document A/C1/PV38, 21 November 1979.

efforts in the region: horizontal transfer of nuclear technology and growing evidence of convergence of the nuclear policies of Argentina and Brazil.

Horizontal transfer of nuclear technology

International attention has generally focused on complications or potential proliferation dangers arising from transfer of nuclear technology by the more advanced countries to countries with developing nuclear programs. Indeed this continues to be a central preoccupation of U.S. policymakers with respect to transfer of European technology to Argentina and Brazil. However, there is growing awareness of possible implications of horizontal transfer of nuclear technology between developing countries (or alternatively retransfer of advanced nation technology from one developing country to another). While it is beyond the scope of this paper to consider in a comprehensive manner this topic as regards Latin American countries, several cases are briefly discussed.

Argentina has been particularly active in seeking to develop nuclear relationships with its Latin American neighbors, including the promotion of heavy water technology. Argentina fully intends to become a regional supplier of heavy water, research (test) reactors, and other nuclear material. A 1977 agreement (supplemented in 1979) with Peru has spurred considerable interest. Under the agreement Peru has received an Argentine-built zero power reactor, the transfer of U.S.-supplied enriched uranium, a 10-MW test reactor to be in operation by 1982, resulting in close cooperation between the CNEA and the Instituto Peruano de Energia Nuclear (IPEN). While the arrangement is fully covered by IAEA safeguards (Peru is a party to Tlatelolco and the NPT), it has nonetheless been greeted as the beginning of a new pattern of horizontal spread of nuclear know-how and material.

Brazil has not stressed bilateral nuclear programs of cooperation to the extent Argentina has, having until recently limited agreements to neighboring states of Uruguay and Paraguay. However, impelled primarily by economic factors, Brazil has undertaken a dramatic acceleration of its program of nuclear cooperation since 1979. The principal economic factors are a need to better utilize partly idle heavy nuclear manufacturing capability imported from Germany and a hope of trading advanced nuclear technology for oil.

In 1979 Brazil initiated a potentially significant cooperative program with Venezuela, a country with which it has not traditionally enjoyed good relations. In a series of official visits culminating with President Figueiredo's November 1979 trip to Caracas, the possibility of oil for Brazilian nuclear equipment and assistance was discussed, and a preliminary agreement reached calling for Brazilian technical assistance in nuclear matters with particular reference to future power reactors.[48] Despite the preliminary nature of the

---

[48] The Brazilian Embassy, *Brazil Today,* 27 November 1979; *O Globo* (Rio de Janeiro, 29 October 1979).

arrangement it represented the first tangible indication of Brazilian interest in reexporting nuclear technology and equipment received in part from more advanced nations.

In response to this and despite growing indications of Argentine-Brazilian nuclear convergence, it is notable that some Argentine officials and newspapers immediately reached geopolitical interpretations. Brazil was viewed as seeking to extend its influence beyond the Southern Cone to a democratic regime as part of an effort to exert political leadership in the hemisphere. To answer this concern Argentina initiated discussions with Venezuela that led to an August 1979 agreement for cooperation and transfer of information on both experimental and power reactors as well as joint prospecting for uranium (in Venezuela) and exchange and training of experts.

Geopolitical concerns and Brazilian need for oil are also factors in the cultivation of nuclear relationships with Chile. It is of interest that despite serious political differences and occasional threatened conflict between Argentina and Chile, the nuclear energy commissions of the two countries have retained a good cooperative relationship including exchanges and training of Chilean technicians in Argentina. Brazil, however, has also initiated steps (in early 1980) to sign a nuclear agreement with Chile whereby advanced technology and training would be transferred as part of an arrangement permitting Brazilian companies to prospect for petroleum on the southern Chilean continental shelf. In a similar fashion, in March of 1980 the Brazilian and Colombian foreign ministers signed a preliminary agreement for nuclear cooperation. This was in the context of a larger arrangement for cooperation in the exploitation of Colombian coal resources, and the Brazilian officials emphasized the desirability of including Venezuela in any future arrangement.

In addition to nuclear relationships between Latin American countries, there are growing instances of cooperation of Latin American countries and developing nations in other regions. Some of these non-Latin American nations, such as India and Spain, have nuclear programs somewhat further developed than Latin American nations, whereas others such as Iraq, Libya, and Romania do not. Among the agreements of interest have been Argentina's with India and Libya and previous Argentine involvement in the Iranian nuclear program. In February 1980 Argentina signed an agreement for nuclear cooperation with another threshold country, South Korea.

Brazil has moved more slowly than Argentina but in 1980 reached a nuclear agreement with Iraq that has stimulated considerable international interest. The Brazil-Iraq agreement raised concern that Brazil might transfer sensitive technology received from the Federal Republic of Germany to a radical country in one of the most turbulent areas of the world. Iraq's leverage on Brazil, from which the latter receives nearly one-half of its imported oil, is viewed with concern by some as raising the prospect of an oil-for-nuclear blackmail relationship.

Under the agreement Iraq will receive Brazilian assistance in prospecting, production, and refinement of uranium and Iraqi technicians will be trained in Brazil. Brazil will also supply Iraq with low-enriched uranium as well as equipment and technology for reactor construction. The ten-year agreement signed in January 1980 is to be subject to IAEA safeguards. Brazilian officials emphasized that it was unnecessary to consult with the Federal Republic of Germany regarding the agreement as it excludes the transfer of know-how or German supplied equipment.[49]

Brazilian officials are not unaware of their vulnerability and, as implied above, are seeking to diversify their oil supply prospects primarily from Mexico and Venezuela. For the next several years Brazil will not have sensitive technology it could retransfer to Iraq or other nations were it so inclined. Yet the Iraq relationship looms as important to the Brazilians; President Figueiredo visited Iraq in early 1980 and has named the previous Chief of Staff of the Brazilian Armed Forces to be Ambassador to Iraq. Brazil will remain dependent on Middle Eastern oil for much of the 1980s and could experience difficulty resisting persistent efforts by Iraq to gain access to advanced nuclear technology.

The accelerating horizontal transfer of nuclear technology is adding a new and unpredictable factor to the nonproliferation picture in Latin America. It will become far more prevalent by the mid-1980s. All of the Latin American countries likely to cooperate with Argentina and Brazil (with the exception of Chile) are covered under full scope safeguards, either through Tlatelolco or the NPT. Thus there are positive aspects to this trend whereby an expanded role for the Tlatelolco regime and OPANAL could be developed. Oil producing Latin American countries such as Mexico and Venezuela, both strongly supportive of Tlatelolco, could encourage a more favorable Brazilian attitude toward cooperation with Tlatelolco. However linkages between Latin American countries and countries in more troubled areas (such as South Korea, Iraq, Libya, South Africa) may have a very different potential.

Argentina and Brazil: nuclear convergence

In May 1980 Argentina and Brazil signed an agreement for nuclear cooperation on the occasion of President Figueiredo's state visit to Argentina. The agreement represented a historic step toward more orderly and predictable bilateral relations, as well as a dampening of the two nations' long nuclear rivalry. If fully implemented the agreement could contribute significantly to peace and security in the Latin American region and to the overall goal of nonproliferation.

---

[49] The full text of the Brazil-Iraq agreement is reproduced in *FBIS*, op. cit., 4 March 1980, 33. Iraq officials were candid in their statements that Brazilian support for the U.N. General Assembly resolution equating zionism with racism as being an important factor in their decision to develop a nuclear relationship.

Geopolitical rivalries have been and remain an important element in Argentine-Brazilian relations as manifested particularly by competition in the Southern Cone. The geopolitical impetus of the foreign policy strategies of both nations have also found definite expression in the nuclear area. Both have tended to view nuclear energy as a major contributor to their national development effort *and* in the context of bilateral competition. The latter point is of particular significance to Argentina, because nuclear power application has remained the one important area where it still maintains clear superiority over Brazil.

While competition in nuclear matters is incontestable, it is, nonetheless, of an almost "gentlemanly" nature. In contrast to other regions of the world facing potential proliferation, there has been a near total absence of official rhetoric, and a considerable degree of mutual restraint. Yet the competition—including the previously discussed competition for influence and nuclear relationships with other Latin American countries—is considered as very important by officials of both nations.

The critical issue separating the two nations throughout the decade of the 1970s was border-related disputes in the very rich River Plate Basin. Observers in both countries had long believed that nuclear cooperation could be possible following solution of the perennial problems surrounding the hydroelectric development of the area. The agreement announced 19 October 1979 between Brazil, Argentina, and Paraguay apparently represented a final settlement of the protracted dam disputes on the Parana River and as such was the essential prerequisite to further cooperation in a number of areas. Subsequent events in early 1980 confirmed this, including an exchange of visits by the Argentine Air Force Commander and the Brazilian Aeronautics Commander, and a decision by the two nations to jointly cooperate in the production of commercial and military aircraft.

The apparent move toward cooperation in the nuclear area builds on past unsuccessful efforts by compatible military governments in both countries. In a number of international forums the two countries adopted a damage limiting type of cooperation whereby they sought to limit impediments or restraint on their nuclear development. An example includes Argentine-Brazilian cooperation during the Tlatelolco negotiations following the 1964 Brazilian revolution when they worked to stiffen the ratification procedures and develop a common position on PNEs. A similar pattern of coordination became prevalent in the Geneva disarmament talks and within the IAEA Board of Governors.

The theme of nuclear cooperation was repeatedly stressed by retired Argentine General Gugliamelli in the influential journal *Estrategia* in the late 1960s and early 1970s, but the unstable domestic situation in Argentina made progress difficult. However in 1976, at the 20th IAEA General Assembly Conference in Rio, Brazilian officials reportedly accepted the idea of bilateral nuclear cooperation as a tentative but desirable future goal.

The U.S.-Brazilian disputes relative to the German sale of the nuclear fuel cycle in 1976 prompted Argentine statements of support for Brazil and suggestions for cooperation. Talks did occur between the two countries in January 1977 and a communique was released by then Foreign Ministers Guzzetti of Argentina and Azeredo da Silveira of Brazil stressing cooperation in nuclear matters. While the Argentine continued to push the idea of technical exchanges in early 1977 the Brazilians once again held back in lieu of a solution of the River Plate disputes and, no doubt, to extract additional concessions from Argentina.

A number of factors can be identified as contributing to the trend toward Argentine-Brazilian nuclear convergence. Personalities are clearly an important factor. CNEA President Castro Madero, a respected and influential military figure, has long been deeply committed to developing an arrangement for peaceful cooperation with Brazil. The May 1980 agreement is in many ways a result of his individual persistence both within his own government and in bilateral discussions. Also Brazilian President Figueiredo came into office strongly committed to establishing a system of permanent negotiations and consultations with Argentina. Having lived in Argentina for many years with his father, who was a political exile, Figueiredo was the first Brazilian president to visit Argentina since Getullio Vargas thirty-five years before.

There are also economic incentives impelling the Brazilian nuclear establishment to favor linkages with Argentina. In 1979 and 1980 budgetary pressures and problems experienced in the nuclear program were causing resources to be diverted toward other energy sources, particularly hydroelectric development. Brazilian nuclear officials confronted with a loss of government resources, an idle NUCLEP (the joint company established with Germany for heavy nuclear industry), and pressure from private Brazilian companies designed to service the nuclear industry, welcomed the possibility of nearby Argentina as a customer. The prospect of supplying parts for several planned Argentine reactors to be built over the next twenty years would more than compensate for a possible slowdown in Brazil's once ambitious program.

The agreement was developed in three steps beginning with a visit by Castro Madero to Brazil in January 1980 in which he met with the foreign minister and all appropriate nuclear officials including the minister of mines and energy and the president of NUCLEBRAS and toured nearly every Brazilian nuclear facility. The second step was a return visit by NUCLEBRAS President Batista and the President of the Brazilian Nuclear Energy Commission Caravelho to work out the details of the formal nuclear agreement which was signed in May during President Figueiredo's visit to Argentina.

The most substantive portion of the nuclear agreement was the formalization of an arrangement negotiated earlier in 1980, whereby the joint Brazilian-German company NUCLEP will construct the core vessel for Argentina's third reactor (which is also to be supplied by the Federal Republic of Germany). Other aspects of the agreement, which is to be implemented in stages, include an exchange of technicians and personnel training, and exchanges of information on component fabrication, nuclear plant security, physical protection of nuclear material, exploration and production of uranium, nuclear safety, and research reactor design (an area of Argentine leadership). An item of particular interest to Argentina is access to the Brazilian Computerized Information Center which obtains and disseminates much of the Western world's technical-scientific information in the nuclear field (which could be connected to a data processing center in Argentina). It is also anticipated that Argentina will supply zirconium to Brazil and eventually Brazil will supply enriched uranium for Argentine research reactors. Finally cooperation is also expected to proceed in basic and applied nuclear physics research and in advanced nuclear technology including thorium utilization and breeder development.

The implications of the nuclear agreement are several. A major benefit perceived by the two parties is a greater ability to resist nuclear supplier pressure and to counter restrictions on advanced technology. In this regard the cooperation could take the form of a "Latin American nuclear bloc" as suggested by Castro Madero to "defend the right of access by the region to nuclear technology and to vigorously express its common points of view."[50] Brazilian involvement in the Argentine-led nonaligned nuclear consumers group is a possibility. The group, designed to coordinate policies relative to the nuclear suppliers, held its preliminary session in Belgrade in 1978 and its first regular meeting in Buenos Aires in June 1980. Of a related nature Argentine-Brazilian coordination regarding international nonproliferation agreements such as the NPT and Tlatelolco may well be enhanced.

A major contribution of the Treaty is its likely nonproliferation benefits. While there are a variety of factors which could impel either country to develop nuclear explosive devices, the most important dynamic is their bilateral competition. In this view the major payoff of the agreement is increased security: a greater degree of confidence and mutual understanding of the other's actions and a reduced danger of misconception and miscalculation. An appreciation of the need to avoid destabilizing and expensive nuclear competition is a strong motive for policymakers in both countries.

The agreement may also lead to more substantive bilateral cooperation in the back end of the nuclear fuel cycle. Eventual creation of a plutonium storage facility is a requirement of Brazil's contract for enriched uranium with URENCO. Cooperation with Argentina for establishment of such a unit in a buffer country, such as Paraguay or Uruguay, is conceivable with the support of the more advanced countries.

Finally it should be noted that the cooperation has a potential, however unlikely, to take a negative turn. While both countries have emphasized that explosives are not a part of their nuclear agreement it could, nonetheless, lay

---

[50] *FBIS*, op. cit., 35, p. 18.

the foundation for joint development and utilization of PNEs. In such an event Tlatelolco could take on a new and important function.[51]

The German role in the current and future course of Argentine-Brazilian nuclear convergence is of considerable importance. Cooperation between the two Latin American neighbors is clearly favored as a prudent business goal by the Germans. Assuming continued cooperation the Federal Republic of Germany could look forward, with reasonable confidence, to a favored role in the supplying of advanced nuclear technology, as well as trade opportunities in other areas.[52]

While Argentine-Brazilian cooperation may be in Germany's economic interest, nonproliferation concerns have been less prevalent in its nuclear policies toward the two countries. This is evidenced in the Federal Republic of Germany's sale of enrichment and reprocessing equipment to Brazil and its refusal to require full scope safeguards from either country over the objections of the United States. Better consultation and coordination between the United States and the Federal Republic of Germany is important in the years ahead, so as to support positive elements in the Argentine-Brazilian nuclear relationship while minimizing the proliferation dangers which could arise.

Future of the Tlatelolco regime

The Tlatelolco regime can make an important contribution to the goal of nonproliferation for the Latin American region in the 1980s. However the support of the advanced nuclear countries, primarily the United States, is essential. Early U.S. ratification of Protocol I will provide needed momentum for completion by other non-Latin American (e.g., France) and Latin American (e.g., Argentina, Cuba) countries. It would also provide reassurance to Latin American supporters of Tlatelolco (such as Mexico, Colombia, Venezuela, and Peru) and to Brazil, which has given support in principle.

Tangible offers of support by the U.S. and other Protocol signatories would strengthen Tlatelolco's machinery, OPANAL. OPANAL's General Conference has called for creation of a voluntary fund for signatories which

---

[51] The Tlatelolco Treaty includes a method for managing and minimizing the political impact of an Argentine or Brazilian PNE. Article 18 restricts the means and methods whereby PNEs can be detonated in Latin America, establishing procedures which are public and calls for a distinct international presence at any such explosion by OPANAL and the IAEA. The important point is that the Treaty represents a convenient regional mechanism for containment of the military and strategic impact of a nuclear explosion in the Latin American region totally absent in other more volatile regions of the world. Moreover once having contained the effort within a set of regional procedures it might short-circuit the final step toward production of actual nuclear weapons.

[52] A more negative speculation is that in the context of Argentine-Brazilian nuclear cooperation Germany might encourage activities (PNE development, etc.) it feels it cannot undertake in its own national territory. The Soviet Union has, in the past, advanced such charges relative to German-Brazilian rocket development and testing in northern Brazil.

could be used to support its operations, training, and to expand staff and to plan for future evolution. An alternative would be a special IAEA fund earmarked for OPANAL support including technical assistance and staff training.

Coordination of the nonproliferation policies of those countries generally considered principal nuclear suppliers to Latin American countries (Federal Republic of Germany, U.S., France, Canada, and, on a lower level, Japan, Sweden and Spain) is desirable. The goal should be common positions on IAEA safeguards, Tlatelolco, transfer of nuclear materials, and equipment. A continued unilateral U.S. approach to Latin American countries is clearly counterproductive in terms of its intended objectives and as regards unacceptable trade-offs in the wider range of bilateral relations. A more productive approach will focus on consensus seeking and emphasizing to all nuclear suppliers the U.S. position that the Latin American region has certain special nonproliferation attributes which should be preserved and encouraged.

In regard to Tlatelolco the policies of the U.S. and other supplier countries should be exercised with restraint. It is undoubtedly an error to tie Tlatelolco ratification directly as a quid pro quo for supply of nuclear materials or equipment. This may well diminish Latin American support for Tlatelolco and convey an image of the agreement as something imposed by outside powers. There are indications that Argentina's view regarding Tlatelolco has been impacted by this perception.

It is also self-defeating for nonproliferation supporting countries to avoid full support for Tlatelolco due to the remaining ambiguities in its requirements. While there are different interpretations of Tlatelolco's requirements it should not be forgotten that the large majority of Latin American countries interpret the agreement as requiring de jure full scope safeguards and prohibition of PNEs. Rather the United States and other advanced supplier countries can best encourage Latin American support for Tlatelolco by giving tangible demonstration of respect for the commitments the parties have undertaken. This can be achieved by avoiding confrontations and unilateral restrictions on the transfer of nuclear material and equipment to full parties. The Tlatelolco pledge of abstention should be accorded complete trust, until such time as trust is no longer warranted.

7

Pariah States and Nuclear Proliferation

Robert E. Harkavy

Introduction: pariah states in historical context

In recent years, a seemingly entirely new type of international actor, the pariah state, has entered the consciousness of scholars and policymakers. Some nations have been deemed deserving of such an appellation because of their precarious diplomatic isolation, the absence of assured, credible security support or political moorings within big-power alliance structures, and because they have become the targets of obsessive and unrelenting opprobrium and censure within international forums such as the United Nations.[1]

The matter is not, of course, merely one of theoretical curiosity. What has become increasingly apparent is that some pariahs, whose diplomatic isolation has deepened amid anxieties over unfavorable regional conventional military imbalances, have been taking the first steps, or strong hints of such moves, toward nuclear weapons status. Israel, South Africa, and Taiwan feature most prominently in this regard, while South Korea also exhibits some crucial characteristics of a pariah status. Under some circumstances, Chile might join the select circle of pariahtude, as well as Pakistan, which in some important

---

[1] George Quester used the term "outlaw states" in discussing pariahs. See his "What's New on Nuclear Non-Proliferation" (Aspen, Colo.: Aspen Institute for Humanistic Studies, 1975). Richard Burt refers to them as "outcasts" in "Fear of Nuclear 'Outcasts' Intensifies Control Debate," The *New York Times,* 28 October 1979, p. 4E. For a discussion amid a more complex typology, see Richard K. Betts, "Paranoids, Pygmies, Pariahs, and Nonproliferation," *Foreign Policy* 26 (Spring 1977): 157–83.

respects—i.e., anxieties about territorial legitimacy and dismemberment—can be discussed within this category.

Furthermore, the thrust toward nuclear status by pariah states threatens the long-dreaded unraveling of the nonproliferation regime through a "domino" or "chain" effect, so that the nuclear drives of Iraq, Libya, Iran, Japan, and India (already partly over the threshold) may ultimately be affected. For all these reasons the pariah state problem is now considered by many to be a linchpin of the nuclear proliferation question.

There is no obviously forthcoming definition of pariah status; one deals with tendencies and often arguable nuances. That caveat notwithstanding, a contemporary pariah might display several or most of the following characteristics. It would be:

1. A rather small and weak nation, actually or potentially outnumbered by its surrounding adversaries, in an exposed position due to weak, waning, or nonexistent support from its big-power benefactor(s) to which it may be—or is—a liability.

2. A nation whose national origins and legitimacy—or present constitutional status—is widely questioned, variously on grounds of borders, the splitting of a "nation," or a conflict over self-determination, racism, ethnic minorities, etc.; that is, its present national status, within its own defined borders, is at issue.

3. A nation with objectively poor diplomatic leverage and, therefore, not considered a good alliance partner by major powers (to the contrary, a liability). It relies primarily on the momentum or credibility of relationships formed earlier, on mere sentimentality, on fears by a big power that its (the pariah's) demise might lessen its overall credibility, or perhaps weakly on some objective factor such as the availability of strategic bases.

4. A nation with precarious, perhaps sole, sources of conventional arms supply and which is too small or underdeveloped to provide a significant portion of its arms needs through indigenous production; also, very vulnerable in a crisis to cutoffs of spare parts or to denial of weapons resupply.

5. A nation faced with adversaries having solid support from a major power, whose support it cannot match.

In summary, the pariah state is a small power with only marginal and tenuous control over its own fate, whose security dilemma cannot easily be solved by neutrality, nonalignment, or appeasement, and lacking dependable big-power support. Under contemporary conditions, pariahtude crucially involves estrangement from the numerically dominant Soviet and Third World blocs—in conjunction with poor leverage which translates into weak, clandestine, or nonexistent support from reluctant Western powers—and perhaps some spillover from the overall anti-Western bias of numerous Third World nations. Thus, it is by combining the various criteria in the list that the pariahtude of Israel, South Africa, Taiwan and, to a lesser degree, South Korea stands out and constitutes a definable national-actor type.

By utilizing the above criteria, other examples drawn from the present or recent past might be found. Weimar Germany and Bolshevik Russia immediately after World War I, and Czechoslovakia in the late 1930s readily come to mind.[2] But, some of these were great powers, none had serious problems in acquiring arms (either because they produced them indigenously or could rely on an essentially laissez-faire arms market—up until 1940), and, most importantly, none could have thought of compensating for diplomatic weakness by acquiring weapons of mass destruction.[3] Rhodesia, Portugal (before the 1974 revolution), Spain (particularly during the early postwar period), Chile, Pakistan, Libya, Uganda, Cuba and even the PRC have at various times fitted by some criteria. But in none of these cases (with the possible exception of Pakistan) has there been that critical conjunction of isolation, smallness, and conventional military insecurity which has triggered the now familiar syndrome toward nuclear weapons assumed increasingly perceived by the current pariahs, if not by others, as vital to their sheer survival. Chile, since the overthrow of the Allende regime, has come the closest to becoming an addition to the pariah group; indeed, as measured by the level of global opprobrium directed at it, it might well outrank South Korea. But, it does not now face an ominous external security threat—certainly none portending massacres of populations or elites—nor does it face any significant global questioning of its approximate borders or national existence.

The present pariah phenomenon seems to defy some traditional maxims about the behavior of the international system—specifically about the operation of the balance of power.[4] There have allegedly been somewhat natural, even near automatic, tendencies toward balance which have allowed weak states to survive by seeking protection from the strong, by moving or threatening to move in ways which would equilibrate the system.[5] This norm, associated with the workings of the much romanticized classical system of Europe, may have withered somewhat with the onset of collective security myths in the twentieth century, not to mention its overriding by the ideological locus of global conflict. But, from the perspective of the modern pariah, the

[2] For a discussion of an asserted analogy between 1938 Czechoslovakia and present Israel, devoid of the term pariah, see Norman Podhoretz, "The Abandonment of Israel," *Commentary* 62, 1 (July 1976): 23–31.

[3] For discussion of the implications (for small as well as large states) of the primarily private-controlled pre-World War II arms markets, see Robert E. Harkavy, *The Arms Trade and International Systems* (Cambridge, Mass.: Ballinger, 1975), esp. chapter 2.

[4] See Hans Morgenthau, *Politics Among Nations,* 5th ed. (New York: Knopf, 1973), pt. 4. Among the myriad other general analyses of the balance of power, see Frederick H. Hartmann, *The Relations of Nations,* 4th ed. (New York: Macmillan, 1973), chaps. 16–19, and A. F. K. Organski, *World Politics,* 1st ed. (New York: Knopf, 1958), chap. 11. For an analysis of the many empirical and normative definitions of "balance of power," see Ernst Haas, "The Balance of Power," *World Politics* 5, 4 (July 1953), 440–77.

[5] For historical analyses of small or weak states' conditions and behavior within the international system, see Robert Rothstein, *Alliances and Small Powers* (New York: Columbia University Press, 1968); and Marshall Singer, *Weak States in a World of Powers* (New York: The Free Press, 1972).

collective security principle has become transmuted in a painfully ironic way. At least as measured by majority or near-unanimous votes in international organizations, a new internationalist ethic of sorts—a sort of inverted collective security principle—has developed and one result has been the placing of great pressures on states deemed to operate outside its pale, along with their, by now, few reluctant supporters. For such states, collective security has become collective damnation, and this has had practical consequences when filtered through the behavior of major states reluctant to be identified with beleaguered and hated small nations laboring under the cloud of delegitimization.[6]

In some cases, then, what once might have been a tendency toward equilibrium in the older balance-of-power system has been replaced—from the perspective of pariahs—by an ominous tendency toward accelerating, destabilizing disequilibrium. States with inherently weak leverage ("moral" issues aside—note the case of Pakistan from 1965 to 1980), far from finding opportunities to trade-in on their balancing potential, are perceived by potential patrons or protectors as liabilities, as burdens. The big powers compete for the best customers, those of highest strategic value—i.e., those with money, raw materials, large markets, and close connections with still other desirable clients.[7] Hence, there are both "willing" and "reluctant" arms supply relationships, since becoming or remaining an arms supplier to an Israel, a Taiwan, or a South Africa may involve high costs elsewhere, where the stakes are larger.[8]

The resulting disequilibria, contrary to balance-of-power tradition, force some small nations to rely precariously upon tenuous or even clandestine support, perhaps based primarily upon sentiment or perhaps banking on a big power's fears about the blow to its overall credibility which might result from too many abandonments of former dependents. For pariahs, those may be thin reeds to cling to, and the not unexpected result may be recourse to an "equalizer"—the nuclear equivalent of a pistol for a scrawny man in a menacing neighborhood.

Some measures of pariah status

The nature of the isolated situations facing Israel, South Africa, Taiwan, and South Korea varies considerably, thus vitiating somewhat the comparative

---

[6] On the collective security principle, in its theoretical and normative senses, see Inis Claude, *Swords into Plowshares* (New York: Random House, 1956), chap. 12; and E. H. Carr, *The Twenty Years' Crisis, 1919–1939* (New York: Macmillan, 1947).

[7] For a discussion of recent assumptions about strategic value, see Harriet Critchley, "Defining Strategic Value: Problems of Conceptual Clarity and Valid Threat Assessments" in *American Security Policy and Policy-Making,* R. Harkavy and E. Kolodziej, eds. (Lexington, Mass.: D. C. Heath, 1980), pp. 45–65.

[8] For a survey of historical changes in the extent and nature of small-power leverage in the arms market, and a discussion of "reluctant" and "willing" arms suppliers, see Harkavy, *The Arms Trade and International Systems,* chapter 4.

utility of the pariah concept. The variations pertain to their relationships with the big powers, their vulnerabilities regarding conventional arms sources, the nature of the regional conventional military threats they face, the intensity with which they are scorned or hated by much of the world at large, and the degree of legitimacy or resigned acceptance accorded them by other nations. The circumstances in each case are too familiar to require elaboration, although a few points deserve emphasis because they impinge upon nuclear proliferation.

First, South Korea's isolation is clearly less serious and profound than that of the other three, ranking it as merely a "quasi-pariah." Like Taiwan, it is scarcely tarred with the brush of racism or colonialism; rather, its image throughout much of the Third World suffers merely from its past American tutelage and from its somewhat antiradical ideological stance. Furthermore, unlike Taiwan, it does not labor under the severe disadvantage that derives from the immense counterleverage of a major power antagonist, applicable over a whole range of diplomatic transactions.

The cases of South Africa and Israel, different from each other, are also distinct as a pair from the cases of South Korea and Taiwan. While white South Africa's 300-year history gives it, in many eyes, some legitimate basis for remaining, there is a near-total concurrence of world opinion on the necessity for, and justice of, majority rule. It remains to be seen whether even that will suffice, for the mere presence of lingering, large white populations on the African continent, in any status, clearly must present a powerful symbol of the past to black Africa. The symbolic equivalent to Israel's presence in the Middle East is plain, and the emotions related to this matter of "incompleteness" or "unfinished business" are widely shared throughout the Third World, even where there are no local Western remnants.

In short, while both South Africa and Israel are the subjects of very widespread hatreds, Taiwan and South Korea are broadly viewed in more benign and perhaps instrumental ways, reflecting the deeper emotional bases of ethnic, religious, and racial conflicts as contrasted with essentially ideological or merely territorial ones. The Korean and Chinese conflicts involve, after all, the same peoples—i.e., they are basically interelite conflicts. That may yet prove to be an important distinction.

An overriding similarity among the four pariahs is that each suffers from widely-held external perceptions of it as a temporary state scheduled for history's rubbish heap (all the more so as the once more formidable U.S. protective shield gradually evaporates). To the extent that these expectations of doom connected to the absence of perceived "permanent" legitimacy are fully comprehended and internalized within the pariahs, of course, they cannot help but militate toward desperate measures, toward "final solutions" involving the familiar mixed imagery of suicide and final revenge. Israeli insistence upon the distinction between Masada and Samson, and comparable South African attachment to the stubborn "laager" myth (and its application to a nuclear solution) should perhaps not be ignored.

A number of fairly objective measures can be used to gauge the political isolation under which the pariahs labor: the number and identity of nations with which they maintain formal diplomatic relations, the outcomes of critical UN votes (particularly those pertaining to the legitimacy of pariah regimes), membership in intergovernmental organizations (IGOs), and overall trade relations are good indices, at least when used in combination. A few illustrative points are merited.

As measured by formal diplomatic ties, South Africa and Taiwan are seen to be the most seriously isolated, exchanging ambassadors with only some fifteen and nineteen states, respectively (the PRC, by contrast with Taiwan, now has diplomatic relations with some 114 states).[9] And in both cases, the trends have been remorselessly downward. Both retain some ties in Latin America, while South Africa's other formal relations are mostly in Western Europe, and Taiwan's are scattered among a few conservative states in Africa, Asia, and the Middle East. Israel still has a much broader network of diplomatic ties (some sixty-five, plus some additional consular arrangements), despite its continuing near-total estrangement from Africa. South Korea has formal relations with some ninety-three states (contrasted with eighty-eight for North Korea) including a considerable number of left-leaning Third World states, and the trend here has been sharply upward in recent years for *both* Koreas, even accounting for the impact of entirely new states. This seems to denote a significantly higher level of legitimacy than is the case for the other three pariahs, whatever the practical consequences.

All of the four pariahs are, to one degree or another, disconnected from the web of regional IGOs, as well as from the various organizations and periodic conferences of the developing and nonaligned nations. Israel and South Africa, however, despite their endless problems within the various organizations of the UN complex (and despite periodic threats of their removal from all of them), do remain members of the UN and virtually all of its subsidiary organs, including the IAEA. South Korea is outside the UN (it does have special observer status), but is a member of most other important IGOs (WHO, WTO, FAO, GATT, IMF—and IAEA), where its status has not caused serious controversies. Taiwan, long expelled from the United Nations and all of its subsidiary organs, retains merely a few lingering minor IGO memberships. Hence, by this measurement, Taiwan is *the* pariah. Its recent expulsion from the Lake Placid Olympic games, which is not surprising in view of its loss of American protection of its memberships, could be contrasted, for instance, with Israel's support within the International Labor Organization.

Each of the pariahs (but much less so in the case of South Korea again) has fared very poorly in crucial UN votes related to its essential legitimacy. In Israel's case, the 1975 resolution entitled "Elimination of All Forms of Racial

---

[9] The data on the formal diplomatic relationships of the pariahs were gathered from the resources of the respective desk officers in the U.S. State Department and from the Washington embassies of the four pariah states.

Discrimination," which determines that "Zionism is a form of racism and racial discrimination," received 72 yes votes, 35 against, and 32 abstentions. There have been many other near-monolithic votes against Israel in recent years, for instance, with regard to the occupied territories. Over the years, South Africa has suffered a cascade of negative votes in the UN on issues related to apartheid and majority rule, arms embargoes, trade relations and investments, "bantustans," and the like. One mandating an arms embargo passed 110-8-20, another on Namibia by 117-0-24. Taiwan, in 1971, was finally expelled by an overwhelming vote of 76-35-17 (though the preceding "important question" resolution passed only narrowly), but has since ceased to be an obsession in UN forums. Meanwhile, UN discussions and votes on the "Korean question" have virtually petered out in the past five years, after an earlier series of referendums that essentially measured respective support for the two Koreas indicated roughly even backing. All in all, nowadays, as measured by menacing barrages of UN disapproval, South Africa followed closely by Israel would rank as the most clear-cut pariahs.

International trade statistics present a somewhat different picture. All of the pariahs have far wider trading networks than those of diplomatic relations; each conducts extensive trade with numerous nations with which it does not exchange ambassadors. Israel maintains important, albeit clandestine, trading (and also technical assistance) relationships in black Africa. There are those statistically surprising categories of "Other Africa" and "Africa not Specified" in the World Bank's trading data for South Africa, not to mention the openly published Soviet–South Africa trade statistics.[10] Taiwan, of course, continues its booming trade with the United States, Europe, and elsewhere despite the breaking of virtually all formal diplomatic ties. All in all, none of the pariahs has been severely disadvantaged economically by its political isolation, although both Israel and South Africa have suffered from some distortions of trading patterns, from boycotts, etc. South Africa, however, may suffer more in the future from cutbacks in foreign investment or more comprehensive economic sanctions.

In a psychological sense, all these aspects of pariahtude may be important to the extent they may translate into subtly lessened inhibitions regarding the development of nuclear weapons. By themselves, even in combination, they would not necessarily constitute a mortal threat. What is more important, of course, are the "conventional" security situations of these states: regional military balance projections, arms transfers, and outside security arrangements and guarantees (or lack of same), as _they_ perceive them. But, the constant drumbeat of UNGA excoriations, organizational expulsions, and diplomatic breaks may not be altogether irrelevant to those considerations, to the

---

[10] For pariah trade data on aggregate, regional, and bilateral bases, see the serial, annual editions of _Direction of International Trade,_ published annually and jointly by the United Nations, International Monetary Fund, and International Bank for Reconstruction and Development, New York.

Table 1: The pariahs and their regional foes: some basic data

Country	Population	Armed Forces	Military Expenditures	Gross National Product	GNP per Capita	MILEX/ GNP
	(millions)	*(thousands)*	*(million dollars)*	*(million dollars)*		
Israel	3.6	165	2781	9777	2708	28.4
Egypt	38.9	350	1154	11698	285	10.4
Syria	7.9	225	960	6773	862	14.2
Iraq	12.0	140	1819	17246	1437	10.5
Jordan	2.9	70	170	1831	642	9.3
Saudi Arabia	7.6	60	6912	46464	5795	15.7
Libya	2.7	30	260	16837	6354	1.5
Taiwan	16.8	460	1517	18509	1102	8.2
PRC	983.0	4300	33200	353377	359	9.4
South Africa	26.8**	67	1764	32298	1205	5.5
Mozambique	9.6	26	45	1439	149	3.1
Angola	6.3	47	94	1822	289	5.2
Zambia	5.2	20	67	2280	437	2.9
Tanzania	16.3	31	116	2814	173	4.1
Botswana	0.7	1	0	271	373	0.0
South Korea	38.2	600	1633	27676	725	5.9
North Korea	17.6	520	2002	10219	581	19.6

*Source: U.S. Arms Control and Disarmament Agency, World Military Expenditures and Arms Transfers (Washington: U.S.G.P.O., October 1979). Data are for 1977.
**Note: white population is approximately one-fifth of total population.

extent that they serve to "delegitimize" the pariahs, weaken their outside supports, and hence reinforce fears and imagery related to final doom.[11]

Regional military balances, pariah arms acquisitions, and the "dove's dilemma"

Each pariah state in its own eyes faces a serious, external military threat, in conjunction with (to varying degrees) insecure sources of conventional weapons and only very tenuous (virtually nonexistent for South Africa) promises of big-power support in crises, or even in the event of direct big-power intervention. The threats facing the four pariahs are sufficiently well-known so as not to warrant extensive description here, although the seriousness of the threats may well be argued over. See Table 1 for summary data.

There is an important fault line dividing the four pariahs into two groups

[11] On the important matter of the legitimization function of international organizations (i.e., the UN), particularly germane to the situation of pariah states, see Inis Claude, "Collective Legitimization as a Political Function of the United Nations," *International Organization* 20, 3 (Summer 1966): 367–79.

with respect to the nuclear proliferation question and having to do with the possible, if not probable, consequences of conventional battlefield defeat.

Taiwan and South Korea, if overrun, can anticipate "merely" a change of regime, a *Gleichschaltung*, in which the high side costs might involve elimination or forced reindoctrination of present elites, and a considerable change in lifestyle for the masses. Serious but not ultimate matters are presumably involved. Israel and South Africa, on the other hand, face specters of a different order. Assuming, at the final moment of defeat, great difficulties in evacuating a significant percentage of their populations, these two states must contemplate the possibility—even the significant probability—of wholesale massacres, perhaps of genocidal proportions. Unavoidably, then, the South African and Israeli governments must deal in worst-case scenarios, and they certainly do.

Although South Africa's evolving security situation is most difficult to analyze and predict (particularly regarding the timing of what appears almost inevitable), it will probably face a gradually escalating conflict (in the classic Maoist mode, reminiscent of Algeria), with operations escalating from urban guerrilla to conventional warfare. Among the critical imponderables: the long-term possibilities for significant military involvement by Mozambique, a black-controlled Zimbabwe, Angola, Zambia, Tanzania, Namibia, et al. regarding either guerrilla havens or actual joint operations; and, of course, the possibility of Cuban and/or Soviet involvement.

Israel's present and longer-term conventional situation is, meanwhile, not easily gauged. Curiously, it has received very little recent scholarly or press analysis.[12] Internal U.S. government analyses apparently continue to wax optimistic on Israel's behalf, whether based on serious and objective analyses, mere extrapolations from the past, or for "political" reasons (i.e., to justify restraining further arms shipments to Israel) is much argued. Future U.S. military support (both before and, if necessary, during conflicts), the quality and quantity of future Arab weapons acquisitions, the degree to which the Arabs can translate oil revenues into much larger operational armies, possible Soviet intervention, the impact of new weapons developments on offensive and defensive strategies and tactics in possible future conflicts, and Israel's preemptive capabilities—all are among the relevant imponderables. There are also questions of whether future possible conflicts would see Egyptian involvement (resupplied during the conflict by the United States along with Israel?), whether they might begin with a PLO state installed on the West Bank, and whether they might see significant Iranian or even (postrevolutionary) Turkish involvement.

---

[12] One recent exception is Geoffrey Kemp, "A Nuclear Middle East," in *International Political Effects of the Spread of Nuclear Weapons,* John Kerry King, ed. (Washington, D.C.: U.S.G.P.O., 1979), a collection of essays from a colloquium sponsored by the CIA and the Department of Defense. See also W. Seth Carus, "The Military Balance of Power in the Middle East," *Current History* 74, 433 (January 1978): 29–32.

Clearly, Israel has vastly improved its defense structure, in an absolute sense, since 1973, banking on the numerous "lessons" it apparently learned in reversing its initial setbacks.[13] Field artillery (necessary to suppress infantry carrying antitank missiles) has been greatly bolstered, numbers of antitank warfare weapons expanded and tactics altered, aircraft avionics and stand-off capability improved. Tactical innovations have apparently been striven for which might again allow Israel to use its once vaunted armor and tactical air power for blitzkrieg operations.

But then, Arab capabilities have also greatly expanded, even if they may be temporarily masked by Egypt's cut-off from Soviet weapons. Iraq and Syria have acquired newly massive and qualitatively improved Soviet (and French) arsenals; Saudi Arabia may now increasingly be a force to be reckoned with; Lebanon presents another battlefront; and Egypt, Camp David notwithstanding, may be acquiring F-15s, F-16s, M-60 tanks, TOWs, and HAWKs.[14]

Rarely mentioned openly looms another specter for Israel: its primarily M-60 and Centurion-based tank force may later face advanced Soviet T-72s in Syria and Iraq which are superior to anything Israel now possesses. Israel would have trouble affording the new U.S. XM-1 tank, even if it should become available.[15] All in all, the weapons and force ratios facing Israel in the future appear more ominous than in the past, and it is not clear whether this can be overcome indefinitely by qualitative personnel superiority and still more innovative tactics and strategies.

South Korea, on the basis of a rather large advantage in GNP and population, has the easy potential for military preponderance over its now better armed (in aircraft and armor) rival, assuming a continued high level of U.S. military aid in the wake of the CIA's revisions of its estimates of the North Korean order of battle. In this sense too, the ROK is anomalous among the pariahs in that it has the objective potential for regional balance and more. Taiwan, of course, is hugely outnumbered, and no amount of maximizing

---

[13] Among the numerous works analyzing the military meaning of the October 1973 war and the subsequent evolvement of an Arab-Israeli military balance, see Martin van Creveld, *Military Lessons of the Yom Kippur War: Historical Perspectives* (Beverly Hills: Sage Publications, Washington paper no. 24, 1975); "Both Sides of the Suez," *Aviation Week & Space Technology,* special ed., 1975; Dale R. Tahtinen, *The Arab-Israeli Military Balance Since October 1973* (Washington, D.C.: American Enterprise Institute, Foreign Affairs Study no. 11, 1974); *The Middle East and the International System: The Impact of the 1973 War* (London: International Institute for Strategic Studies, 1974), Adelphi Paper No. 114; and various articles in *Aviation Week & Space Technology,* 10 March 1975.

[14] For recent analyses of impending Egyptian arms acquisitions, see, inter alia, "Egypt Reported to Say U.S. Will Sell It Any Arms," The *New York Times,* 22 February 1980, p. A8; and "Egypt: Maintaining an Arsenal of Soviet Equipment," *Middle-East Intelligence Survey* 7, 10 (16–31 August 1979).

[15] For a hint of the implications of forthcoming Syrian acquisition of Soviet T-72 tanks, see "Role of Tanks Clouded by New Arms," The *New York Times,* 27 March 1980, p. A6, wherein details are conveyed of the ongoing technological race pitting new tank armor versus new antitank technology featuring the "millimeter wave detection" system.

economic and population resources can significantly reduce its disadvantage. It relies on its water barrier to offset the numerical imbalances, and on the PRC's continued nugatory naval capacity for a large-scale amphibious (perhaps abetted by airborne operations) assault across the Taiwan Straits, as well as on the PRC's need to deploy much of its forces against the USSR. But, there is also the oft-mentioned threat of a PRC naval blockade, now seemingly without fully credible assurance of a forthcoming, countering U.S. response.

The precariousness and diversity of the pariahs' arms-supply sources varies. South Africa's situation (with, at present, lesser requirements) is the most precarious; Israel's and Taiwan's are perhaps next; and South Korea appears to have relatively assured sources, aside from the matters of quantity and financing.

South Africa faces a very insecure situation with respect to external arms supplies, which is only partly mitigated by its modest requirements for the most sophisticated systems and its now fairly extensive indigenous arms production.[16] The UN-sponsored arms embargo has essentially been adhered to by the United States and the United Kingdom since 1964. Between then and recently, Pretoria's arms sources were narrowed, but a flow of sophisticated arms from France (including Mirage jet fighters), trainer/attack jet aircraft from Italy, and licensed small arms from Belgium, filled the gap. Now, however, France has apparently joined the embargo, bowing to black African pressure given force by Nigerian oil and others' mineral resources. Israel, too, has apparently been prodded into acquiescence by U.S. pressures, after some earlier transfers. Pretoria may still be able to assemble some Mirages and can build its own light attack aircraft, armored cars, small arms, and ammunition, but in some of these areas crucial dependence for component parts is a problem. One recent report cited several impending weaknesses: in armor, where South Africa relies on an aging force of some 500 British Centurions, and in antitank and antiaircraft missiles.[17]

As Israel was to learn during the Yom Kippur War, the capacity for indigenous production of a portion of one's arms may not be sufficient.[18] Few,

---

[16] All the arms-trade data here and in subsequent pages come from the various publications of the Stockholm International Peace Research Institute (SIPRI) and the International Institute for Strategic Studies (IISS). In particular, I have relied on the arms-trade registers in the IISS's annual _Military Balance_; SIPRI's annual yearbook, _World Armaments and Disarmament;_ and SIPRI's _Arms Trade Registers._ The last-mentioned chronologically lists, by major weapon categories, all global arms transfers in the postwar period up to 1973.

[17] See "South Africa Reviews Defenses as Rhodesia Votes," The _New York Times,_ 3 March 1980, p. A4. The article's tone is pessimistic on behalf of South Africa's indigenous defense capabilities, at some variance with standard, recent analyses which may, in particular, have ignored the parallel with the PRC's position after 1961 once cut off from a major power's transfer of licenses.

[18] For a good review of current small nations' indigenous arms development efforts and associated barriers to same, see M. Moodie, "Defense Industries in the Third World: Problems and Promises," in _Arms Transfers in the Modern World,_ S. Neuman and R. Harkavy, eds. (New York: Praeger, 1979), pp. 294–312. See also G. Copley, M. Moodie, and D. Harvey, "Third World Arms Production," _Defense and Foreign Affairs Digest,_ September 1978, pp. 10ff;

if any, small nations can produce all the components needed for sophisticated systems, even where full assembly capability exists. And then, the sheer volume requirements for ammunition and spare parts during a war can cause massive equipment attrition. Even given the fact that South Africa appears to have time to further develop its own arms industries, and that a large-scale war is not likely to occur there any time soon, the specter of serious shortages looms. Certainly there is little prospect for external resupply if push should come to shove.

Israel, once a favored French client, and at one time aided by German and British arms as well, has come to the point of near-total reliance on the United States, particularly for those arms in the most sophisticated categories. This is not to mention Israel's dependence on outright grant aid (in order to counter Arab arms purchases) or its resupply requirements during a crisis. U.S. arms supply to Israel has seemingly been less forthcoming in the past few years (even if this has not received much publicity), as Saudi pressures and America's growing reliance on Egypt as the linchpin of its regional influence have had their inevitable impact. Matmon C was whittled down, Israel's F-16 aircraft requests vastly reduced, and numerous other requested transfers of high technology items quietly denied or delayed, often under the cover of the arms control restrictions of Presidential Directive 13.[19]

Israel has developed indigenous production in many areas—small arms and ammunition, artillery, various electronic and avionic accessories, some air-to-air and air-to-surface missiles—and is now believed to produce some 30 to 40 percent of its own requirements.[20] It has also designed and produced its own fighter aircraft (Kfir), tank (Merkava) and missile-firing patrol boats (Reshef and Saar class). Each, however, is dependent on foreign engines.[21]

Prospects for Multilateral Arms Export Restraint, U.S., Congress, Senate, 96th Congress, 1st session, April 1979, p. 34; and Stephanie Neuman, "Into the Crystal Ball: Indigenous Defense Production and the Future of the International Arms Trade," paper delivered at meeting of International Studies Association, Los Angeles, 19–22 March 1980.

[19] For a general discussion of the U.S.-Israel leverage relationship with respect to arms transfers and military and economic aid (and the withholding of them), see Thomas R. Wheelock, "Arms for Israel: The Limit of Leverage," International Security 3, 2 (Fall 1978): 123–37. On Matmon C and related matters, see Foreign Assistance Legislation for Fiscal Year 1979: Economic and Military Aid Programs in Europe and the Middle East, U.S., Congress, House of Representatives, 95th Congress, 2nd session, pp. 199–269.

[20] For earlier information on Israel's weapons-development programs, see World Armaments and Disarmament: SIPRI Yearbook, 1975 (Cambridge: MIT Press, 1975), p. 236; SIPRI, The Arms Trade with the Third World (New York: Holmes & Meier, 1975), pp. 768–78; The New York Times for 23 April, 15 September and 19 September, 1971; and "Israel Revisited," Aviation Week & Space Technology, 10 March 1975, pp. 9–22. See also "Israeli Arms Industry Has Grown Fivefold Since '73," The New York Times, 15 January, 1977, p. 3; and Louis Kraar, "Israel's Own Military Industrial Complex," Fortune, 13 March 1978, pp. 2ff.

[21] Israel's Kfir aircraft and Merkava tanks rely on U.S. engines, its naval craft primarily on West German engines. The new fighter aircraft it plans for the 1980s, the "Lavie," may possibly be built around the General Electric F-404 engine, as reported in "Israel Unveils Plans to Build New Fighter-Bomber," Jerusalem Post Weekly, 2–8 March 1980, p. 3.

Crucial dependence for high performance aircraft, helicopters, heavy artillery, various missiles, and a large variety of avionics and other crucial components remains. For a nation of some 3 million people, with a necessarily specialized industrial structure, to overcome this dependence is virtually out of the question.

Taiwan, too, remains crucially and inescapably dependent on the United States for arms, though it does now license-produce F-5 fighters and Bell helicopters (partly assembly production), and has developed some indigenous capability to produce less sophisticated arms.[22] However, the one-year moratorium on U.S. transfers emerging from the U.S.-PRC deal on establishing relations may signal a more restrained U.S. supply policy toward Taiwan—an impression reinforced by heretofore American denial of F-4 aircraft and Harpoon antiship missiles.[23] Whether the United States will keep the arms pipeline sufficiently open to ensure Taiwan's ability to repel an invasion or break a blockade is not clear, though that is being promised. Taiwan has no discernible alternatives to U.S. arms (and Israeli transfers of Gabriel and Shafrir missiles provided only a minor mitigation of its problem); European suppliers must concern themselves with relations with a larger power on the mainland which is also potentially a more lucrative arms market.[24]

South Korea now seems to have a serious U.S. commitment to move toward rectification of its imbalances vis-à-vis its formidable northern rival (which has some 2,600 tanks, 1,000 APCs, 4,000 field artillery pieces, 450 combat ships, and 750 combat aircraft, far more in each category than the ROK possesses).[25] With its Force Improvement Plan, and assisted by the United States, it plans a vast increase in defense spending relative to GNP, involving some $4 billion per year spread out over numerous projects. Involved are acquisitions of TOW, Harpoon, Maverick, and Hawk missiles; helicopters, patrol boats, F-5 aircraft, and the upgrading of hundreds of old M-48 tanks, which will require massive foreign exchange outlays beyond the aid assistance and credits the United States will provide.

The United States apparently aims at increasing the ROK's self-sufficiency via licensed production, though one source reported earlier that

---

[22] See "Nationalists Update Fighter Force," *Aviation Week and Space Technology,* 29 May 1978, pp. 14–16; and "Taiwan Center Designs Two Aircraft," ibid., pp. 14–16.

[23] The perhaps crucial U.S. denial to Taiwan of advanced fighter aircraft such as the F-4 or F-18 and of the Harpoon ship-to-ship missile is cited in "U.S. to Sell Taiwan Defense Missile," The *New York Times,* 4 January 1980, p. A4. Therein, the Carter administration is said to have turned down the requests for the F-4 and F-18 "because providing them would have violated the President's arms transfer policy."

[24] For one noting of Israeli arms supplies to Taiwan, see "Taiwan Forces Reportedly Buy Israeli Missiles," The *New York Times,* 6 April 1977, p. 1; and "Taiwan Looks Beyond U.S. for Arms," The *New York Times,* 20 June 1977, p. 17.

[25] These data and information on the ROK's "Force Improvement Program" are drawn from the State Department's annual unclassified report, "Report on Korea," provided the author by State's South Korea desk.

"the U.S. has been reluctant to allow South Korean production of sophisticated weaponry, lest it create additional instability in the heavily militarized peninsula."[26] But despite Seoul's intention to develop something of an indigenous arms industry, it will continue to be crucially dependent on U.S. arms, occasional purchases of, for instance, Italian Fiat APCs aside.[27] North Korea, unlike the Arabs, Africans, or the PRC, does not wield sufficient economic or political leverage to ward off those who would supply arms to its rivals. Then, too, the United States has learned in recently threatening its now aborted pull-out from Korea, that it must also take Japan into account. The ROK worries nonetheless about the future of U.S. security support. In that connection, it has virtually threatened to go nuclear, and as such, its situation has been compared with that of Israel and Taiwan.[28]

The nuclear status of pariah states: capabilities, strategies, rationales

In view of the pariah states' threatening conventional security situations, it should not be surprising that each would at least consider the acquisition of nuclear weapons. Each has given strong signals or is the subject of widespread rumors about an intent to produce atomic weapons.

Israel, of course, is widely considered to have possessed actually deployed weapons for at least ten years, its continuing public disclaimers about not being the first state to introduce nuclear arms into the Middle East notwithstanding.[29] The recent flurry of speculation surrounding its possible role in what some analysts believe to have been a weapons test in the remote southern Indian Ocean has merely added to widespread assumptions about its "bomb in the basement" posture.[30] The long unsafeguarded Dimona reactor, the Jericho

[26] "Korea Asks $1.5 Billion in U.S. Loans for Arms," *Washington Post,* 29 December 1975, p. A2. See also "Schlesinger Minimizes Seoul Peril," *Washington Post,* 28 August 1975, p. A25.

[27] For information on ROK indigenous weapons programs, see Bruce A. Smith, "Koreans Seek New Military Air Capability," *Aviation Week & Space Technology,* 22 October 1979, pp. 62–63, wherein its intentions to coproduce or coassemble Hughes helicopters and F-5 aircraft are discussed along with modifications to the Nike-Hercules SAM. It is noted that the ROK has also recently launched its first destroyer.

[28] See "Official Hints South Korea Might Build Atom Bomb," The *New York Times,* 27 May 1977, p. 3, based on a statement by Foreign Minister Park Tong Jin; and "Glenn Asks Probe of Korea Arms Plan," *Washington Post,* 4 November 1978, p. 16.

[29] Among the numerous publications on the Israeli nuclear weapons program, see Fuad Jabber, *Israel and Nuclear Weapons* (London: Chatto & Windus, 1971); Robert J. Pranger and Dale R. Tahtinen, *Nuclear Threat in the Middle East* (Washington: D.C. American Enterprise Institute, Foreign Affairs Study no. 23, 1975); "How Israel Got the Bomb," *Time,* 12 April 1976; Robert Tucker, "Israel and the United States: From Dependence to Nuclear Weapons?," *Commentary* (November 1975): 29–43; Robert E. Harkavy, *Spectre of a Middle Eastern Holocaust* (Denver: University of Denver Press, 1977); and S. Aronson, "Nuclearization of the Middle East," *The Jerusalem Quarterly,* no. 2 (Winter 1977): 27–44.

[30] See, among other press reports, "Israel Reported Behind A-Blast Off South Africa," *Washington Post,* 22 February 1980, p. A6; and "Neutron Bomb Suspected in Africa Blast," *Washington Post,* 9 March 1980, p. A7.

SRBM missile program, and the persistent (but still publicly unsubstantiated) reports about Israel's earlier alleged thefts of weapons-grade U-235 provide, in combination, much circumstantial evidence. American intelligence agencies by now appear convinced that Israel is the seventh (or is it the sixth?) nuclear power, and have virtually ceased being reticent about it.

South Korea's *present* intentions would seem to be less clear. Its earlier aborted (by U.S. pressures) move to purchase a plutonium reprocessing plant from France raised widespread concern, particularly given the supposed economic infeasibility of such a purchase, even given the ROK's ambitious civilian reactor program.[31] Then, too, there were strong hints—virtually threats—leaked by South Korean officials in response to the Carter administration's now lapsed plans for a near-total withdrawal of U.S. troops from Korea. Those plans are now reversed and the United States seems committed both to retaining a strong military presence and to aiding in upgrading the ROK's forces. Within the past year, news and hints about South Korea's nuclear ambitions have been correspondingly muted.

Taiwan, like South Korea, is in the process of acquiring a number of power reactors (each badly needs to reduce oil imports for balance-of-payments reasons), under stringent safeguards still being conducted by the IAEA, despite Taiwan's expulsion from that organization. It was earlier rumored to have developed a small reprocessing operation, and possesses a 40-megawatt Canadian research reactor of the same type that enabled India's nuclear test. The earlier publicized imbroglio over its scientists studying missile guidance technology at MIT raised the specter of a match to Israel's Jericho program, particularly as conventionally armed surface-to-surface missiles would appear to have only limited military value to Taiwan as well.[32] But, Taiwan's nuclear program is now widely considered to have been brought under U.S. surveillance and control, and similar to the South Korean situation, speculation about weapons development has recently been dormant.[33]

Finally, South Africa, with a scientific and technological infrastructure not much inferior to Israel's and in some areas, such as specialty steels, superior, has apparently succeeded in independently developing the Becker nozzle method for separating U-235 from natural uranium. Pretoria's stated intentions are to use the nozzle facility to produce fuel for the reactors it intends to acquire from France (the United States will not provide fuel short of

[31] In the *Washington Post* article cited in footnote 28 above, it is claimed that the ROK embarked on a weapons program in the early 1970s under President Park, but which was halted or delayed after the French cancellation of the reprocessing plant venture in 1976 and under pressure from the U.S. Park was quoted, however, as saying that "if the U.S. nuclear umbrella were removed, we have to start developing our own nuclear weapons capability." See also, "Official Hints South Korea Might Build Atom Bomb," The *New York Times,* 1 July 1977, p. 4.
[32] See "Taiwanese Program at MIT Ended," *Washington Post,* 16 July 1976, p. A5.
[33] For analyses of the Taiwanese nuclear capability, see "Taiwan Develops Nuclear Industry, Weapons Capacity," *Washington Post,* 27 February 1977, p. 21; and "Taiwan's Nuclear Plans Concern U.S. Officials," *Washington Post,* 20 December 1978, p. 21.

South Africa's acquiescing in full-scope safeguards), and to become a significant exporter of reactor fuel. It is assumed, however, that such a facility, by
having stages added, could (or may already) produce material usable for
weapons, and, if so, South Africa is virtually home-free on the way to
weapons status.[34] The facts (and what they meant) regarding the alleged 1977
South African feint at a nuclear test in the Kalahari Desert (claimed to have
been thwarted by a joint U.S.-Soviet démarche) have never been made publicly
clear, nor, for that matter, have those relating to a possible South African role
in the still mysterious event over the nearby ocean.[35] However, if South Africa
has indeed acquired the (unsafeguarded) ability to produce weapons-grade
material, it would seem that only the thin barrier of weapons-design
knowledge stands between it and the possession of atomic weapons. For a state
with its technological-scientific base, that is a minor barrier, particularly with
respect to primitive weapons, portable by aircraft. The purchase of the
French-supplied Koeberg reactors, expected to go onstream in 1982–1984,
would appear effectively irrelevant to its weapons acquisition capability.

Regarding the utilities or rationales for nuclear weapons possession, it is
usually averred that it would not necessarily assure the security or survival of
the four cases in question; indeed, arguments have been made for each case
that it might actually be counterproductive. The actual use of nuclear weapons
would raise the prospect of an overwhelming response from some quarter (not
precluding joint U.S.-Soviet nuclear sanctions), which in turn begs questions
about credible deterrence. However, since each pariah has clearly considered
making the move, its own apparent perceptions of utility should be taken
seriously, and there may be a tendency in the West, based on wishful thinking,
to underestimate the deterrence possibilities.

In gauging the potential usefulness of a small nuclear force to the pariah
state, one must examine a range of possible strategic doctrines, not necessarily
to be made formally explicit. Variously, last resort deterrence, deterrence-by-
uncertainty, massive retaliation, or "trip wire" doctrines, tactical battlefield
use, or threats in order to cover wholesale population withdrawals (Exodus!)
may come into play.[36]

[34] For earlier analyses of South Africa's nuclear prospects, see Edouard Bustin, "South Africa's
Foreign Policy Alternatives and Deterrence Needs," in *Nuclear Proliferation and the Near-
Nuclear Countries,* O. Marwah and A. Schulz, eds. (Cambridge, Mass.: Ballinger, 1975), pp.
205–26; and J. E. Spence, "The Republic of South Africa: Proliferation and the Politics of Out-
ward Movement," in *Nuclear Proliferation: Phase II,* R. Lawrence and J. Larus, eds. (Lawrence,
Kans.: University of Kansas Press, 1974). Among numerous items discussing the South African
U-235 nozzle facility at Pelindaba, see "South Africa's Secret Atom Plant Suspected of Working
on a Bomb," The *New York Times,* 30 April 1977, p. 1, and also Robert S. Jaster, *South Africa's
Narrowing Security Options* (London: IISS, 1980), Adelphi Paper No. 159, pp. 44–48.
[35] On the Kalahari Desert episode, see, inter alia, "France Says Data Show South Africa Plans
Atomic Test," The *New York Times,* 23 August 1977, p. 1.
[36] For a good review of nuclear weapons doctrines potentially applicable to new or small nuclear
powers, see Lewis A. Dunn and Herman Kahn, *Trends in Nuclear Proliferation, 1975–1995*
(Croton-on-Hudson, N.Y.: Hudson Institute, 1975).

The obstacles and dangers are legion and inhibiting. Each pariah must worry about getting across the nuclear threshold to a deployed nuclear force in the face of possible preemptive attacks by antagonists who may worry about time running out. The pariahs must also be concerned about (a) big-power responses, ranging from nuclear preemption to withdrawal of lingering economic and political support, (b) the encouragement of rival nuclear development (most serious in the case of Israel, not relevant for Taiwan), (c) the possible limited usefulness of nuclear deterrence in the face of conventional "salami" tactics, and (d) still deeper global political isolation.

In the cases of Taiwan and South Korea, the specter of nuclear use against people who are their conationals must act as an inhibiting factor—one absent in the Middle East and South Africa, where racial and ethnic hatreds and fears of genocide abound. Still, there is the possibility of deterrence-by-uncertainty in these cases, of what credibility no amount of scenario-writing can easily determine.

Each case can be discussed according to a variety of standard criteria: the value of last-resort, counter-cities threats, possible tactical uses, problems of nuclear force survivability and penetration under last-resort circumstances, psychological rationales regarding the achievement of others' weary resignation about the costs of final solutions, deterrence of big-power intervention into regional conflicts, "blackmail" against major powers in connection with continuing conventional arms shipments, and so forth. We may merely summarize the generalizations proffered by analysts regarding the four cases.

Israel's case is habitually discussed in the light of a grim last-resort scenario portraying the imminent overrunning of its territories by Arab armies bent on wholesale massacres, accompanied by American unwillingness or inability to intervene. At such a juncture, nuclear threats, demonstrations, or counter-cities salvoes would be anticipated (some reports about the opening phases of the 1973 war see this having then come close to actuality), whether for practical deterrence or war-fighting purposes, or as a suicidal act of final vengeance. Penetration of Arab airspaces is considered virtually assured by a mixed force of nuclear-configured aircraft, Jericho missiles (if operational despite rumored guidance problems), and perhaps other more exotic methods (surface-fired missiles from patrol boats, torpedoes from submarines, etc.), though if Israel's air force were whittled way down by this point in the scenario, the viability of a nuclear threat might be weaker than often assumed in "static" analyses.

Some analysts consider the virtual certainty of a Soviet nuclear riposte to render Israel's nuclear threat less than credible, but others point to the varied possibilities of missile hardening, airborne alert, mobile missiles, launch-on-warning, and the use of Palestinian populations as hostages against a Soviet "area" response, as providing potentially viable deterrence. The capacity of Israel to "absorb" a Soviet strike and to retain the capability to knock out some Arab cities ("triangular second-strike capability") is central to all such analyses.[37] It might be asked, moreover, whether Israel would ever have embarked on such a (presumably) expensive and (with regard to the U.S.) politically dangerous nuclear weapons program if it had not felt reasonably optimistic about the technical possibilities for effective deterrence, despite the Soviet counterthreat.

Israel may also envisage deployment of tactical nuclear weapons to the extent allowed by its quantitative production of bomb material, and if the conventional military balance should deteriorate to its disadvantage, might even contemplate a (not necessarily credible) "tripwire doctrine," with all the problems faced by the United States in Europe and for many of the same reasons. If the explosion over the southern seas was, as has been speculated, Israel's, its reportedly determined megatonnage—2-3 megatons—is intriguing in connection with possible tactical weapons (perhaps neutron weapons) testing. Other Israeli nuclear rationales might involve deterrence against use of chemical weapons (note Egypt's allegedly large nerve gas stockpiles) and of massive conventional bombing of cities, and the possible need to cover withdrawal of Jewish populations from the Middle East if the state's destruction is conceded and a massacre anticipated (the latter might be used as a form of threat vis-à-vis the United States).

Whether Israel's assured possession of a nuclear stockpile was a part of the reason for Sadat's 1977 peace initiative bears reflection in connection with the aforementioned "psychological" rationales. Perhaps above all, there is the relation to America's "dove's dilemma," as Arab oil pressure makes an accommodating (for Israel) U.S. arms supply policy more and more difficult, costly, and (in the long-run) questionable.

South African nuclear weapons, should they become a reality, would seem to have high survivability—again with the advantage of hostage populations. For the foreseeable future, too, there is little reason for Pretoria to anticipate problems in penetrating the urban airspaces of surrounding nations, not to mention the possibilities for sea-borne delivery. But, there are the imponderables: (a) the future Soviet regional role (including perhaps the countering of South African nuclear weapons) and (b) the strategic or tactical utility of weapons of mass destruction in a guerrilla warfare environment. Soviet Scud rockets might still end up in Mozambique or elsewhere. Still, South Africa appears to have a time cushion, and there is little immediate prospect of a regional nuclear balance of terror, as promised before long for

---

[37] I have coined the term "triangular second-strike capability," referring here to the three-way relationship among Israel, the USSR, and the Arab states, since no suitable phrase exists in the strategic literature. Basically, the following questions are involved for Israel: could it absorb a Soviet first-strike and still carry out a countercities strike against the Arabs sufficient to cause "unacceptable" losses? *and* would the Israeli ability to do so be perceived, beforehand, by the Soviets and the Arabs? If a phased-array radar capability could be developed, launch-on-warning might provide such a deterrent, albeit with the cost of greatly increasing structural instability and the chances for accidental nuclear war. See Harkavy, *Spectre of a Middle Eastern Holocaust,* esp. pp. 59–64.

Israel, by current activities in Pakistan (the "Islamic bomb"), and perhaps Iraq.[38]

It remains to be seen whether Pretoria will follow the "bomb in the basement" route. Because it no longer receives arms from western sources, it may have less to lose from outside sanctions by going to an overt nuclear status than would Israel.[39] It could be made to suffer economically from a full trade embargo and cut-off of further investments, though its gold hoard and possession of other strategic materials (chrome, platinum-group metals, etc.) give it more counter-leverage than Israel, domestic American politics aside.[40] Most likely, South Africa will continue to keep the world guessing about its capabilities in order to provide itself with the maximum leverage in warding off further pressures about racial liberalization. But, if the Mugabe regime in Zimbabwe should become a menacing Soviet base, there could be surprises if South Africa comes to see a clearer specter of further unraveling of its security situation.

Many analyses of South Africa's nuclear activities argue their lack of strategic utility in confronting what would be expected to be a guerrilla conflict, perhaps abetted by invasions from neighboring countries, and where Pretoria would be impotent in the face of Soviet nuclear counter-threats (and the lack of any prospect of a countering American threat to that). On the contrary, it is argued that South Africa, like Israel, might devise a triangular second-strike deterrent against Maputo, Salisbury, and other cities, might bank on a psychological deterrent to induce caution in its foes, or might, like Israel, contemplate a nuclear cover for exodus of its white populations at a moment of impending collapse. Those are widely considered thin reeds, yet, if the South African government has indeed already gone nuclear or intends to, it must presumably have thought such things through and come (rightly or wrongly) to some "optimistic" conclusions.

Taiwan, perhaps more so than South Africa or Israel, might contemplate tactical as well as countervalue rationales for a small nuclear force, even admitting the dangers of nuclear escalation against a better-armed foe. A PRC amphibious invasion fleet headed for Taiwan, or its assembly points in coastal

---

[38] On the matter of the Pakistani centrifuge installation, see, inter alia, "Zia Denies Pakistan Builds Nuclear Bomb and Urges U.S. to Resume Aid," The *New York Times,* 23 September 1979, p. 14; and "Pakistan is Offered a Choice on A-Arms," ibid., 17 April 1979, p. A3. On the Iraqi nuclear program, see "Iraq Said to Get A-Bomb Ability With Italy's Aid," The *New York Times,* 18 March 1980, p. 1; and "Magazine Reports Israeli Agents Sabotaged Iraqi Nuclear Reactor," *Oakland Tribune,* 15 March 1980, p. A12.

[39] For a synopsis and analysis of recent U.S. nonproliferation legislation, particularly as pertains to sanctions, see W. Donnelly and D. Kramer, "Nuclear Weapons Proliferation: Legislation for Policy and Other Measures," Issue Brief No. IB77011, The Library of Congress, Congressional Research Service, August 1978.

[40] The impact of the recent gold price increase on the South African economy (hence, also, perhaps its political leverage), is noted in "South Africa Cuts Income Taxes Because of Rise in Price of Gold," The *New York Times,* 27 March 1980, p. A22. See also "Gold's New Turbulent Role," The *New York Times,* 28 January 1980, p. D1.

cities beforehand, would present very inviting targets, as would an established
beachhead of the Normandy or Iwo Jima types.[41] And, if Taiwan's elites were
to face last-resort circumstances, there would be the possibility of counter-city
strikes which could be conducted by nuclear-armed F-104 aircraft or by
missiles, if such should be developed (later development of cruise missiles cannot be ruled out).[42] Cover for withdrawal of the Taiwanese government amid
bargaining over a U.S. rescue airlift is a fairly plausible scenario, use for com-
pellence purposes to break a possible PRC naval blockade appears only weakly
credible. In last-resort circumstances, the problem of aircraft penetration into
the Chinese mainland might be a formidable one, as attackers would face
swarms of alerted defense interceptors. If Taiwan were to go nuclear, its
development of surface-to-surface missiles might be considered crucial. One
with the reach of Jericho, about 300 miles, could bring coastal cities such as
Swatow and Amoy within range. Longer-range missiles with a 500-mile reach
would be required for attacks on Canton or Shanghai; Peking, however, is
over 1,000 miles away.

For now, Taiwan's nuclear ambitions, such as they are, seem thwarted—
blocked by U.S. pressures underpinned by the threat of cut-offs of conventional weapons and enriched uranium needed to fuel Taiwan's power reactors.
Like Israel, Taiwan has moved just far enough along so that it has implicitly
signalled the United States and others of one possible ramification of pushing
it too far—that is, it banks on a favorable resolution of the "dove's dilemma"
to keep its arms pipeline open and a still implicit U.S. security guarantee
operative.

South Korea, though not blessed with a formidable geographic barrier to
invasion, could hypothetically expect to use tactical nuclear weapons to good
effect on its narrow, mountainous peninsula (not without fall-out danger to its
own populations), and where a nuclear counterthreat may not soon be present.
Further, a counter-cities threat against nearby Pyongyang or Wonsan may well
be technically possible, with aircraft or short-range ballistic missiles. The
credibility of such nuclear threats, however, might be weakened by the ethnic
ties, the lesser seriousness of last-resort circumstances, and their uselessness
against "salami" tactics. The ROK now appears to bank primarily on the
threat of its going nuclear (also on the possible impetus that that might lend to
development of Japanese nuclear ambitions) to deter a withdrawal of the U.S.
security commitment; indeed, the strategy appears to have been successful up
until now.

---

[41] See Jonathan D. Pollack, "The People's Republic of China in a Proliferated World," in op.
cit., John Kerry King, ed. pp. 132–33.
[42] It should be noted, however, that on several occasions, Taiwanese leaders have said they
would never develop nuclear weapons because the idea of unleashing them against "Chinese com-
patriots on the mainland" was unthinkable. See "Taiwan Develops Nuclear Industry, Weaponry
Capacity," op. cit.

If there is a single thread which connects these cases, it is that which relates to the continuance of external arms acquisitions and military support during crises. What others, pejoratively, might deem a form of nuclear "blackmail," may be perceived by the pariahs as a precarious bit of remaining leverage. South Africa is here a partial anomaly. Having already lost its (at least overt governmental) arms suppliers and any reasonable hope of military support during crises, its "blackmail" may retain some usability to deter more stringent economic pressures.

The limits of a "pariah international"—reality or fantasy?

For a number of years, there have been nascent hints that the isolated pariah states, in various bilateral combinations or *in toto,* were moving toward some low-key semblance of an implicit, clandestine alliance. These rumors have been given some credence by persistent reports about growing Israeli-South African conventional military ties, and by odd bits of information bruiting the possibility of east-west pariah linkages. Speculation about joint Israeli-South African nuclear activities in Kalahari or out over the southern ocean have dramatically brought the notion of a "pariah international" into recent prominence.

Historically, it might be claimed, small-state alliances, have been of dubious value; the Little Entente of the interwar period is a classic example.[43] And a geographically far-flung alliance, such as would be defined by the pariah four, would seem to be quixotic, given the virtual absence of any plausible mutual assistance in crises or regional conventional conflicts (the Taiwan-South Korea combination here excepted). But there are possibilities for collaboration regarding conventional arms transfers (including possible coproduction ventures), strategic basing or staging assistance and—germane to the primary focus of this paper—nuclear cooperation. Beyond that, inter-pariah relations might provide trade and investment outlets—particularly if boycotts and embargoes should become more serious.

There have already been some indications of arms-transfer patterns linking some of the pariahs. Israel has sold missile patrol boats to South Africa, is reported to have assisted it with electronic surveillance gear for counterinsurgency warfare, and may also have aided in refurbishing and upgrading Pretoria's large Centurion tank force (Israel has had much experience extending the lives of its own old Centurions). South Africa also uses Israeli small arms, probably Belgian-produced on license and obtained through private dealers. The possibility of a Kfir fighter deal was earlier adum-

---

[43] See Robert Rothstein, *Alliances and Small Powers* (New York: Columbia University Press, 1968).

brated, but was squelched because of American restrictions on retransfer of Kfir's J-79 engine.[44]

No reciprocal South African transfers have been reported, though its license-production of some French systems creates possibilities.[45] During the 1976 Vorster visit to Israel, the press noted the potential for South African investment in Israeli arms industries—presumably intended to result in transfers to the former, which would also give the latter greater economies-of-scale.[46] South Africa's capabilities for producing heavy steel armor have been the subject of rumors in connection with Israel's indigenous tank development efforts. Then, too, South Africa may, at times, have provided refueling stops for Israeli ships making the long trip around the Cape of Good Hope.

So far, Israel's sale of Gabriel and Shafrir missiles to Taiwan has been the only significant "east-west" arms transfer among the pariahs (though reported large-scale South African raw uranium sales to Taiwan are worth noting here). Israel almost achieved a deal for Kfir fighters to Taiwan at one point, which was first temporarily thwarted by the United States, then given the green light but subsequently aborted by Taiwan, presumably under pressure from Saudi Arabia.[47]

To date, South Korea and Taiwan, even with their fairly advanced scientific and technological infrastructures, have had only small indigenous arms-production programs and have not participated significantly in supplier markets. This may change, however, and if it does, some reciprocity with the other pariahs could develop; for instance, South Korea, aside from its licensed production, now has some indigenous capacity to produce patrol boats.

General trade among the pariahs increased dramatically between 1970 and 1977.[48] Taiwan's exports to the other three increased many-fold during that period, and the two-way figures for all possible combinations except Israel-ROK were not far behind. South Africa has recently announced major technical exchange and trade deals with both Israel and Taiwan. Still, there are

[44] On the Israel-South Africa arms link, see, inter alia, "South Africa Gains Arms and Trade as Israel Link Hardens," The *New York Times,* 21 May 1977, p. 6; and "South African Jews: Cautious, Vulnerable," *Washington Post,* 15 February 1977, p. 9.

[45] This author was recently informed by a (not to be named nongovernmental) source that South Africa has recently improved the avionics for its Mirage fighters, and that the improved technology may also have been transferred to Israel. See also, inter alia, "Israeli Tours South Africa as Arms-Trade Furor Grows," The *New York Times,* 10 February 1978, p. 2.

[46] See the *Johannesburg Star* around 15–17 April 1976; also, "South Africa Link to Israel Grows," The *New York Times,* 18 August 1976, p. 9.

[47] See "Taiwan Using Unofficial Diplomatic Ties to Avoid Becoming an Outcast," The *New York Times,* 17 September 1977, p. 2; "Taiwan Rejects Israeli Plane Offer," The *New York Times,* 7 July 1978, p. 3; and "U.S. Decides to Permit Israeli Sale of 50 to 60 Jet Fighters to Taiwan." The *New York Times,* 5 July 1978, p. 1.

[48] See *Direction of Trade: Annual 1970–1974* (Washington, D.C.: IMF/IRBD, 1975) for full data on trade involving the pariahs, by exports and imports, regions and individual countries. On Israeli-South African economic relations, see "South Africa Gains Arms and Trade as Israel Link Hardens," The *New York Times,* 21 May 1977, p. 6, wherein Israel's exports of chemicals, textiles, and electronics is said matched by South Africa's exports to it of sugar, coal and steel.

severe limits on the extent to which the pariahs could substitute for other trading relationships by building up commerce among themselves. Their markets are limited, and the distances are great. Even with the great increase in South Africa's exports to Israel, Taiwan, and South Korea over the past five years, the combined imports of the three from South Africa represent only a fraction of the imports from any one of their major Western trading partners. And, Taiwan and South Korea have far more extensive trading relationships with the combined Arab OPEC countries than they do with Israel. Israel's exports to South Africa are now only about 25 percent of those to Switzerland.

In recent years, there has been considerable speculation about a possible Israeli-South African nuclear axis. Much, to begin with, has been inferred from the seeming complementarity of the two nations' nuclear capabilities and resources. Israel presumably has (perhaps advanced and varied) weapons-design capability and may possess at least small-scale reprocessing facilities. South Africa has vast raw uranium reserves, the nozzle process for physical separation of U-235, and open spaces and proximity to remote ocean areas usable for testing. Moreover, Israel has the Jericho missile program and has been reported working on a missile with greater range (perhaps in excess of 500 miles). Even in the absence of transfers of material and equipment, there are the obvious possibilities for less visible transfers of technical information, which could possibly result in a synergistic growth in the two nations' nuclear capabilities. One can merely cite here again the rumors about the explosion over the ocean. Whether it was a nuclear test, and whether it involved either or both Israel and South Africa is not publicly known, and hence can be speculated upon only with great caution.

Less likely, but not to be ruled out, is future nuclear collaboration between Taiwan and South Korea or between them and the other two pariahs. ROK missile technology and a possible Taiwanese reprocessing capability could, hypothetically, be shared. Uranium-235 from South Africa, plutonium from Israel, and Israel's Jericho technology are all conceivable items of exchange in a "gray market," although the certain displeasure of the United States, should such transactions come to light, might well give the pariahs pause, all the more so now given the deterrent of recent Congressional legislation. But, clandestine possibilities exist, and one might speculate wildly, for instance, about the possible coincidence between Israel's alleged guidance problems with Jericho and the incident at MIT concerning Taiwanese attempts at acquiring apparently related technology in the United States.

Still, the political and security ties among the pariahs are inherently unstable—they are uneasy bedfellows at best. In some cases, their relationships may even constitute overall liabilities. Israel recognizes that its growing links with South Africa may jeopardize its chances for resuming formal diplomatic ties in black Africa (this issue arose at the time of the CBS leaks on the alleged ocean test), not to mention their impact on the more crucial U.S.-Israeli relationship, including the matter of black American opinion. For

South Africa, the Israeli connection decreases the chances of leapfrogging Africa to establish ties in the Middle East or in the broader world (it is presumably only an ironic twist of fate that recent massive Arab sell-offs of dollars have contributed to a gold price-rise bonanza for Pretoria). Similar generalizations may be made about South Korean-Taiwanese ties with the other two pariahs, if not about links between the former two.

Interpariah ties may, of course, also provide pariahs leverage for reducing the surrounding hostility and concomitant isolation. Israel's alleged nuclear nexus with South Africa may actually have impelled, paradoxically, some black African states to try to detach the two by improving relations with the former.

Then, there have been the strenuous efforts made by some Arab oil states to split the ROK and Taiwan off from any relationship with Israel. Taiwan not only has technical assistance and agricultural teams in some Arab countries, but its companies have been given some $500 million in construction contracts, including one for $150 million to build a power station in Saudi Arabia.[49] South Korea not only also has construction contracts there, but also some 100,000 contract laborers in Arab lands (some 19,000 alone in Saudi Arabia), the combined remittances of which are important for Seoul's payments balances.[50] The Arab efforts at detaching the Asian pariahs from Israel have succeeded, among other things, in prodding Taiwan not to buy Kfir fighters (and perhaps other possible follow-ons) and in South Korea's actual closing of Israel's embassy in Seoul (announced by Israel as a financial stringency measure).[51] The arms sale denial diplomacy is important in relation to Israel's efforts at achieving economies-of-scale and financing for its indigenous arms industries. These developments do not, of course, necessarily preclude continuing quiet, clandestine east-west pariah links, which could possibly involve nuclear transactions.

The amelioration of pariahtude: "quasi-proliferation" as a conflict control mechanism

The pariah statuses of these four states are extremely difficult to resolve, in great part because of these nations' inherent lack of political leverage within the international system in its present constellation. Nonetheless, none of these situations is necessarily permanent, nor need one posit an ineluctable trend towards nuclear proliferation. Indeed, it is just possible that the pariah status

[49] See "Visit By Taiwan Leader to Saudis Underlines Bond Between Nations," The New York Times, 11 July 1977, p. 35; and "Taiwan Using Unofficial Diplomatic Ties to Avoid Becoming Outcast," The New York Times, 9 September 1977, p. 2.

[50] The data derived from conversation with State Department's South Korea desk officer.

[51] See "Israel Says It Will Close Embassy in South Korea," The New York Times, 16 February 1977, p. 7, wherein it is said that the ROK was taking an increasingly pro-Arab position, to win friends in the Third World and to further its economic penetration of the Middle East.

of some of these states may be resolvable through exploitation of mere rumors of potential weapons development, though other avenues of escape are also obviously possible—i.e., new alignments or amelioration of underlying political conflicts.

As noted, the Egyptian move toward peace with Israel in 1977 is considered by many to have been impelled, at least in part, by recognition that Israel's nuclear stockpile may nearly preclude the "final solution" long sought in the Arab world. That would now presumably at least be far more costly. However, whether such a shift in attitudes can further be internalized in the remainder of the Arab world remains to be seen. There is some evidence of a more open recognition of the ultimate consequences of Israel's nuclear program. Whether that will militate towards a peaceful solution or toward matching nuclear efforts by the Arabs so as to neutralize the Israeli nuclear threat and hence allow continued pursuit of conventional strategies, is not yet clear.

Recent numerous hints of a softening of the PRC's long attempt to eliminate the remnants of the Kuomintang might be ascribed to similar considerations, particularly given the former's seeming near-term inability to carry out an invasion, and the latter's presumed relatively short time-frame for weapons development, if it should decide to move ahead.

South African and South Korean relations with their antagonists, however, do not seem yet to have been ameliorated for similar reasons, unless it might be claimed that periodic, sporadic discussions about Korean unification might be related (from the North Korean perspective) to nuclear activities and expectations. Indeed, South Africa has seen a serious recent upsurge of guerrilla activity, highlighted by the attacks on its SASOL installations, which might appear to presage a new stage of conflict.[52]

In the long run, however, constant reminders of the ultimate possible costs of attempts at eliminating one or more of the pariahs might produce, in some cases, a weary resignation that might assist resolution of long-festering disputes. It might also produce a more sober perspective on certain conflicts by major powers prone to assisting efforts at eliminating pariah states, and by others prone to abandoning pariahs as unwanted burdens.

Each of the pariahs would, of course, prefer to achieve outside security arrangements (with a great power or through regional alliances) to preclude sole reliance on nuclear deterrence. The possibilities vary from case to case. Israel, now shorn of useful regional connections with Iran and Ethiopia and increasingly isolated from support in Western Europe, relies almost solely on American ties. Not altogether precluded is the possibility of an implicit alliance with Egypt, faced off against the radical Arab states aligned with the USSR. That appears unlikely, and as Arab oil and monetary leverage over the

---

[52] "Attack on South African Oil Plants Expected to Bring Stiff Retaliation," The *New York Times,* 3 June 1980, p. 1.

United States increases, Israel seems ever more reliant on the leverage held by Jews and their political allies within the United States.

Taiwan's situation is somewhat paradoxical. While it fears the loss of the U.S. security umbrella, it may also come to rely upon American leverage over the PRC (i.e., the latter's need for backing vis-à-vis the USSR), which may be enhanced if China should become reliant on U.S. military technology. Curiously, however, Taiwan has complained bitterly about hints of U.S. arms transfers to the PRC. Otherwise, Taiwan's economic power is valuable in mitigating its isolation, pertaining to its role as a trade outlet and investment locale, a matter germane to Japan, Europe, and some of the Arab countries as well as to the United States.[53]

South Korea's pariah status is, in a major sense, self-inflicted. Though its present defense posture is precarious and it relies heavily on American conventional and/or nuclear deterrence, the economic and population wherewithal for regional predominance, if not balance, is at hand. A more extensive defense effort, coupled with Chinese inhibitions about risking their American tie over Korea, could promise amelioration of its situation, though the possibility of Soviet instigation of another North Korean assault may not altogether be precluded.

South Africa's situation, perhaps more than the others, appears particularly unresolvable. It has come to rely on western fears about loss of its vast raw materials (as fears about a Soviet resource denial strategy mount) as well as its strategic position astride the Cape maritime route along which much of the Persian Gulf oil passes. No reasonable possibilities exist, however, either for new regional alignments or those with major powers, and periodically bruited security ties with the nations of South America's southern core are not likely to become significant.[54] Barring a Zimbabwe-like final outcome, or a much fairer separation or partition policy than that promised by the present Bantustans, the specter of a protracted and lonely conflict for white South Africa appears inevitable.

If one or more of the pariahs has come to rely upon a "quasi-proliferation" posture, that raises the question of how long such an ambiguous position can be maintained. Israel has remained in this state for about a decade, unless the event over the southern ocean may be interpreted as a deliberate move towards a more open posture. If it is moving towards a large-scale and variegated nuclear arsenal, however, pressure from the Israeli military concerning testing (perhaps more necessary for tactical than for large counter-cities devices) may have quietly mounted.

Pariah moves toward an unannounced or "bomb in the basement" posture might, contrary to the foregoing, impel their rivals toward preventive war strategies intended to produce a "final solution" before the "sands run out" and a permanent stalemate is produced. There is some inconclusive

---

[53] See "Taiwan Prosperity Unmatched in Asia," The *New York Times,* 28 March 1980, p. A6.

[54] One recent report of undetermined accuracy does report on South African sales of armored cars to Morocco for use against the Polisario. See *Africa Confidential,* 9 April 1980, p. 8.

evidence that Nasser's instigation of the 1967 crisis had such considerations in mind, and one analyst at least claims that the Soviets may have considered a preventive attack on Dimona at the time of the 1969–1970 "attrition war."[55] The Soviets might conceivably still consider preempting South Africa's nuclear facilities, just as they apparently earlier considered a similar solution for the then nascent Chinese nuclear threat in the 1960s. Such considerations may not yet be germane for either the PRC or North Korea, though the latter's recent instigation of a number of border and sea incidents could presage a preventive war threat. For these reasons, some pariahs might likely wish to produce small arsenals quietly, *before* using them as political weapons, postponing testing until a small stockpile is amassed.

The foregoing dilemma involving the political uses of merely rumored or clandestinely existent nuclear stockpiles brings us to an important fault line dividing the four cases, concerning the matters of time-frames or "fuses." For Israel and South Korea, there is an obvious immediacy to potentially mortal threats, underscored by the vivid memories of 1967 and 1973 for the former and 1950 for the latter. For these two pariahs, weapons made operational with a "turn of the screw" might be deemed immediately necessary if the bluff of merely rumored nuclear ambitions should suddenly be called. South Africa and Taiwan, by contrast, appear to have longer fuses, as increasingly ominous security situations would presumably be signalled over longer periods, respectively, by escalating guerrilla war and by a necessarily protracted buildup of PRC naval amphibious capability.

Cross-cutting the above pairings, however, it is noted that Israel and South Africa, both possessing unsafeguarded facilities, have the capacity to go nuclear on their own (if they have not already done so) without much external interference. South Korea and Taiwan, on the contrary, would presumably have to engage in clandestine efforts to acquire nuclear weapons which most likely would be detected by American intelligence services, hence producing almost certain, severe sanctions. In combining the above two criteria, thus, it is apparent that South Korea's situation is particularly difficult, even if its conventional defense potential may be stronger than that of the other three pariahs.

In a related vein, it might be speculated that pariah states' nuclear programs—or their threat—might be useful items of leverage regarding arms supply or resupply during future possible conventional conflicts.[56] The U.S.

---

[55] Regarding Nasser's preventive war threats in response to Israeli nuclear developments, see the following *New York Times* 1966 articles: "Warning on Bomb Given by Nasser," 2 February, p. 8; "Nasser Assails U.S. and Britain," 23 February, p. 2; "Nasser Threatens War on a Nuclear-Armed Israel," 18 April, p. 6; and "Nasser Cites Need for Nuclear Arms," 9 May, p. 8. On the 1969–1970 preventive war possibility, see Avigdor Haselkorn, "Israel: From An Option to a Bomb in the Basement?" in *Nuclear Proliferation: Phase II,* R. M. Lawrence and J. Larus, eds. (Lawrence, Kans.: University of Kansas Press, 1974).

[56] This matter is elaborated upon in R. E. Harkavy, "Arms Re-Supply During Conflict and the Carter Administration's Arms Control Policies," paper delivered at the International Studies Assoc. meeting, Los Angeles, 19–22 March 1980.

airlift to Israel in 1973 after more than a week's delay (said to have resulted from American desires for a limited Arab victory and an *"in situ"* ceasefire) is frequently claimed to have been initiated only when Israel's invoking of a nuclear threat was feared.[57] If another Arab-Israeli conflict should erupt, that specter will doubtless again affect U.S. resupply decisions (Israel is now, however, widely considered more capable of fighting a lengthy war with pre-existing inventories than it was in 1973). Taiwan, South Korea, and even South Africa might one day be imagined subject to the same considerations. And, of course, a pariah denied, or seriously delayed arms resupply during conflict, if it should survive, will subsequently have still more incentive to build nuclear weapons. That threat might make resupply more likely beforehand, to the extent it was taken into account by otherwise reluctant big-power arms suppliers.

There is another possible long-term dénouement here, which could result if the United States, in particular, were to downgrade the priority of nuclear proliferation vis-à-vis other goals and to concede the inevitability of significant nuclear spread. In that event, the United States might more readily decouple from one or more of its dependent pariahs, the better to compete—with the USSR and Western Europe—for influence with more strategically valuable states. General discouragement with arms control might well contribute to such a shift.

The major powers, the world, and the pariahs

The nuclear aspirations of the pariahs, whatever they may be, produce some painful dilemmas for policymakers in the United States and, for that matter, in Europe, the USSR, and much of the rest of the world. The increasing desperation of the pariahs comes in a period of intense concern over a possible breakdown of the nonproliferation regime, at a time when there appears to be a considerable convergence of U.S. and Soviet policy in this area, as evidenced by the recent nuclear suppliers' conferences. (Indeed, the Soviets are considered by many to be even more concerned about proliferation than is the United States if for no other reason than because some of the most likely proliferators are located around their borders.)[58]

On the one hand, a further decoupling of the United States from Israel, South Korea, and Taiwan, particularly if in the context of growing overall U.S. military and economic weakness, can scarcely help lending greater impetus to proliferation incentives. Edward Luttwak has referred to recent U.S. security policies including those revolving about Salt II as a "counter-nonproliferation policy."[59] In South Africa's case, however, the "dove's dilemma"

[57] See the Insight Team of the *London Sunday Times, The Yom Kippur War* (Garden City, N.Y.: Doubleday, 1974), pp. 282–85.
[58] For a discussion of this point, see Geoffrey Kemp, "The New Strategic Map," *Survival* 19, 2 (March/April 1977): 50–59.
[59] Edward Luttwak, *U.S. Foreign Policy in a Proliferating World* (Santa Monica, Calif.: 1975), California Seminar on Arms Control and Foreign Policy, Discussion Paper No. 68, p. 14.

no longer applies, since no one can now envisage a resumption of U.S. arms sales. The nature and magnitude of future U.S. economic and diplomatic pressures on South Africa will presumably be relevant, however.

For the other three cases, being a virtual sole source of support affords the United States considerable leverage, since some or all of that support can be withdrawn (arms aid, and also enriched uranium fuel sales for the ROK's and Taiwan's reactors). A difficult bargaining situation is thus implicit in the U.S. relationship with its dependent pariahs, with both sides retaining some leverage despite the seeming massive asymmetries involved. While the United States can threaten to withdraw support if a pariah goes nuclear or even hints at doing so, the pariah can "proliferate" if its support is diminished, perhaps moving to overt testing or even to an enunciated "trip wire" or "massive retaliation" doctrine if its conventional means of defense are then left to wither.

Some other aspects of this problem, in the realm of pure conjecture, are worth noting in connection with U.S. and Soviet policies. Some analysts have suggested that the United States should provide assistance regarding "failsafe" technology (i.e., permissive-action links, etc.) to new nuclear states in order to reduce the chances of their accidentally initiating nuclear war.[60] Others, however, have begun to hint at contingency planning for joint U.S.-Soviet nuclear sanctions against states guilty of "first-use" of nuclear weapons.[61] The pariahs would appear jointly to constitute the core of problem states potentially subject to such measures, all the more so as in each case (more so for Israel and South Africa) the USSR would not likely be very reluctant to join such an effort (India or Cuba, for example, would no doubt be different stories). Such a prospect, however, might well drive one or another pariah to still more desperate contingency planning (clandestine suitcase insertion of atomic weapons in major powers' territories, for instance) if it felt that the superpowers together were bringing it to the brink of final checkmate.

The United States, in short, faces some painful dilemmas regarding the pariahs. Some vital U.S. foreign policy interests (Arab oil, Nigerian oil, the China card) may come to clash head-on with U.S. nonproliferation goals. The recent impasse over arms to Pakistan may have previewed—or merely reinforced—the nature of a more widespread dilemma. For much of the remainder of the world, there is the question of whether continued belaboring of the pariahs in the UN and elsewhere will prove to be rational and prudent given the obvious implications for possible nuclear conflict, if not merely proliferation.

---

[60] This idea was earlier bruited by William Bader in *The United States and the Spread of Nuclear Weapons* (New York: Pegasus, 1968), pp. 109–10.

[61] See, for instance, Richard Garwin, "Declaratory Posture for the Second Nuclear Regime," in *Nuclear Weapons and World Politics,* David C. Gompert, et al., eds. (New York: McGraw-Hill, 1977), pp. 130–31.

8

India and Pakistan:
Nuclear Rivals in South Asia

Onkar Marwah

Introduction

The literature on nuclear nonproliferation has informed us of the dangers resulting from the horizontal spread of nuclear weapons, the rate and sequence in which it might occur, and the rationales or inequities which justify national decisions to "go nuclear." There is, however, scant analysis of what happens when actual nuclearization takes place, especially in a region where states have a history of violent antagonism towards each other. Among the non-OECD nuclear threshold states, few have had as troubled a relationship as India and Pakistan. They are, unfortunately, among the first two threshold states clearly approaching the capability to make nuclear weapons. Since both these states exist primarily outside of the central strategic balance, no guidelines are available in strategic doctrine or experience as to how their future relationship will be worked out, and as to what may be the likely effects in subcontinental, regional, and global terms of a nuclearized South Asia. What follows is speculative, but it is based on hypotheses plausible in the special circumstances of the subcontinent.

Background

The operational aspects of the nuclear nonproliferation debate have been concerned with preventing the horizontal spread of nuclear weapons to states beyond the five allowed to possess them under the Nuclear Nonproliferation Treaty (NPT). In practice, anxieties have existed with respect to the intentions of a small number of Third World and "pariah" states which for one reason or another refused to sign the NPT. These anxieties turned to alarm after India's nuclear explosion in 1974, where a civilian nuclear program was used to provide what is widely perceived as a weapons option. In its capacity as the major state concerned with the problem of nuclear proliferation, the United States took the lead in consulting with other nuclear technology supplier states for the establishment of international restraints that would curb other threshold states from following the Indian example. Connoting technical, legal, and institutional measures that would internationalize sensitive segments of the nuclear fuel cycle, these restrictions are enshrined in nuclear-related export guidelines adopted by all the major nuclear supplier states—of both socialist and nonsocialist persuasion—convening as the London Suppliers Group (LSG). In addition a number of the supplier states have undertaken unilateral or bilateral actions to supplement the preceding multilateral arrangement for restraints—e.g., the U.S. Nuclear Nonproliferation Act of 1978 (NNPA Act), and the Australian and Canadian regulations to govern the supply of uranium ores or fuel.

The framework of what may be termed the "new international nuclear regime" in the post-Indian explosion stage devolves from the following:

1. *Accession to full scope safeguards*
   States outside of the NPT regime but seeking nuclear cooperation, technology, supplies or materials from a member of the LSG, must accede to a system of full scope safeguards. Full scope safeguards provide for the inspection and continuous monitoring of all current and future nuclear facilities and materials in the consumer states in return for the supply of nuclear equipment and technology.

2. *Assessment of the International Nuclear Fuel Cycle Evaluation (INFCE)*
   The INFCE deliberations provided a two-year breathing spell in decisions relating to the most appropriate technical path for the future exploitation of nuclear energy. Despite its findings in favor of the breeder reactor and the future use of plutonium, supplier states were encouraged to reexamine their policies with regard to the export of equipment and technology to support plutonium-fuelled reactors abroad.

3. *Control over the front-end of the nuclear fuel cycle*
   This is being undertaken through the policies or laws of individual states so as to oversee the international supply of uranium ores and enrichment services.
   The only exceptions to such control are natural uranium-fuelled power plants in Argentina (1), Pakistan (1), and India (2, plus 2 under construction).

4. *Control over the middle of the nuclear fuel cycle*

This is being undertaken through the rules tacitly or formally developed by the LSG to govern all future nuclear plant equipment exports. Long lead times in actual transfers are envisaged once agreements have been made between suppliers and the consumer states. Additionally, technical changes in the nature of the nuclear fuel—to lower or increase its radiation count and in the design of the plant—are underway so as to reduce the incentive for the clandestine diversion of delivered sensitive nuclear materials.

5. *Control over the back-end of the nuclear fuel cycle*

This has so far not been achieved. If present efforts at some acceptable form of international plutonium and nuclear waste storage are successful, then the institutional framework of the new nuclear regime would be completed.

Apart from the international measures described above, the United States opened a special dialogue with the Indian government to probe the latter's intentions. More importantly, the U.S. government sought to persuade the Indians to accede to some internationally acceptable measures which could vindicate their professions of peaceful nuclear intent in the postexplosion stage. The Indo-U.S. discussions centered on the following issues:

1. An Indian undertaking, preferably formal and public, to abstain from any further nuclear explosions.
2. Indian accession to the system of "full scope safeguards" on all its nuclear facilities as an alternative to signing the NPT.
3. U.S. application of the terms of the NNPA Act, 1978 whereby earlier American agreements relating to the supply of low-enriched uranium fuel for India's Tarapur nuclear power station would be voided if the Indians did not accede to "full scope safeguards."

The course of the Indo-U.S. negotiations between 1975 and 1979 has been detailed elsewhere and need not be repeated here.[1] U.S. efforts at gaining Indian acquiescence to the measures outlined were constant throughout the period. It was expected that following Indira Gandhi's defeat in the 1977 elections, the new Indian government, led by Morarji Desai and professing "genuine nonalignment" in foreign affairs, would be more amenable to the American point of view. These hopes were only partially vindicated. The Desai government did agree to India's abstention from further nuclear explosions, but remained adamant on the question of the country's accession to full scope safeguards. While Mr. Desai personally professed skepticism about India's need to conduct nuclear tests and, indeed, downgraded the activities of the Indian Atomic Energy Commission, he could not—and as a strong nationalist,

[1] Paul F. Power, "The Indo-American Nuclear Controversy," *Asian Survey* XIX, 6 (June 1979): 574–96.

would not—bring about fundamental changes in nuclear policies that had a wide and long consensus within the country. Full scope safeguards would have required India to open up all its existing and future nuclear establishments to continuous inspection and monitoring by outside agencies. Although presented as a less painful alternative, the system of full scope safeguards was judged by the Indians as even more stringent than that of the NPT.[2] The attempt to convince India in favor of full scope safeguards through delaying or withholding fuel supplies for the Tarapur nuclear power station probably made it more difficult for the Desai government to deal with domestic critics of its negotiations in nuclear matters with the Carter administration. In any case, the tenures of the Desai-led and later Charan Singh-led Janata governments in India were too short. Towards the end they were given over to so much political squabbling that it would have been unreasonable to expect any substantive redirections in any Indian policies. In early 1980, Mrs. Gandhi swept back to power with a parliamentary majority greater than when she herself was defeated in 1977. A few days later, and significantly, after 10 March 1980—the cutoff date for all nuclear supplies under the U.S. NNPA Act to countries that had not signed the NPT or acceded to full scope safeguards—Mrs. Gandhi announced that India would carry out nuclear tests if they were in the national interest.[3]

The objectives of the preceding sets of actions—those undertaken internationally and those pursued in relation to India—were twofold. The international measures were designed to prevent the use of civilian nuclear facilities for military purposes while maintaining the availability of the technology as an energy option. The actions with respect to India were, in a way, unavoidable and strictly logical since its activities had been the catalyst for the international measures. Unlike the other threshold states, however, the Indians already possessed a large, diversified, and almost-integrated nuclear establishment. Indian deficiencies in the nuclear field were not so significant that they could not be overcome through local effort over a short period of time. The dilemma from the American point of view was obvious: the Indians could neither be ignored in the application of sanctions, nor be restrained from achieving their goals despite the sanctions.

Of the greatest importance from the viewpoint of the *other* threshold states—prime among them being Pakistan—was that civilian nuclear materials, technology, and equipment became increasingly difficult to acquire in the *open* international market as the rules of the new nuclear regime came into

---

[2] The "scope" of fullscope safeguards has never been precisely defined, perhaps as a measure of deliberate policy. That is probably due to the fact that a finite application of the safeguards would *limit* the extension of the system to equipment and technology which, currently safe, might *later* be considered sensitive.

[3] "India gets bolder on nuclear tests: they will go ahead." *Christian Science Monitor,* 19 March 1980, p. 4.

force. Pakistan, then under the stewardship of the late Prime Minister Bhutto, sought, soon after India's nuclear explosion of 1974, to negotiate the purchase of a plutonium reprocessing plant from France. Over a period of time, the effort was aborted by the U.S. success in dissuading France from supplying the plant to Pakistan.

Pakistan adopts an alternative route to a military nuclear option

The underside of the nonproliferation debate has always been that a determined country could achieve a military nuclear option at less cost through a production reactor and dedicated facilities rather than through the circuitous route of a civilian nuclear program. The Israeli and South African nuclear weapon programs—presuming their existence—are based on the concept of dedicated facilities, since neither of these states possesses a commercial nuclear power plant or most of the other attendant civilian nuclear facilities. Indeed, stories abound of the latter two states' surreptitious collaboration with each other; with a number of the major nuclear-supplier states; and of the sustained transfers to them of sensitive nuclear materials, equipment and technology to support their focused drives for nuclear weapons.[4] Whatever veracity one attaches to these stories, they appear to have enough currency to suggest that a special nuclear market for special bidders has existed for sometime. It is not surprising, therefore, that new entrants could appear in that market in novel ways.

The Cascades of Kahuta

Beginning sometime in 1975—and soon after India's nuclear explosion—Pakistan seems to have adopted the dedicated-facilities approach to a nuclear weapons program. The centerpiece of that program was the attempt to acquire an independent source of fissile nuclear material. The means were, as we now know, to seek the purchase abroad of plants for *both* the reprocessing of plutonium *and* the enrichment of uranium. The method was to look for a public vendor of the plutonium reprocessing facility, but to back-stop that effort with the disaggregated, surreptitious, and therefore more certain purchase of equipment to construct a small centrifuge uranium-enrichment facility. Through dummy corporations the major items of equipment for the enrichment plant were acquired, at last count, in countries as varied as Britain, Holland, Belgium, Germany, Switzerland, Japan, and the United States. By present information, the plant comprising 400 "enriching" cascades, is in an

---

[4] For South Africa, see a monograph by Dan Smith, *South Africa's Nuclear Capability* (New York: U.N. Center Against Apartheid, February 1980).

advanced stage of construction at Kahuta, 15 miles south of the city of Rawalpindi under the direction of a Special Work Organization.[5] The construction site is surrounded by SAM missile batteries and guarded by a special detachment of the Pakistan army. Neither the complexity of the task nor the question of costs—which must run to some hundreds of millions of dollars—has deterred the Pakistan government from pursuing its goal. Apart from the Kahuta plant, it is known that Pakistan had received most of the blue prints for a reprocessing plant from the French before the deal fell through. The country has possessed a hot-cell laboratory at the Institute for Nuclear Science and Technology in Islamabad for some time, and it had also been working on a pilot-scale enrichment plant at Sihala prior to the Kahuta operation.

Unconfirmed reports suggest that A. Q. Khan, the metallurgist responsible for the technical aspects of the cloak-and-dagger operations that led to the worldwide location and delivery to Pakistan of the Kahuta enrichment plant machinery, is now working on a trigger mechanism for a nuclear explosive device. Current information is that, if no technical or other difficulties beset the successful operation of the cascades at Kahuta, Pakistan could successfully detonate a nuclear device any time after 1982. If, as many observers claim, financial support for the whole undertaking has been shared by Pakistan with other countries such as Libya and Saudi Arabia, then it is plausible that the results will also be shared. As will be shown, the latter event may be of greater consequence than a Pakistani bomb vis-à-vis India.

The "tenderness" of the Kahuta plant

It is worth remembering at this stage that, despite their impressive clandestine technical coup in acquiring the equipment for the Kahuta enrichment plant, the Pakistani attempt at a nuclear capability is essentially an "erector-set" approach to acquiring the bomb. There are bound to be some missing parts in technology or in equipment. If an accident were to damage the existing plant, the equipment, presumably, could not be replaced as easily as it was bought on the first occasion. Then there is the matter of operationalizing the equipment, synchronizing the cascade series, and running the plant for some time to obtain the weapons-grade enriched uranium. There is no reason to denigrate Pakistani competence in that respect, but some aspects of the operation of a centrifuge plant will have to be learned on the job. Japan, a more technologically sophisticated country than Pakistan, took almost ten years and encountered many mishaps, before it was able to bring its centrifuge plant into successful operation. In the end, however, one must assume that Pakistan will succeed in its effort as long as its basic enrichment plant equipment is safe from sabotage, serious accident, and the like. Time alone rather

---

[5] See Colin Smith and Shyam Bhatia, "How Dr. Khan Stole The Bomb For Islam." *The Observer* (London), 9 December 1979, p. 11; and, "Atoms For War," *The Observer* (London) 16 December 1979, p. 12.

than competence remains the unknown quantity before a nuclear Pakistan emerges in South Asia.

It is interesting to speculate as to whether Pakistan would have attempted the acquisition of a nuclear explosives capacity if India had not carried out its 1974 test or subsequently acceded to a system of full scope safeguards. The Indian argument has been that Pakistan has always felt the need to match Indian capability in a variety of fields. In nuclear matters, the Pakistanis initiated the attempt to overtake Indian competence well before the 1974 explosion—as claimed by Bhutto before his execution, and by his supporters thereafter.[6] There is little doubt, however, that the Indian explosion spurred the Pakistan government, under Bhutto's guidance at the time, to a more focused and determined effort at acquiring a similar capacity. Given the knowledge that the clandestine Pakistani attempt to obtain reprocessing and high-enrichment facilities began in 1975 and continued through the whole period over which the United States sought to persuade Indian accession to full scope safeguards, it is moot as to whether Indian assent to the safeguards would have made any difference to Pakistan's secret effort to match India. During the intervening period Pakistan also proposed a nuclear-weapon-free zone for South Asia, even as it determinedly sought the means to manufacture nuclear fissile materials within its own territory. On their part, the Indians could hardly object to the public stance of the Pakistanis to the effect that the Kahuta facility was for peaceful purposes since it duplicated the Indian stance of separating intent from capability. As a consequence, the Indians—boxed in by the Pakistanis on the basis of their own logic—have had few options other than to blandly accept Pakistani professions of peaceful intent, to feign indifference to the construction at Kahuta, or to imply future changes in its own nuclear policies to keep up with events in Pakistan.

A nuclearized South Asia

A single nuclear explosion does not automatically connote an operational weapon, and even less so a nuclear weapons system. It is widely understood that seven years after their own nuclear test the Indians have not taken steps to convert their explosives capacity into a militarily usable weapon. This may be due to a variety of reasons peculiar to India's domestic and foreign situations: the weakness and fractiousness of the country's internal political situation, the advice and pressure of major states, the awkwardness of changing from a peaceful to a military stance in the absence of any immediate nuclear threat to the country. With some modifications, the preceding conditions could be as applicable to Pakistan in a postnuclear explosion stage as they have been to India. Thus, if a subcontinental nuclear arms race is to be avoided it would

---

[6] Zulfiqar Ali Bhutto, *If I Am Assassinated.* . . . (New Delhi: Vikas, 1979), passim.

seem desirable that both India and Pakistan quickly seek a comprehensive dialogue to prevent their falling into the inexorable trap of an action-reaction syndrome. Despite their differences, and given their continuing mutual suspicions, it is still possible to imagine that both states could be impelled to carve out rules of behavior to common pragmatic advantage early enough, and thereby preclude the immediate resort to a nuclear-weapons buildup by both sides.

A subcontinental system of mutual assurances

Following upon a Pakistani nuclear test, it would seem appropriate that states friendly to both sides persuade the two subcontinental neighbors to independently seek to create a system of mutual assurances. The measures could include bilaterial on-site inspection arrangements, verification procedures, permanent consultation machinery, a "hot-line" communication system, internationally-deposited instruments and guarantees against surprise attack— and any other processes and understandings peculiar to the needs and anxieties of the two states. It is to be assumed that the proximity and cultures of the two states permit the near-complete availability of intelligence on each others' activities. Both might agree, in the circumstances, to turning a blind eye to whatever increases in that function are dictated vis-à-vis each other by their individual perceptions of military safety in the future.

Linking the subcontinental system of mutual assurance to a wider system of restraints

The preceding subcontinental system of mutual assurances could also be locked into a wider system of assurances, and indeed, sanctions. Neither India nor Pakistan exist by themselves, and each is beholden in a variety of ways to other states, regions, or international groups. Both belong to and are especially sensitive to the opinions of the nonaligned countries or groups within the nonaligned. A formal resolution by that group, and its significant constituents separately, to the effect that any use or threat of use of nuclear weapons *under any circumstances* by either state against the other would lead to the incumbent's immediate expulsion and an outcast status vis-à-vis the nonaligned group, would have some measurable impact. The resolution could be fleshed out by formal groups within the nonaligned through an automatic system of sanctions—e.g., OPEC, on whose oil and markets both India and Pakistan are heavily dependent. Proceeding further, one could visualize a third stage of preventive-automatic nonmilitary sanctions being triggered at the behest of groups such as the EEC against a wayward nuclear act by either state of the subcontinent. A final layer of uncertainty and caution could be imparted to the calculations of subcontinental decision makers through a joint and unilateral declaration by the nuclear superpowers: any threatened escalation of a local hostility to the nuclear level would bring in the superpowers, and any actual use of nuclear weapons by either state would run the risk of a selective superpower counterattack against the offending state.

A nuclearized South Asia without institutional restraints

While the benign environment of an interlocking system of restraints is plausible, it is more realistic to assume that drift, uncertainty, and lack of control will characterize the policymaking function in respect of a postnuclear South Asia. It is entirely possible that behind a facade of symbolic assurances of peaceful intent, alarm bells will ring loudly in the chanceries and defense establishments of the two subcontinental states. And it is more than likely that a Pakistani nuclear explosion will lead to an immediate reappraisal of the Indian nuclear program's objectives to include an operational military option. In that case, and presuming Indian reappraisal, the Pakistani's would undoubtedly follow suit without the delay in moving towards an operational weapon that has occurred in the Indian case since 1974. The bottom line of security assessments will be that, given their proximity and lengthy borders, neither state could ever in the future rest assured against a successful surprise nuclear attack by the other. Because of the short distances to be covered to likely targets, there would literally be no warning time available to either side against a sneak attack. With both states in formal possession of only first-strike capabilities, the strategic environment of South Asia would become highly unstable. In the circumstances, other states in the region may wish for little more than physical isolation from a potential South Asian conflict. Likewise, the major or global powers, not directly threatened by the modest nuclear capabilities of the two South Asian states, may merely wash their hands of the internecine quarrels of India and Pakistan. With their overwhelming military superiority, the global powers would in any case retain the right to intervene were their local or regional interests ever endangered. To that end, both India and Pakistan would—if they are not already—become targeted by the nuclear forces of the global powers.

Rather than the "automatic deterrence" envisaged by Pierre Gallois in such situations, the initial years of a post-nuclear South Asia could more appropriately be described as one of a wild-eyed and wary deterrence. On both sides the temptation might lurk for preemptive strikes, but—barring the irrational move—it would be modified by the assessment that neither state could utilize a sneak attack as a war-winning measure. A massive first-strike capacity would not be available for some time to either state. Both countries would secrete and disperse their few nuclear weapons so as to maintain a retaliatory capability. Delivery would present no problem to either side. It is unknown for the moment what numbers of weapons in the possession of one state would be sufficient to "deter" the other, but it is safe to assume that the numerical threshold would be low. Thus, India might possess fifty nuclear weapons to Pakistan's ten. The threat, however, of even half the latter getting through to Indian population centers in case of hostilities could give pause to any malevolent intent on India's part despite its bigger inventory of weapons. The calculation would work in reverse, too. The implication is that South Asia's second nuclear explosion—carried out by Pakistan—will lead to more of the same. Or, at the very least it will lead to a buildup of weapons inventories in the two countries, whatever shall be the public stance of their respective leaderships. The effort will probably be concealed, but it is hard to believe that it will not be made. A sort of standoff stability overlayed by constant alertness on both sides would be the hallmark of this phase in Indo-Pakistani relations—somewhat similar to the U.S.-Soviet nuclear relationship in the early fifties.

A nuclearized South Asia over the long-term

In an extended period of time, the imbalance between India and Pakistan would be manifested in nuclear matters as it exists in other fields. India would be able to manufacture significantly more weapons than Pakistan, disperse and emplace them for retaliatory strikes across a larger expanse of territory, and be able to hold a counterthreat of greater destruction as a riposte to a Pakistani nuclear strike. Later this year or early in 1981, India's space program is scheduled to launch an indigenously-manufactured space launch vehicle carrying the country's third satellite into synchronous orbit at 30,000 kilometers. The missile is guidance-controlled and has a range of approximately 2,500–3,000 kilometers. It could obviously provide the basis for a relatively safe and probably overwhelming "second-strike" capacity. India's research establishments have also experimented successfully with remotely-piloted vehicles, so that it is possible to foresee the later development of cruise missiles in the country. The point being made is that India's scientific, technological, and industrial structures are substantially more diversified and larger than Pakistan's. They could—and in the condition of a nuclearized South Asia, probably would—be employed in the long-run to create a significant margin of strategic capability in India's favor.[7] Indeed, at some point in time, India's pursuit of decisive strategic superiority over Pakistan will inevitably lead to the creation of a strike capability extending beyond the subcontinent, to China, and beyond. That event lies some years down the line so that it may be unreal at this stage to conjecture about its wider implications. The logic of the situation—with the spur provided by a nuclear Pakistan and the absence of any system-generated restraints—points inexorably to an Indian reach for "enoughness" in strategic terms. "Enoughness" in military matters, as we know from the experience of more powerful states, is a seldom-satisfied

[7] For Pakistan, see Zalmay Khalilzad, "Pakistan and the Bomb," *Survival* XXI, 6 (Nov–Dec, 1979): 244–50; for India, see, Onkar Marwah, "India's Nuclear and Space Programs: Intent and Policy" *International Security* 2, 2 (Fall 1977): 96–121.

quest. India's ability to pursue that objective would be modest by the standards of the major nuclear powers, but it would greatly outdistance that of Pakistan's.

The results would be twofold. In interactions with the major nuclear powers India's political flexibility would be enhanced in direct proportion to increases in its strategic reach. As a consequence, its ability to maneuver within the subcontinent would also be greater. The other states would find it less of a nuisance not to interfere in that area. India, it should be noted, would still be deterred by Pakistan's nuclear capability. To the extent that fear of attack or absorption by India determines Pakistan's policies it would be an improvement in subcontinental security perceptions for the latter's anxieties to be dispelled. In the context of overall strategic changes, however, Pakistan's choices would be no better than they are today. In fact, its range of actions may be lowered since it would no longer be able to seek coalition arrangements with external powers to press its demands upon India.

There are three caveats to the preceding assessment of long-run Pakistani choices. In the first place, Pakistan may seek to enlarge its area of maneuverability by spreading its nuclear know-how to selected states in the Middle East and Persian Gulf regions. Over 50 percent of Pakistani budgets in the past few years have come by way of grants-aid from countries like Saudi Arabia, Iran, the United Arab Emirates, and Libya.[8] The decision to provide the results of its nuclear capability to other Islamic states would not, however, come easily to Pakistan.[9] To provide the technology or the weapon to Libya would create difficulties with Egypt. In bestowing nuclear favor on Saudi Arabia, the Pakistanis would have to contend with the reactions of the Iraqis and the Iranians. While the choices would not be easy, it is likely that pressures to divulge its nuclear secrets could be mounted on Pakistan by several of its munificent donors. If the Pakistani choice fell on withholding its nuclear capability from *all* Islamic states to avoid enmeshment in the latters' intranecine rivalries, then it is also likely that Islamabad would be boycotted by its major financial donors and treated as any other, rather than as a special state within the Islamic family of nations. The latter situation, coupled with the reluctance of the major nuclear powers to come to its aid against India, would enjoin an "almost-pariah" status on Pakistan. There is no reason to assume that Pakistan would place itself in such a position. On the contrary, lacking any significant raw materials, Pakistan's strongest quid pro quo with other states, especially within the Islamic community of nations, would be its superior technological and industrial base. Therefore, the impact of Pakistan's

[8] For instance, up until May 1980 Pakistan had already received assistance worth $1,700 million from donor countries in the Islamic world. *Hindustan Times* (New Delhi), 26 June 1980, p. 6.

[9] General Zia ul-Haq, President of Pakistan, has denied the possibility of nuclear-related transfers to other states in the following words: "Do you honestly think we'd go around giving other people our nuclear secrets?" (quoted in Colin Smith and Shyam Bhatia, "How Dr. Khan Stole The Bomb For Islam." *The Observer* (London), op. cit., p. 11.

acquisition of nuclear weapons is likely to be greater on the quarrels and disputes of the Middle East in the long-run than on those of South Asia.[10]

The second problem modifying assessments about the "neutral" effect of Pakistani nuclear weapons concerns the country's political and state structures. Like India, Pakistan has strong disruptive and disintegrative forces at work within the body politic. Unlike India, the Pakistani decision-making structure is militarized, cannot be changed through elective processes, and does not respond routinely to the institutionalized forms of political protest and compromise permissible in India. Thus, despite the recent large-scale disturbances in India's north-east region, there is little fear in Delhi about the emergence of secessionist demands, except as they have existed among the small Naga and Mizo tribal communities. In contrast, there are strong disintegrative forces active in the Baluchistan and the North West Frontier provinces of Pakistan. The execution of Zulfiqar Ali Bhutto could not have endeared the country's military leadership to the people of Sindh, the late Prime Minister's home state. These three areas—Baluchistan, the North West Frontier Province, and Sindh—comprise 70 percent of the territory of Pakistan and 40 percent of its population.

The third imponderable with regard to Pakistani nuclear weapons relates to developments that may result from the Soviet military intervention in Afghanistan. Depending on Pakistani responses to the events in Afghanistan, and perhaps irrespective of them, the Soviet Union now has the opportunity and may soon arrogate the incentive to stoke the resentments of strongly disaffected minority communities in Pakistan, beginning with the Baluchis and the Pashtuns. Pakistan recently rejected an American offer of $400 million in military aid, and the close embrace with western military plans for the region that the offer implied. Any changes in the Pakistani position—consequent, say, to increases in the amount of military aid provided—would occasion strong reactions by both India and the Soviet Union, separately if not jointly. Since Pakistan possesses little oil, it should be a troubling question for that country's military planners to gauge how far, in what way, and for how long the western states would support Pakistan against a hostile Soviet Union and India. In the circumstances, it is not surprising that Pakistani thinkers already speak of their prospective nuclear weapons as necessary to avoid a crunch between the Soviet Union and India.[11] While the preceding logic may appear unreal to some external observers, what is important is the Pakistani perception in this matter. A nuclear-armed Pakistan threatened with disin-

---

[10] It remains to be seen as to whether the transfers, if they occur, would consist only of nuclear technology and materials. Given the currently-modest levels of technical capability in states such as Libya and Saudi Arabia, the demand and the supply might well include *completed* nuclear weapons.

[11] Pervaiz Iqbal Cheema, *Pakistan's Quest For Nuclear Technology* The Strategic and Defence Studies Centre, Research School of Pacific Studies. Working Paper No. 19 (Canberra: The Australian National University), pp. 6–7.

tegration, led by a fundamentalist military leadership, fearful of collusive action by the Soviet Union and India, and suspicious of the staying power of western states in the region, would be a very unpredictable and therefore a dangerous Pakistan.

A nuclearized South Asia: probable and ideal outcomes

The actual postnuclear environment of South Asia may come to exist somewhere in between the two extremes of a benign sanitization through system restraints and an absolute quarantine imposed by the global powers. A system of world-community-initiated restraints, if at all possible, is likely to come slowly. On the other hand, and despite their joint interest in stemming proliferation, the global powers have too many conflicting purposes to be able to ignore or neutralize by their superior power, the disruptive potential of a nuclearized South Asia—for South Asia and also for regions skirting South Asia. The modesty of the two subcontinental nuclear arsenals would itself impart a measure of unpredictability, even convey the threat of irrational behavior, to the actions of either or both states. The situation would then be one of mutual terror in the subcontinent, tempered by the realization that any wayward nuclear act by either India or Pakistan *could* bring retribution from outside the region. That, in the short-term at least, would be the measure of "stability" which South Asia could expect, and it would not be a sanguine situation for either India or Pakistan.

It would be to the security advantage of the more powerful states to create an institutional cushion against their being dragged into local disputes once regional nuclearization does take place in South Asia, or elsewhere. Despite their nuclear weapons, countries like India and Pakistan would, for many years, remain modest nuclear powers, and novices in the control and safe deployment of these weapons. In the circumstances, it might seem appropriate, even if contradictory otherwise, for them to be provided with the command and control equipment necessary for a nuclearized environment. Relieving some of the burdensome aspects of regional nuclearization would be to the mutual benefit of the local states, who may not have considered these questions so far, and the major powers, whose noncooperation in these matters would ill-serve their own larger interests in maintaining global stability. Indeed, the larger context of discussions once regional nuclearization does take place should be one in which the "older" nuclear powers search for ways to sanitize the turbulence created in the international environment by the entry of the new nuclear states. A pragmatic approach to policy would require convincing the new nuclear states that they themselves are likely to be the first and major beneficiaries of an institutionalized system of restraints. The emphasis in that scheme is on understanding and perhaps acceding to the inevitable dynamics of change, yet managing its onset in a manner that dampens the potential for conflict. It is important to note that the framework of restraints is "institutionally-neutral" and could just as well be made applicable to other regions where putative nuclear rivals exist.[12]

The probable nuclearization of South Asia—and the inevitable need to adapt it to the world political system—could form the basis for a fresh approach to international institutions, and to rules that remain frozen in a post-World War II mold, while the global security environment has continued to change. The preceding view is particularly applicable to the Gulf region which skirts South Asia and where, after the Afghanistan events, the superpowers are in a state of open and high competition to reassert their interests. The problem arises that in these regions, as elsewhere, firebreaks need to be created between the unpredictable vindication of superpower interests, and the uncertainties they could occasion for local states, particularly if the latter acquire nuclear arms. The framework of restraints proposed herein is not subject to the ideological choices of powerful states or the military might and shifting preferences of today's superpowers between one or another potential nuclear-proliferator state. It deliberately relies upon the application of sanctions, pressures, and reinforcing norms by a wide variety of actors and organizations cross-cutting across the economic, political, and strategic dimensions. As a consequence, the system of constraints is not dependent on the whims of the superpowers, and on its neutral inspiration can be adapted to any region facing nuclearization.

Conclusion

The approaching nuclearization of South Asia provides both general and unique lessons to understanding the problem of nonproliferation. Despite the greater restraints under the new nuclear regime on the availability of civilian nuclear technology and materials, determined states have the choice and will adopt the path of dedicated facilities to a nuclear capability. A market to respond to the needs of states in that category, through negligence, connivance, or commercial considerations, will come into existence. Costs and expenditures will be of little concern to a nation determined to "go nuclear." If such a state is able to purchase most of the equipment abroad, it may not require a particularly sophisticated industrial structure to fabricate nuclear weapons.

The number of states with nuclear weapons "options" may increase. The conversion of those options into weapons, however, is not an automatic process engulfing all the threshold states. The decisions to that effect are more

---

[12] Unlike for instance the well-intentioned but stillborn attempt to create a nuclear-weapon-free zone in South Asia on the example of the Latin American nuclear-weapon-free zone. The institutional analogy is artificial inasmuch as South Asia, unlike Latin America, cannot be separated from areas to the north and south of the subcontinent where exist nuclear weapon powers and their armed might.

likely to be based on individual national assessments of threats to security, as in the case of Pakistan. When those calculations or miscalculations have been made, the state concerned will not be willing to solve the "dove's dilemma" by forswearing nuclear weapons in return for the supply of sophisticated conventional weapons. It will seek both categories of weapons, as did Pakistan. The number of states outside of the OECD group who might actually seek nuclear weapons is, nonetheless, quite small, and only a few of them appear presently as candidates in search of nuclear weapons. For those which could be included in the latter category—Libya, Iraq?—there exists a vast gap between intent and capability.

South Asia will be a very different place after Pakistan goes nuclear. While there is no need to look forward happily to the prospect of two nuclear powers cheek-by-jowl in the subcontinent, the dangers can be contained through a variety of system-imposed restraints. The effort and experience in applying such restraints to South Asia could be useful for other regions of threatened proliferation. If these restraints cannot be imposed, then a period of short-term strategic uncertainty will ensue for the states of South Asia. Over the long haul, however, the current general imbalance in resources and capabilities between the two countries will continue to work in India's favor in nuclear matters. India would be "deterred" by Pakistani nuclear weapons, but that concept has meaning only if India had designs to destroy Pakistan. Despite Pakistani fears or assertions to that end, India remains, at least territorially with respect to Pakistan, a status quo power. It did not seek to absorb Bangladesh into India, and its military power in the best of times would hardly be sufficient to conquer *and* subdue a nation of 75 million people. The real dangers to the continuance of the Pakistani state are internally generated, and they seem to possess a life of their own irrespective of any malicious Indian intent.

If it is assumed that India has few incentives to *initiate* changes in the subcontinental status quo, then Pakistani nuclear weapons would not materially alter the local situation. The total security environment of the area would, of course, be more precarious in the presence rather than in the absence of nuclear weapons. The NATO and Warsaw Pact countries, especially their central European components, have learned to live and prosper in that troubling reality. India and Pakistan could probably accomplish the same tasks, with guarantees to the currently constituted status quo effected by India's bigger, more diversified, and safely dispersed nuclear barricade in comparison with Pakistan's.

A threat of greater proportions than to South Asia would arise, however, if there were a lateral diversion of Pakistani nuclear technology and materials to states in the Middle East and the Persian Gulf regions.

9

Some Reflections on the "Dove's Dilemma"

Lewis A. Dunn

Slowing the spread of both conventional arms and nuclear weapons has traditionally figured prominently on the list of arms control objectives. However, with the development during the late 1960s and early 1970s of advanced conventional weapons that seemed to promise a greatly improved defense against attack, attention increasingly focused on possible tensions between pursuit of these two arms control goals.[1] References to a "dove's dilemma," of the necessity to choose between efforts to slow conventional arms transfers abroad and to head off more widespread nuclear weapon proliferation by using arms transfers as an instrument of nonproliferation policy, were frequently encountered.

The effects of the new conventional weapons

Often referred to as precision guided munitions or PGMs, these new weapon technologies included TV and laser guided bombs, wire guided anti-tank missiles, precision guided antiaircraft missiles, and remotely piloted

Parts of this paper draw on a recently completed study of life in a world of more widespread nuclear weapon proliferation undertaken for the Twentieth Century Fund.

This paper represents the views of its author and in no way should be attributed to the Hudson Institute.

[1] One of the first and most helpful discussions remains Richard Burt, "Nuclear Proliferation and Conventional Arms Transfers: The Missing Link," presented at the California Seminar on Arms Control and Foreign Policy, September 1977.

vehicles for identifying and tracking targets.[2] Each of these new technologies held out a high probability that, once the target was acquired and the weapon fired, the target would be destroyed with a single shot. Other important battlefield developments of the time were the production of advanced scatterable land mines and area denial munitions, improved mechanisms of command and control permitting more rapid responses to the shifting flow of battle, and remote sensors for better monitoring of enemy troop movements and activities.

In the early 1970s many analysts argued that these new conventional technologies would enhance defense against conventional attack. For example, by permitting a substitution of technology for manpower and of cheaper defensive weapons for large numbers of expensive tanks and aircraft, they were thought likely to increase the capacity for self-defense of weaker countries or alliance groupings. In particular, defense against large armored spearheads supported by aircraft was believed to be greatly improved by the new antitank and antiaircraft weaponry. Further, precision guided munitions, to take another example, were thought likely to increase significantly the defender's ability to destroy key bridges, railheads, and command centers in the rear, hindering reinforcement of an attacking army, while scatterable land mines and area denial munitions would slow the forward edge of the assault. As a result, the attacker's force would begin to lose critical momentum.

On further analysis and with the emergence of tactical innovations to counter the new weapons, some of the more excessive claims, of course, were moderated. For instance, more cautious observers noted that, even though at the "strategic" level the distinction between defender and attacker in a given conflict might be clear, that distinction could easily break down at the tactical level: territory seized by an attacker then has to be defended, while defense might easily require counterattacks or even preemptive strikes across the original frontier. There was an element of uncertainty about which side would be most helped by the new weapon technologies. Nevertheless, the consensus by the end of the decade was that these new conventional weapon technologies did have an important role to play in buttressing key countries' and alliances' defensive capabilities.[3]

Selective arms transfers as a nonproliferation tactic

It was but a short step from that tempered analysis of these new technologies to the proposition that their selective transfer could be a useful non-

---

[2] See, for example, Richard Burt, "New Weapons Technologies: Debate and Direction," *Adelphi Paper* No. 126 (London: International Institute for Strategic Studies, 1976); James Digby, "Precision Guided Weapons," *Adelphi Paper* No. 118 (London: International Institute for Strategic Studies, 1975); John J. Mearsheimer, "Precision-guided Munitions and Conventional Deterrence," *Survival* 21, 2 (March/April 1979): 68–76.

[3] See Mearsheimer, op. cit., passim.

proliferation tactic, strengthening the military security of certain prominent prospective proliferators. Indeed, in some important cases arms transfers are likely to be one among several measures that might be taken to hold down key countries' proliferation incentives.

For instance, notwithstanding the Carter administration's abortive offer of military assistance to Pakistan after the Soviet invasion of Afghanistan, the provision of such assistance and the transfer of selected advanced conventional arms—if of a sufficient scope—still may be necessary elements of a package of measures to check Pakistan's continuing march toward the bomb.[4] Assistance for modernizing Pakistan's logistics network as well as arms transfers ranging from the sale of new technology antitank and antiaircraft weaponry to replacement interceptors for Pakistan's outmoded F-86 fighters could greatly augment that country's capability to resist conventional military incursions across its frontiers—at least for long enough to provide an opportunity for outside diplomatic intervention to stop the conflict short of a Pakistani dismemberment. Arms transfers and assistance sufficient to provide that improved defensive capability in contrast with the offer of January 1980 would symbolize the existence of a restored U.S.-Pakistani security connection. Consequently, pressures on Pakistan to match India's nuclear test out of fear of becoming a victim of nuclear blackmail might be significantly ameliorated.

Of course, other Pakistani proliferation incentives, not least of all a desire to show that Pakistan, too, could detonate a nuclear explosion, will still remain. Moreover, selective arms transfers would be only one part of a broader package which might have to include, for example, passage of a Presidentially supported Congressional resolution pledging U.S. support against nuclear blackmail to both Pakistan and India; substantial additional unilateral and multilateral economic assistance to Pakistan to deal with what its leadership sees as the longer-term threat to Pakistan's security; and a continuing, even if low key, threat of hostile multilateral economic, political, and other responses if Pakistan detonated a nuclear device. But by going far to assuage those incentives related to Pakistan's security, utilization of conventional arms transfers could shift the balance of the internal debate over nuclear weapon acquisition and greatly reinforce those other possible complementary nonproliferation measures. And, in that regard, though impossible to tell, more than a few close students of the evolution of the Pakistani nuclear weapon program believe that the U.S. failure to respond favorably to Pakistan's request, after India's test in 1974, for closer U.S. security ties and the supply of advanced arms was a turning point in that country's nuclear weapon decision making.[5]

The continued sale of advanced conventional arms also would help to

---

[4] On Pakistani activities and incentives, see Zalmay Khalilzad, "Pakistan and the Bomb," *Survival* 21, 6 (November/December 1979): 244–50, esp. 245–48.

[5] See, for example, Khalilzad, op. cit., p. 246.

dampen security related proliferation incentives in South Korea.[6] Those sales not only are critical to that country's defense capability against numerically superior North Korean forces, but they also symbolize the U.S. alliance connection. Nevertheless, by themselves, even heightened arms sales probably would not be able to compensate for any future weakening of the other two pillars of South Korea's security—the presence of U.S. ground forces and the U.S. alliance. On the contrary, should those troops be withdrawn, South Korea's leaders—out of fear of a deterrence gap which could lead to miscalculation by the North—are likely once again to take steps towards a nuclear weapon capability. Similarly, arms transfers alone would not be a sufficient substitute for the alliance connection as a means of buttressing the South Korean public and elite's morale, thereby checking other arguments for "going nuclear."

Similarly, the sale of limited advanced arms to Taiwan, now that the United States has recognized Peking, is important not only as a buttress for that country's defenses, but also as a symbol of residual U.S. concern for Taiwan's security. Nevertheless, arms transfers are only one part of the needed package of measures. Had the U.S. Senate not taken the lead in providing new security assurances after full normalization, it is quite likely that pressures would have been intense for resumption of Taiwan's earlier nuclear weapon activities. If the United States succumbs to renewed Chinese pressures for terminating all arms sales,[7] Taiwan would be left without any prospect of hampering a Chinese use of force to absorb it, while fears of further erosion of the remaining, if more ambiguous, U.S. security commitment would grow. One consequence easily could be heightened incentives to acquire nuclear weapons, both for defense against invasion and as a symbolic replacement for the U.S. connection.

In the Middle East as well, arms transfers are an important component of continuing U.S. efforts to influence whether Israel openly deploys nuclear weapons. Confidence in the capability of its conventional defenses to handle local military threats is one of the factors underlying Israel's current nuclear status[8]—but without supplies of U.S. arms, that favorable conventional balance could not be maintained. At the same time, however, a belief in the readiness of the United States to deter Soviet military involvement and the nonacquisition of nuclear weapons by Israel's Arab opponents are equally important determinants of whether the Israeli government decides to change its policy.

---

[6] On those incentives, see, for example, Young-sun Ha, "Nuclearization of Small States and World Order: The Case of Korea," *Asian Survey* 28, 11 (November 1978): 1134–51.

[7] "China Steps Up Protest of U.S. Arms for Taiwan," *Washington Post,* 22 June 1980.

[8] See Robert Harkavy, *Spectre of a Middle Eastern Holocaust: The Strategic and Diplomatic Implications of the Israeli Nuclear Weapons Program,* Monograph Series in World Affairs (Denver, Colo.: University of Denver, 1977), pp. 59–64.

In addition to that apparently low fungibility with other security related nonproliferation measures, there are several other caveats concerning the utility of selective arms transfers as a nonproliferation tactic. The transfer of conventional arms will not enhance security against nuclear blackmail or nuclear use by a regional rival that had just acquired nuclear weapons. For example, in the event of an Indian decision to deploy a full-fledged nuclear force, pressures on Pakistan to acquire its own crude deterrent capability are likely to be strong in the absence of a reliable external nuclear umbrella or guarantee.

Moreover, there are compelling proliferation incentives and motivations other than pursuit of enhanced security that will be left unaffected by arms transfers. The quest for regional status or global prestige has been a factor in the past and could eventually animate nuclear weapon programs in, for example, Argentina or Brazil. Arms transfers will not alleviate the possible uncertainty in these two countries about the "true intentions" of the other; but such uncertainty could fuel steps towards acquiring the bomb, lest the other get a jump on it. In yet other countries, acquisition of nuclear weapons may be viewed as a means of supporting a more ambitious foreign policy whose goal is to overturn an existing regional status quo. For instance, while partly a response to Israel's reported possession of nuclear weapons, in all probability Iraqi acquisition of nuclear weapons also would be intended to upset the Middle East diplomatic status quo, force a great-power imposition of a comprehensive peace settlement, and enhance Iraqi influence in the Persian Gulf. Selective conventional arms transfers also are unlikely to have much relevance where internal bureaucratic and political considerations are the motivating factors, as apparently was the case with Mrs. Gandhi's decision in 1974 to test a nuclear explosive device or as might occur with any ultimate South African decision to "go nuclear"—in part to boost domestic public morale.

Identifying the risks

Thus, using conventional arms transfers as a nonproliferation tactic, finally, entails significant risks. Among the more important are a heightened danger of local conventional conflict and the prospect that, if the recipient decides to acquire nuclear weapons anyway, past arms transfers will have enhanced its nuclear posture. The magnitude of these risks is likely to depend heavily, however, on the particular regional situation.

In some instances even transfers of primarily defensive weapons such as new technology antitank and antiaircraft systems could augment the risk of conflict. Their availability might embolden the recipient to take a more stubborn or adventuresome position in an ongoing dispute. Alternatively, such transfers could lead to preemption by the other side before the balance of forces had been changed. It also might provide critical equipment needed for an attack or to modify the technical characteristics of the local military balance in such a manner that, henceforth, there would be a considerable premium on being the side to strike first.

Illustrations of each of these relationships are easy to find. For example, partly emboldened by the build-up of their armored forces with U.S. assistance and by those forces' initial successes in the Rann of Kutch, the Pakistani government in 1965 adopted an intransigent position vis-à-vis India after that initial clash; it made only limited efforts to avoid the war that broke out between them several months later.[9] In turn, it is widely acknowledged that the Soviet decision in 1955 to supply arms to Egypt via Czechoslovakia—auguring a shift in the pattern of arms sales to the Middle East—triggered Israel's preemptive strike in 1956.[10] Similarly, without the build-up of Soviet arms aid to Egypt after the 1969–1970 War of Attrition, Egypt's 1973 offensive across the Suez Canal would have been precluded.[11] Likewise, Soviet assistance to North Vietnam in 1974–1975 contributed critically to the final North Vietnamese offensive.[12] And until the recent Egypt-Israel peace treaty, some observers argued that with the deployment of advanced, long-range aircraft the Middle East military balance was becoming increasingly preemption-prone on account of the reward for striking first.[13]

However, the relationship between transfers of advanced conventional arms and the risk of conflict is more complex than suggested by this mere recitation of supporting illustrations. Underlying each of these conflicts were fundamental and long-standing conflicts of interest, tradition, and/or ideology. Had those basic sources of tension and conflict been more muted, as may be the case now in the Indo-Pakistani dispute, arms transfers' impact probably would have been quite different. Moreover, in yet other examples the transfer of advanced arms actually may dampen the risk of conflict. Supplies of advanced arms to South Korea in conjunction with a continuing U.S. security connection serve as a deterrent to North Korea and a restraint on South Korean adventurism. Similarly, though admittedly accompanied by what seems to many to be Israeli intransigence on West Bank issues, Israeli access to high performance U.S. military equipment helps maintain a balance of military forces conducive to a reduced risk of conventional Middle East conflict.

[9] William J. Barnds, *India, Pakistan, and the Great Powers* (New York: Praeger Publishers, 1972), pp. 197–208, esp. p. 200.

[10] Edward Luttwak and Dan Horowitz, *The Israeli Army* (London: Allen Lane, 1975), pp. 136–37.

[11] A. J. Barker, *The Yom Kippur War* (New York: Random House, 1974), pp. 62–66.

[12] See Frank Snepp, *Decent Interval* (New York: Random House, 1977), pp. 137–39.

[13] Dale R. Tahtinen, *The Arab-Israeli Military Balance since October 1973* (Washington, D.C.: American Enterprise Institute, 1974), passim.

Thus, what stands out from these respective sets of examples is the extent to which the impact of the transfer of advanced arms on the risk of local conflict will vary from case to case. While such transfers may augment that risk, that is unlikely to be uniformly so.

Transferring selected advanced conventional arms as a nonproliferation tactic, however, also risks exacerbating U.S. relations with the remaining countries in the particular region. Recent U.S. arms diplomacy in South Asia suggests that even when efforts are made to reassure those neighbors, other interests may be adversely affected. On occasion, increasing military assistance and sales to one country may even enhance nonrecipients' motivations to acquire nuclear weapons. For example, to the degree that U.S. arms transfers to Israel contribute to a rigidification of the Middle East status quo or symbolize in Arab eyes U.S. unwillingness to pressure Israel to make concessions, nuclear weapon acquisition could come to be seen (not without cause) by Iraq or other Arab countries as the last available means for diplomatically shattering the status quo. For such acquisition probably would trigger renewed efforts to reach an overall Middle East settlement as the United States and other countries came under pressure to take ''new initiatives'' before events and proliferation momentum got out of hand.

In still other situations, transferring late model conventional arms may fail to have the desired influence on the prospective proliferator's calculations and eventuate, instead, in its acquiring useful components for a nuclear *force de frappe*. Already, transfer of high performance aircraft over the last decades has provided most prospective proliferators with adequate delivery systems. Continued and future transfers of short range surface-to-surface missiles, naval missiles, and possibly large surface-to-air missiles subject to reconfiguration for use in a surface-to-surface mode threatens to exacerbate this aspect (assuming the capability on the part of these countries to design warheads to meet the weight, volume, and related constraints). Other new conventional military technologies with applications both for conventional defense and as elements of a nuclear *force de frappe* include airborne and other early warning systems (to lessen the chances of a surprise first strike on the new nuclear force), precision guided bombs (to help carry out such a first strike), remotely piloted vehicles (for reconnaissance), and enhanced command and control mechanisms (to increase the usability of the new nuclear force).

Finally, by using arms transfers to support nonproliferation policy, the United States also risks undermining even further the recent efforts to foster a global policy of arms restraint. Other potential suppliers of arms are likely to be even less ready to exercise restraint in approving customers. In addition, those individuals in the U.S. Congress, the bureaucracy, and industry arguing for ''adjusting to reality'' and adopting a less restrained approach on sales may be better able to press their case in such an environment. Conversely, because of the precedential impact of selective transfers, it may be more difficult to resist other arms requests from countries claiming that interests other than nonproliferation are at stake.

Weighing the risks: nuclear versus conventional conflict

The preceding delineation of the varied risks of transferring arms as a nonproliferation tactic does not, of course, resolve the question of their use in that manner. To put the issue most starkly, even assuming that the price of so using arms transfers was a very high risk of local conventional conflict, that risk still might be worth accepting, the dilemma of choice more readily resolved than usually thought. The level of destruction of past regional conflicts in the Middle East and South Asia has been measured at most in the thousands or tens-of-thousands of casualties. While a local nuclear conflict could take many forms, not all of which need entail attacks on population centers, there would be a serious risk of escalation to attacks of that character as well as of accidental or stray detonations involving cities in the heat of battle. Thus, the nuclearization of conflict-prone regions poses the risk of a one or even two orders-of-magnitude jump in the destructiveness of local conflict. Nor can it be assumed, as some would have it, that this very prospect will bring about a new caution and prudence in conflict-prone regions: the high stakes, the presence of many flashpoints for conventional conflict, the risk of escalation where geographically contiguous rivals confront each other, and potential technical weaknesses all suggest the need for greater skepticism about the self-limiting effects of access to nuclear weapons.

However, it would be taking the preceding line of argument a step too far to conclude that avoiding the risks of proliferation should automatically take precedence, and that any decision to transfer arms should be approved in the name of nonproliferation. Rather, what is needed are rules of thumb or an analytic approach for deciding on a country-by-country, region-by-region basis whether or not to use arms transfers as a nonproliferation tactic and to assume the risks involved.

A starting point for a country-by-country determination clearly would have to be careful analysis of the probability that arms transfers would influence the target country. To recall the earlier argument, only some key countries are likely to be able to meet this burden of proof.

Equally important would be a specific assessment for the given region of the likely consequences of proliferation. Would emergence in that region of a fairly stable balance of terror be the probable outcome of proliferation? Or would there be many flashpoints for nuclear conflict? Would local access to nuclear weapons be neutralized by constraints imposed by outside parties? Would those new nuclear weapons be secure from seizure by subnational groups? Having thus begun to set some boundaries to the risks of proliferation in that region, the next step would be to compare those possible costs with those inherent in arms transfers to that region.

The relative importance of arms transfers within the proposed overall package of responses to potential proliferation would be a further consideration. Were its contribution easily made up by other means—whether new security ties, threats of sanctions, or diplomatic initiatives—the justification for arms transfers would be weakened. Conversely, in some cases the readiness to provide a significant level of military assistance and to accept the risks thereof may be seen by the proposed recipient as a bellwether of the seriousness of the U.S. commitment.

Further, whether there are ways of minimizing the risks of arms transfers generally by providing only certain types of equipment and assistance also needs to be considered in determining when their use as a nonproliferation measure is warranted. Though even those more defensive new weapon technologies may lend themselves under some tactical conditions to support of a strategic offensive, the distinction between more offensive and more defensive systems is not wholly devoid of meaning. It could be utilized at least to preclude the transfer of some systems—such as deep penetration attack aircraft—and to shift attention to the provision of others—such as antitank systems. Restrictions as well on the deployment of transferred weapons—say to preclude a build-up of Pakistani forces in Kashmir—could be made a tacit condition of the arms transfer deal and might lessen the impact on neighbors while minimizing the risk of misuse of the new arms. By establishing in advance more clearly than has been done previously, those eventualities for which any necessary logistics support and resupply of spare parts would not be forthcoming, the risk of such more adventuresome uses also might be reduced.

Arms restraint, nuclear restraint, and differing norms

The dilemma of having to choose whether to use arms transfers as a nonproliferation tactic at the expense of sacrificing pursuit of global arms restraint has been overdrawn. Although in theory so using arms transfers risks undercutting efforts at multilateral arms restraint, in practice those efforts have had little success anyway. Indeed, their failure stands in clear contrast with the relative success of recent efforts to restrain the spread of nuclear technology. The record is clear on the comparative results.

In 1977 the incoming Carter administration announced a new arms transfers policy aimed at making arms transfers an exception rather than the rule of U.S. foreign policy and proposed to seek multilateral support for a posture of global restraint.[14] But those calls for arms restraint had little

[14] "Broad Carter Policy Will Restrict Sales of Weapons Abroad," *New York Times,* 20 May 1977.

substantive impact abroad: U.S. allies, such as France and Great Britain, continued to export old and new generations of high performance weapons, even to tension-prone regions, while the Soviet Union did likewise. To make matters worse, even as these calls for restraint among the traditional arms suppliers met with only pro forma responses, a new class of advanced developing-country arms suppliers entered the arena of arms sales competition. Whether typified by Brazilian sales of armored cars, tanks, and maintenance support to Iraq and other Middle Eastern countries, Indian plans to coproduce and sell abroad the *Jaguar* attack aircraft being sold by Britain, South Korean sales of equipment from canteens to patrol boats, or Israeli sales of naval ship-to-ship missiles, avionics, and advanced aircraft, these new suppliers saw their interest to be in increasing, not checking, arms sales.

By contrast, the record, at least so far, in the nuclear field is more encouraging. Past and recent experience evidences a far greater willingness on the part of many countries to exercise restraint. Libya's unsuccessful attempts in the early 1970s to acquire a nuclear weapon from China, as well as its more recent falling out with India over the latter's unwillingness to provide Libya with access to nuclear technology with practical applications[15] are typical of how nuclear weapon states have been unwilling to deal in nuclear weapons. Concomitantly, after much initial controversy, the major nuclear suppliers were able to reach agreement in the London Nuclear Suppliers Guidelines on a framework of rules and restraints for exports of peaceful nuclear technology. And though West Germany proved unwilling to reassess its sale to Brazil of a full fuel cycle, France did shift its position on the sale of a reprocessing plant to Pakistan once the purposes for which that plant was being sought became clear.

This relatively greater success in inducing restraint over the transfer of nuclear technology may have partly to do with the different interests at stake. Both nuclear exports and arms sales are attractive for their potential financial, domestic-economic, and foreign policy benefits. A key difference between them, however, is the greater possible threat to the seller's security and well-being that is likely to accompany the spread of sensitive nuclear technology and, in some instances, of weapons developed from that technology. While the diffusion of advanced arms is likely to increase local powers' capability to attack outsiders entering their region and reduces thereby the great powers' freedom of action, at least for countries like France and Britain any reduced ability to intervene in a region is partly balanced by their lessened desire to do so. In addition, many arms recipients are far removed geographically from their suppliers, reducing again the likelihood of their recipients posing a serious threat to the supplier's security. By contrast, in a more proliferated world, a country such as the Soviet Union might find itself threatened directly

---

[15] "Libya Pressures India to Supply Nuclear Technology," *Financial Times* (London), 1 September 1979.

by several additional nuclear-armed enemies, while even the former great powers would be vulnerable to nuclear threats levied against them either directly or as a means of influencing U.S. policy. Further, in that environment, even the more "isolationist" arms suppliers could not discount the possibility of becoming a target of nuclear terrorism. And one consequence of the further spread of nuclear weapons readily could be easier access to nuclear weapons for subnational groups. Put simply, it is the diffuse but widely shared belief in the higher risks of life in a more proliferated world which probably explains some of the greater readiness to exercise restraint in the nuclear field even at some expense to other interests.

Particularly for the existing nuclear weapon states, status also may lead them toward a more restrained nuclear assistance policy. Historical experience clearly indicates that each new member of the "nuclear club" has sought to close the door after its entrance. Doing so may be important to preserving its newly gained prerogatives and setting itself off from lesser countries.

A further factor, which appears to have played a role at least in the recent agreement among the major suppliers "to exercise restraint" in the spread of sensitive reprocessing technology, has been a reluctant acknowledgment by other suppliers that civilian reactor-grade plutonium can be used to make a nuclear weapon. Earlier doubts or skepticism about this fact contributed to a readiness on some countries' parts to countenance exports of reprocessing technology.

In the final analysis, however, perhaps the most important factors explaining the greater success of recent U.S. efforts to win support for a framework of nuclear exports restraint may be two diffuse but widely accepted perceptions about acquisition of nuclear weapons. On the one hand, there is an increasingly widespread belief or norm that acquisition of nuclear weapons no longer is quite a legitimate international activity. Charles de Gaulle celebrated France's entry into the "nuclear club" as a right accorded it as a great power, while India slipped in under the guise of detonating a "peaceful nuclear explosive." This norm of nonproliferation is codified in the Nonproliferation Treaty, with its over 100 adherents, and reflected partially in both the superpowers' rhetoric of nuclear arms control and the calls for an end to vertical proliferation by developing countries.

On the other hand, the perception that runaway proliferation is avoidable also induces restraint. Without that possibility, such restraint would be a futile symbolic gesture paid for at the expense of other interests. Contrariwise, in a world where conventional arms already are widely spread and many more sources of supply exist, arms transfers restraint is seen by many as no more than such a gesture.

Nevertheless, backsliding even in this nuclear technology transfer area cannot be precluded. There are strong economic, domestic, and political pressures that could erode the existing framework of restraint, particularly over the export of sensitive peaceful facilities and technologies. And ambiguities about just what is a sensitive technology could facilitate that erosion. Consequently, if this key difference between the relative success of recent arms transfers policy and nuclear proliferation policy is to be preserved, it will be especially important in the next years to strengthen the norm that says nuclear weapon acquisition is not quite legitimate and to maintain the perception of the avoidability of widespread proliferation. But to do so it may be necessary, as in those cases discussed, to use arms transfers as one of a package of nonproliferation tactics.

The dove's true dilemma

In the mid-1970s, the availability of a new generation of advanced conventional weapons seemed to offer a new instrument for nonproliferation policy. Quite quickly it became popular to talk of a dove's dilemma, and, as this analysis suggests, there are likely to be instances in which pursuit of nonproliferation objectives will, indeed, conflict with arms sales restraint. But as that analysis also implies, a more serious dilemma often has been overlooked. For checking the growth of quite a few key countries' proliferation incentives, whether in South Asia, the Middle East, or Northeast Asia, partially requires a continuing or strengthened U.S. security connection—whether in the form of a formal alliance, a de facto commitment, or the presence of U.S. forces. The resulting tension between a reduced, if lingering, post-Vietnam desire to avoid U.S. political-military intervention abroad, and the economic burdens of such renewed activism, and a strong demand for efforts to slow the spread of nuclear weapons is the dove's true dilemma.

10

The Future Unlike the Past: Nuclear Proliferation and American Security Policy

Michael Nacht

Given the considerable amount of work done on the nuclear proliferation problem in the last two decades it is surprising that so little attention has been paid to the relationships between the spread of nuclear weapons and the security policies of the principal state seeking to stem this spread—namely, the United States. Most of the analyses that have addressed questions of American policy have focused on the nonproliferation issue per se. The litany of American initiatives—the Acheson-Lilienthal Report, the Baruch Plan, the Nuclear Nonproliferation Treaty, the Carter nonproliferation policies, as well as the Limited Test Ban Treaty, the Seabed Treaty, the Outer Space Treaty, and other bilateral and multilateral arms control efforts—are impressive and familiar reminders of the extraordinary role played by the United States in the diplomacy of nuclear nonproliferation.[1] What is less familiar, however, is how American foreign and military policies and major U.S. defense programs affect and are affected by the process of additional states acquiring nuclear weapons. This essay begins with an examination of what these effects have been in the past in order to anticipate what they might be in the future.

The past

In the thirty-five years since the United States detonated two atomic bombs against Japan, four other states have stockpiled large numbers of

[1] Joseph Nye's essay in this volume examines many of these initiatives and points the way to new developments in American nonproliferation policy.

nuclear weapons and acquired sophisticated means for their delivery, one state has exploded a single nuclear device without evidently fabricating additional weapons, and one state is widely acknowledged to be able to detonate one or more nuclear weapons on short notice. How has American security policy been affected, in the first instance, by Soviet, British, French, and Chinese nuclear weapons programs, in the second case, by the Indian nuclear detonation, and in the third, by Israel's ambiguous nuclear weapons status?

The Soviet Union

The outlines of America's adversarial relationship with the Soviet Union following World War II were clearly in evidence before the Soviet Union acquired nuclear weapons. The famous "long telegram" issued in February 1946 by George Kennan, then *chargé d'affaires* at the U.S. Embassy in Moscow, is widely credited with having shaped thinking in Washington concerning Soviet behavior. Kennan argued that Soviet hostility toward the West was a necessary condition for the Russian leadership to feel secure internally and to justify its totalitarian rule. The conclusion Kennan drew from his analysis could not have been more categorical:

> We have here a political force committed fanatically to the belief that with the U.S. there can be no permanent *modus vivendi*, that it is desirable and necessary that the internal harmony of our society be disrupted, our traditional way of life be destroyed, the international authority of our state be broken, if Soviet power is to be secure.[2]

Subsequently, of course, Kennan articulated his views publicly in the famous "X" article in *Foreign Affairs* that introduced "containment" as the organizing concept of American policy toward the Soviet Union. But the "X" article made no reference to the prospect of Soviet nuclear weapons acquisition. Containment, as seen by President Truman, Secretary of State Acheson, and other high-ranking American officials, was surely predicated on other considerations: the threatening character of Soviet communist ideology, consolidation of Soviet political control of Eastern Europe, the potential threat posed by Soviet conventional forces against Western Europe, the subversive techniques of the international communist movement controlled by Moscow, and the intransigent character of Soviet negotiating behavior on a wide range of postwar issues. Prior to the detonation of the first Soviet atomic bomb on 29 August 1949, it was these concerns that dominated American policy toward the Soviet Union.[3]

---

[2] Moscow Embassy Telegram #511: The Long Telegram, 22 February 1946, reprinted in *Containment: Documents on American Foreign Policy and Strategy, 1945-1950,* Thomas H. Etzold and John Lewis Gaddis, eds. (New York: Columbia University Press, 1978), p. 61.

[3] This judgment is confirmed by the analysis presented in NSC 20/4, a paper approved by President Truman on 24 November 1948 that served as the official articulation of U.S. policy until April 1950. See "U.S. Objectives with Respect to the USSR to Counter Soviet Threats to U.S. Security," 23 November 1948, reprinted in Etzold and Gaddis, *Containment,* pp. 204-11.

The Soviet detonation, however, affected American defense policy in several respects. It influenced significantly the decision to proceed with development of thermonuclear weapons, approved by Truman on 31 January 1950, and it stimulated the formation of an ad hoc study group that outlined the technological parameters for an effective U.S. air defense system against Soviet bomber attack.[4] Moreover, it led directly to the establishment of a special State and Defense Department study group chaired by Paul Nitze that produced NSC 68, a major reassessment of American national security policy. This paper, never formally approved by Truman, called for "a rapid build-up of political, economic, and military strength in the Free World," justified in part on the threat of a Soviet nuclear surprise attack on the United States.[5]

In short, acquisition of nuclear weapons by the Russians was used to confirm rather than redefine the basic assumptions of American policy toward the Soviet Union. But this development did raise issues of strategic vulnerability, stimulating support for enhanced U.S. nuclear and conventional forces, the deployment of active defenses, and the building of passive defenses (i.e., civil defense).

During the thirty years since NSC 68 was written, American defense posture has undergone numerous shifts, and several of them have been related, albeit in a complex fashion, to the quantitative growth and qualitative improvements in Soviet nuclear force deployments. In the variety of force posture decisions that have in fact been implemented over the years, several interrelated questions have been at issue:

1. What U.S. force deployments are required to deter a Soviet nuclear attack?
2. How can secure retaliatory forces best be maintained?
3. What mix of conventional and nuclear forces are needed to extend deterrence to America's allies?
4. What role should active and passive defenses have in the protection of civilian populations, urban/industrial targets, and nuclear forces and their command, control, and communication systems?

As technologies have advanced and the nature of the Soviet military threat has grown, answers to these questions have changed. But these responses have been at the heart of the American reaction to the Soviet nuclear program.

One additional dimension to the American reaction has been the emergence of a strong interest in negotiated arms control, both as a means of stabilizing the Soviet-American nuclear weapons competition and—particularly when American policy was guided by Henry Kissinger—as part of a complex set of levers designed to alter the expansionist aims of Soviet foreign

---

[4] These developments are authoritatively reviewed in Herbert F. York, *The Advisors: Oppenheimer, Teller, and the Superbomb* (San Francisco: W. H. Freeman and Co., 1976), pp. 40–74, 114–15.

[5] See "NSC 68: A Report to the National Security Council by the Executive Secretary on United States Objectives and Programs for National Security," 14 April 1950, first published in the *Naval War College Review,* XXVII, 6/Sequence No. 255 (May-June 1975): 51–108, p. 103.

policy. By the end of the 1970s there were serious questions about the future role of negotiated arms control in satisfying even modest American military, political, or economic objectives. But considerable support for the aims of negotiated nuclear arms control persisted within the executive branch and Congress and among the public generally.

Great Britain

The first British atomic weapons test, code-named "Hurricane," was carried out at Monte Bello, Australia, on 3 October 1952. It was the culmination of seven difficult years in British-American nuclear relations in which American policy moved from an initial position of information denial to one of reluctant and then active cooperation with the British nuclear weapons development effort.

The British government decided in secret to acquire atomic weapons in January 1947 (a decision made public in the House of Commons in May 1948), and there were persistent British efforts to obtain greater American support throughout the late 1940s. Britain was clearly motivated to acquire nuclear weapons in order to maintain great power status at a time when its vast colonial empire was rapidly disappearing and in the face of extremely serious domestic economic problems. From the British perspective, nuclear weapons also made sense to provide a deterrent independent of American control against a Soviet attack on the United Kingdom. And the weapons program served as a means of maintaining a competitive edge on French nuclear weapons acquisitions.

Influential Americans, however, were not keen on assisting the British. Some held out hopes of establishing international control of atomic energy, even after the failure of the Baruch Plan, and did not want the United States to contribute to nuclear weapons proliferation, even if the proliferator was America's closest ally. Others had no particular desire to see Britain retain its great power status, seeing a nuclear-armed Britain as a troublesome competitor to, rather than a close friend of, the United States.[6]

The collapse of any hope of international control of atomic energy and the intensification of hostility in Soviet-American relations swept away much of the American skepticism about cooperating with the British on nuclear matters. In the wake of the Soviet atomic test and then the outbreak of the Korean War in June 1950, the American mood changed sufficiently to warrant amendment of the McMahon Act in October 1950, permitting substantially increased American support for the British weapons program. Although

[6] See Margaret Gowing assisted by Lorna Arnold, *Independence and Deterrence: Britain and Atomic Energy, 1945-1952,* Volume I: Policymaking (New York: St. Martins Press, 1974), p. 265. This work is the official history of the British atomic energy project commissioned by the U.K. Atomic Energy Authority.

difficulties remained, and in fact the United States refused a British request to use American atomic-test facilities, the principal barriers to Anglo-American nuclear cooperation were overcome.

Despite a few rough moments since the early 1950s, particularly the Skybolt affair in 1962 and the flirtation with the multilateral force that ended in 1965, relations between the United States and Great Britain on nuclear weapons matters have been remarkably close. Most significantly, American-built submarine-launched ballistic missiles (SLBM) carried on British-built submarines have served for many years as the backbone of the British nuclear deterrent force. And the nuclear force modernization choices that Britain faces in the 1980s are intimately linked to U.S. SLBM and cruise missile programs.

In the British case, therefore, it is safe to conclude that nuclear proliferation did not affect in any meaningful way close political relations that had long been the normal mode of conduct between the United States and Britain. In defense matters, the impact on American programs has been confined to the sharing of technology and know-how and coordination on selected nuclear policy issues.

France

Relations between the United States and France had had many ups and downs prior to the French acquisition of nuclear weapons in 1958. From the frictions between de Gaulle and Eisenhower at critical stages during World War II to the American unwillingness to assist French troops during the debacle at Dienbienphu in Indochina in 1954, the generally cordial Franco-American political landscape was dotted with a number of instances of disagreement, bitterness, and disappointment.

The watershed in the postwar French relationship with the United States was undoubtedly the Suez Crisis of October 1956, in which French, British, and Israeli forces were forced to withdraw from control of the Suez Canal as a consequence of joint pressure from the United States and the Soviet Union. This experience confirmed to French leaders, if it was at all necessary, that the United States could not be counted upon to serve French foreign policy interests. The plain fact was that throughout the postwar period the United States sought to dominate the policy choices of its allies. But French will, French culture and history, the sense French men and women have of the role France should play in the world, the French mistrust of American policies, and the intrinsic French fear of a militarily-strong Germany once again posing a major threat to France's security all strengthened France's resistance to American domination. With a sophisticated nuclear energy establishment and, most importantly, the leadership exerted by General de Gaulle upon his return to power in 1958, a French nuclear weapons capability was an obvious consequence.

The French military withdrawal from NATO, the ambiguity of the French commitment to the Alliance in the event of war, and the French declaratory policy of *"tout azimuth"* initially caused significant political upheavals in Franco-American relations and led to a nontrivial redeployment of NATO's conventional forces and to the assignment of several U.S. ballistic missile submarines for NATO use. But, in the longer view, these were relatively modest disturbances. The oscillations between cooperative and competitive phases in the relationship between the two powers have continued since France joined the nuclear club. De Gaulle, after all, was a major supporter of President Kennedy's actions during the Cuban missile crisis and, more recently, France endorsed vigorously the early phases of American détente policy with the Soviet Union and the strategic arms control agreements signed in May 1972. Moreover, French cooperation in NATO military affairs continues in several important respects, while being carried out in a singularly unobtrusive fashion. Alternatively, the French were consistently critical of American policy in Vietnam, and have pursued strikingly independent foreign policies from the United States with reference to the Arab-Israeli conflict and sub-Saharan African affairs. While the French *force de frappe* has had profound effects on French strategy and force planning, overall it has made strikingly little impact on American defense planning.

China

The features of American policy toward China from 1949 through the mid-1960s are highly familiar. U.S. policymakers saw Communist China as, other than the Soviet Union, the most powerful threat to American security interests, especially in Asia but in other regions of the developing world as well. The decade of the 1950s included the Sino-American armed conflict in Korea and the several major crises over Taiwan and the neighboring offshore islands. The 1960s began with deepening American involvement in Vietnam, justified in part to contain Chinese expansion and to disprove the efficacy of Maoist notions of People's War. The Sino-American relationship, prior to Chinese nuclear weapons acquisition, was wholly adversarial, and those Americans who thought it should be otherwise either had no influence or were summarily discredited if they voiced their views too loudly.

The break in Sino-Soviet relations leading to opportunities for improved Sino-American relations had something to do with nuclear weapons policy, but it would be stretching the point too far to claim that this was the decisive issue leading to the Sino-Soviet conflict. Difficulties between the two giant communist states, it can now be seen, were clearly multidimensional: the personal animosity between Mao and Khrushchev, the differing conceptions of how a communist state should be run, incompatible interpretations of Marxist-Leninist ideology and its meaning for developing societies, competition for leadership of the world communist movement, outstanding Sino-Soviet border differences that predate the Russian Revolution, cultural antagonisms between the Russians and the Chinese, and the sheer tensions produced by the geopolitical reality of two powerful states with large populations sharing a 4,500-mile border.

On top of these difficulties was the unwillingness of the Soviet leadership to make available state-of-the-art expertise and equipment to the Chinese nuclear weapons program, which began in 1954 despite Mao's earlier disparaging observations. Soviet scientists, engineers, technicians, and military advisors all participated in Chinese nuclear weapons research and development until 1960, but the Chinese never received the full benefit of Soviet knowledge, a state of affairs the Chinese leadership came to resent deeply.

It took many years for American policymakers to appreciate the significance and genuine shift in Sino-Soviet relations. Initially, the principal effect of Chinese nuclear weapons acquisition on American policy was as a stimulus to and bureaucratic argument for the deployment of a U.S. antiballistic missile (ABM) system. The U.S. intelligence community anticipated the rapid development of a Chinese intercontinental-range ballistic missile capability, and this prospect was used to justify the Sentinel ABM system in 1967.[7] The emergence of major technical problems and doctrinal concerns about strategic stability subsequently led, however, to American interest in negotiating with the Soviets severe restrictions on ABM deployments, culminating in the 1972 ABM Treaty. Consequently, there are in fact no U.S. strategic nuclear weapons systems in operation, offensive or defensive, whose existence is directly attributable to the threat posed by Chinese nuclear forces, real or imagined.

In foreign policy terms it can be argued that the Chinese nuclear weapons effort was both a cause and a consequence of the Sino-Soviet rift, that this effort contributed significantly to China's independent military posture from and deterrence of the Soviet Union, and that this independence in turn facilitated closer Sino-American cooperation. But nuclear weapons seem in this instance to have been at best a subsidiary consideration to the fundamental axiom of international politics that "the enemy of my enemy is my friend."

India

India detonated a nuclear device in May 1974 and nuclear proliferation in South Asia has been of growing American concern ever since. But, as in the

---

[7] The role of these projections in the U.S. ABM debate is discussed at length in Morton H. Halperin, *Bureaucratic Politics and Foreign Policy* (Washington, D.C.: The Brookings Institution, 1974), especially pp. 297–310.

cases previously examined, it is extremely difficult to identify any direct impact of this event on the fundamental nature of Indian-American relations or on U.S. defense programs.

Coolness in India's relations with the United States dates back at least to the mid-1950s when Prime Minister Nehru sought to lead the movement of newly-independent states on a course between East and West, at a time when Secretary of State Dulles had enlisted arch-rival Pakistan as a member of the anticommunist alliance structure in Southwest Asia. Moreover, India's persistent rivalry with China, which erupted in war in 1962, drew it inexorably closer to the Soviet Union, particularly once the Sino-Soviet rift had become truly serious. An Indian foreign policy emphasizing discord with China and Pakistan and harmony with the Soviet Union (India signed a twenty-five year Treaty of Peace, Friendship, and Cooperation with the USSR in 1971) guarantees friction in Indian-American relations.

These difficulties were seriously exacerbated in 1971 when the United States tilted toward Pakistan in the India-Pakistan war. The aircraft carrier Enterprise and other ships of the Seventh Fleet were sent into the Bay of Bengal, largely to deter India from destroying the sovereignty of West Pakistan after Indian forces had helped transform East Pakistan into the sovereign state of Bangladesh. This symbol of U.S. interference, no matter how noble the objectives as seen through American eyes, has left an indelible mark on Indian attitudes toward the United States.

With a sophisticated nuclear energy establishment that dates back to the early 1940s and with a deeply felt sense that American nonproliferation policies are absurdly hypocritical in light of the enormously advanced U.S. nuclear weapons arsenal, Indian decision makers moved relatively easily to the nuclear detonation decision in 1974.[8] Since the detonation, a variety of controversial issues have been raised in Indian-American relations, particularly with reference to American nuclear fuel supplies for the Indian reactor at Tarapur. The relationship between the two powers has remained cool, with occasional bouts of acrimony, but is far from adversarial. The Indian nuclear explosion and the prospect this raises of a full-fledged Indian nuclear force has yet to influence seriously cultural, economic, scientific, or political ties with the United States.

Israel

The United States has been Israel's principal arms supplier and provider of government-to-government economic assistance only since the 1967 War and the shift in the Middle East policies of several European states, par-

---

[8] Indian perspectives and capabilities are described in detail in Onkar Marwah, "India's Nuclear and Space Programs: Intent and Policy," *International Security* 2, 2 (Fall 1977): 96–121.

ticularly France. The record of American-Israeli relations since has been a complex one. The United States has sought to influence Israeli behavior in order to promote American strategic interests in the region (principally the minimization of Soviet influence, the improvement of relations with Arab oil-producing states, and the preservation of Israeli security), while Israel has tried to manipulate American military, political, and economic support and diplomatic involvement in the Arab-Israeli conflict to promote Israel's perceived security interests.[9]

What is striking about the relationship, however, is the extremely limited and subtle influences exerted on American policy by the prospect of Israeli nuclear weapons. Rumors of Israeli nuclear weapons acquisition have been widespread since the late 1960s, usually associated with weapons-grade material that could be produced at the Dimona nuclear research facility in the Negev desert.[10] But while American leaders have been aware of the Israeli nuclear potential, there is no evidence such awareness directly affected U.S. policy until the 1973 war. Quandt, for example, in analyzing the 1969–1970 Middle East initiatives advanced by Secretary of State Rogers, observes that "no one knew quite what to do about the Israeli nuclear option, but it added to the sense that the Middle East was too dangerous to ignore."[11] And Safran, in analyzing the unfolding developments of the October 1973 war, asserted that "Kissinger, along with a few people at the top government echelons, had long known that Israel possessed a very short nuclear option which it held as a weapon of last resort, but he had not dwelt much on the issue because of the remoteness of the contingency that would make it relevant."[12]

Perhaps the only indirect influence of the Israeli nuclear option on American policy prior to 1973 was the impetus to provide Israel with sophisticated conventional weapons so as to lessen the incentive Israeli leaders would feel to proceed with their nuclear program.[13] In the 1973 war, however, American willingness to resupply Israel with vast amounts of arms early in the conflict seems to have been tied directly to concerns that the Jewish state, seeing itself on the verge of defeat, would indeed resort to the use of nuclear weapons to defend itself. *In extremis,* the dilemma had become an imperative.

The ambiguous status of the Israeli nuclear program has not had any demonstrable effect on the intrinsic strengths or the difficulties of Israel's

---

[9] Two excellent analyses of this complicated relationship with quite different perspectives are Nadav Safran, *Israel: The Embattled Ally* (Cambridge, Mass.: The Belknap Press of Harvard University Press, 1978) and William B. Quandt, *Decade of Decisions: American Policy toward the Arab-Israeli Conflict, 1967–1976* (Berkeley: University of California Press, 1977).

[10] One rather explicit but unconfirmed report of the origins and development of the Israeli capability is contained in "How Israel Got the Bomb," *Time,* 12 April 1976, pp. 39–40.

[11] Quandt, op. cit., p. 80.

[12] Safran, op. cit, p. 483.

[13] This is an example of the so-called "dove's dilemma" treated at length by Lewis Dunn in this volume.

relationship with the United States, nor has it affected U.S. defense programs in any discernible fashion. It has, however, influenced American diplomacy in a time of crisis and presumably would do so again in the future. The pressures for the United States to come to Israel's defense and to pursue means of conflict resolution in the event of war are exacerbated because the price of American procrastination or failure could mean nuclear war.

Toward the future

An examination of the interactions between nuclear proliferation and American security policy demonstrates several propositions:

1. The political relationship between the United States and each new nuclear weapon state was not fundamentally transformed as a result of nuclear proliferation.
2. With the exception of the Soviet Union, no new nuclear state significantly affected U.S. defense programs or policies.
3. American interest in bilateral nuclear arms control negotiations has been confined to the Soviet Union.
4. A conventional conflict involving a nonnuclear ally (Israel) prompted the United States to intervene in ways it otherwise might not have in order to forestall the use of nuclear weapons.

If the future were like the past, there would be remarkably little to be concerned about even as nuclear weapons proliferate to other states. American foreign policy would have to be adjusted with each new nuclear state only to a modest degree. American defense programs would still be tailored solely to the Soviet threat. The likelihood of nuclear weapon use would remain negligibly low. And American diplomacy, when necessary, would be called upon principally to prevent near-nuclear states from having to use nuclear weapons as a last resort. Two emerging conditions suggest, however, that the future will not be like the past. The first is the intensification of the Soviet-American competition generally and shifts in the nuclear balance in particular. The second is the changing character of American regional security policies.

The significance of intensified Soviet-American competition

The historical record of Soviet-American relations suggests an oscillation between warmer and cooler periods since the end of World War II—from the immediate glow of victory with the defeat of Germany to the confrontation over the Berlin blockade; from flirtations with "Open Skies Agreements" and the "Spirit of Camp David" during the Eisenhower period to the Cuban missile crisis but a few years later; from the articulation and implementation of détente in the early 1970s to its virtual collapse by the end of the decade.

It seems highly probable, however, that the next phase of the relationship will be marked by an intensification of competition. The sustained growth of Soviet military capabilities, both nuclear and conventional, and the increased assertiveness of Soviet political-military policies in the developing world have, over time, generated a deepening skepticism among Americans about Soviet motivations. This skepticism has been translated into political pressures for a cooling in relations with the Soviet Union and for increased funding for U.S. defense programs—developments that have a bearing on the nuclear proliferation problem. In particular, three consequences are worth addressing: trends in military programs, effects on negotiated arms control, and impact on regional security policies.

In military programs, technological advances and political pressures both are leading to the development and deployment of high accuracy systems that can carry out selective strikes with limited collateral damage. It can be anticipated that by the end of the 1980s the United States and the Soviet Union would each possess a variety of weapon systems that would place any identifiable fixed target at risk. Nuclear-armed, intercontinental-range, land- and sea-based ballistic missiles would be capable of striking within tens of feet of targets located eight to ten thousand miles from their launch points. Cruise missiles, whether deployed with nuclear or conventional warheads, would, at least in the American case, utilize terrain contour matching guidance systems to attack targets located thousands of miles away with consistent pinpoint accuracy. It is because high-accuracy intercontinental-range systems are now in the offing that the U.S. land-based missile problem has become a major issue in the American defense debate. But more importantly, the vulnerability of fixed-based systems of all kinds places a natural premium on mobility, deception, and defenses as potentially effective countermeasures.

In terms of American strategic nuclear weapons and related programs, prospective deployments reflect these concerns: the shift from hard-silo, fixed-based intercontinental ballistic missiles (ICBMs) to a mobile system utilizing some form of deceptive basing mode; an emphasis on counterforce weapons—including the MX ICBM and, eventually, the Trident II SLBM—that would be useful to attack the enemy's military targets; the deployment of standoff bombers that would fire cruise missiles at targets without the bombers themselves having to penetrate Soviet air defenses; reconsideration of ballistic missile defenses to protect some fixed-based U.S. ICBMs (hard-point defense); greater budgetary support to examine civil defense options, renewed interest in a continental air defense system, and substantially enhanced funding for research and development efforts in the areas of antisatellite weapons, other space-based systems, and the military applications of exotic technologies (high-energy lasers, particle beams and the like).

There are several connections between these developments and the nuclear proliferation problem. In the most general sense, these American military programs are perceived by attentive publics in the developed and developing world not merely as the natural product of evolutionary force modernization planning. Rather they are seen as tangible evidence of the realization that the United States has permitted its position of nuclear superiority over the Soviet Union to slip away, that the United States is now making a concerted effort to redress the military trends of the last decade, but that even a condition of "parity," "essential equivalence," or nuclear stalemate will not be easy to maintain during the next decade given the momentum of Soviet programs and America's seemingly intrinsic economic and domestic political constraints. It is difficult, of course, to demonstrate the precise effect of this shift in the strategic balance on the likelihood of individual states crossing the nuclear weapons threshold. But it is surely the case that the decline of American military power relative to the Soviet Union is not a development likely to strengthen the forces of nonproliferation.

The Soviet-American nuclear balance is, after all, the most significant and most visible symbol of the status of the superpower relationship. The serious decline in America's position, as measured by most static and dynamic indicators, has had, at a minimum, a deleterious effect on the credibility of U.S. security guarantees. While far from decisive by itself, the shifting balance has meant that elites in Germany and Japan, in South Korea and Taiwan, in Israel and Pakistan, are questioning more than ever whether or to what extent they can rely upon U.S. support. And this questioning, in turn, leads some influential figures to look more toward their own defense capabilities, including nuclear weapons, as psychological and military compensation for declining American strength.

Changes in the Soviet-American nuclear balance could be felt in nuclear threshold states in more specific military terms.

—The enormous publicity given to the ICBM vulnerability problem and to the eventual deployment of the MX missile are representative of a more fundamental trend: the development of technological capabilities for and doctrinal justification of nuclear counterforce systems. These systems will, to some, make nuclear war more likely and will serve as a basis for the procurement of large numbers of mobile systems. The acquisition by both superpowers of sophisticated nuclear counterforce systems could make nervous elites in some threshold states even more nervous, and even more desirous of acquiring nuclear weapons "insurance" for their own states.

—Cruise missiles armed with conventional and nuclear warheads are likely to be significant in the Soviet and American military arsenals by the mid-1980s. With intensification of the Soviet-American competition, the United States may not show restraint concerning the transfer of cruise missile technologies to its allies. And in time, cruise missile technologies (including high specific impulse, small engines, and sophisticated, miniaturized guidance systems) may be obtained by large numbers of states. Cruise missiles could than become attractive nuclear delivery vehicles for new nuclear states, especially in view of their low cost relative to manned aircraft or ballistic missiles.

—Soviet-American tensions, as well as technological developments since the early 1970s, could lead to the revision or even the abrogation of the ABM Treaty in the next several years. For the United States, this is a complex issue involving the state of ballistic missile defense technologies (e.g., vulnerability to saturation attack, decoys, jamming), political, economic, and military costs of treaty abrogation, and several other important considerations.[14] But the demise of the ABM Treaty and the deployment of ballistic missile defenses could be a further signal of Soviet-American tensions, stimulating the nuclear debate in nonnuclear states.

—Widespread deployment of air defenses and civil defenses by the United States would again suggest that nuclear war planning in its fine details had replaced deterrence as the cornerstone of American strategic nuclear policy and could, at a minimum, provoke other states to emulate American programs where feasible.

It is not just a matter of U.S. and Soviet nuclear weapons programs perhaps stimulating nuclear proliferation. The interaction is a more complex one. Some of the Soviet and American systems that would be deployed would no doubt also be justified on the grounds that they could strike incipient nuclear forces of hostile new nuclear states (air-launched, sea-launched, or ground-launched cruise missiles armed with conventional warheads) or could defend the superpower homeland against attacks by such states (sophisticated multilayered surface-to-air missile systems or low-altitude ballistic missile defenses). In particular, the prospect or demonstration of nuclear proliferation could be useful in the American domestic defense debate to support politically systems that were primarily directed at the Soviet threat. Moreover, the deployment of a wide variety of such systems by the United States and the Soviet Union would lend credibility to the arguments of proponents of nuclear weapons acquisition in nonnuclear states. These proponents would have additional evidence to support their contention (real or contrived) that the superpowers were indeed hypocritical about nuclear arms control and in fact posed a menace not only to each other but to nonnuclear states as well.

Deterioration in Soviet-American relations would likely halt all serious prospects for bilateral negotiated nuclear arms control, as has already been demonstrated when the Soviet invasion of Afghanistan in late 1979 precipitated American suspension of the Senate ratification process of the SALT II Treaty. Lack of progress in Soviet-American arms control

[14] These considerations are addressed in detail in *U.S. Arms Control Objectives and the Implications for Ballistic Missile Defense,* Proceedings of a Symposium held at Harvard University, November 1979.

negotiations, and indeed the possible unravelling of existing agreements, would no doubt cripple the prospects for multilateral nonproliferation initiatives.[15] The Nuclear Nonproliferation Treaty (NPT) would be weakened, and the feasibility of the Treaty of Tlatelolco entering into force for Brazil or Argentina, and of other nuclear free zone arrangements being completed, would be seriously undermined. Lack of progress on these diplomatic fronts would, in turn, reduce the political barriers to nuclear weapons acquisition in many threshold states.

It has often been observed that the Soviets have the most to lose in a world of many nuclear powers because the vast majority of these states would be hostile to them. As a consequence, it is argued that the Soviet Union has an incentive to maintain cooperation with the United States in this policy area irrespective of the general nature of the relationship. Indeed, it has often been overlooked that one of the most fruitful areas of Soviet-American cooperation has been in the field of nuclear nonproliferation.[16] But this is probably too apolitical a perspective, and it just may not be feasible for the Soviet Union to cooperate on any front if the bilateral relationship takes on confrontational overtones.

Finally, with respect to regional security policies, evidence already abounds that the intensification of Soviet-American competition in the developing world has stimulated the move toward creation of American rapid deployment forces, providing an enhanced interventionary capability. Both states are likely to invest heavily in the years ahead in airlift, sealift, surface navy, and other power projection forces, to provide the capability to intervene in regional conflicts or to preempt or deter intervention by the other side. This exacerbation of superpower regional competition would provide greater opportunities to carry out selective strikes against the military facilities and forces of hostile new nuclear states. But these forces might also pose sufficient threats that they would stimulate rather than retard the pace of nuclear proliferation in developing states. Moreover, in a confrontational atmosphere it would be far more difficult for the superpowers to implement crisis management techniques that would be essential for producing conflict resolution.

In sum, the intensification of the Soviet-American competition is likely to stimulate or at least provide the opportunities for stimulating nuclear weapons

---

[15] Most proponents of American abrogation of the ABM Treaty, for example, are, to be sure, dominated by concerns about the Soviet threat. But the demonstration of nuclear weapons proliferation by one or more states hostile to the United States would strengthen the argument for abrogation substantially in U.S. domestic political terms, irrespective of its technical or military merits.

[16] Recall that the United States and the Soviet Union were important architects of the NPT. And, cooperation was demonstrated as late as October 1979 when the Soviets observed what was thought to be a nuclear weapons explosion in the South Atlantic and relayed the information to American intelligence services.

proliferation. The pace of American and Soviet nuclear weapons deployments would quicken as a consequence of their rivalry and would be justified in part by, and in turn promote, nuclear proliferation. Lack of progress in arms control negotiations would make proliferation politically more acceptable in threshold states. And the prospect of superpower regional confrontation would provide threats that could be used to support new nuclear programs. Intensification of the Soviet-American competition would provide a better excuse for and legitimate cause of nuclear proliferation by third parties.

The changing nature of regional security

Traditionally the United States has rarely articulated the explicit objectives it is seeking to achieve in the various regions of the world. For roughly the first two decades after World War II containment of communist expansion was the overriding rationale behind American actions and declaratory policies. But containment was anything but region-specific. Indeed, its great strength in terms of generating a domestic consensus in the United States was its simplicity in ignoring the highly significant disparities across and within regions. When the universal validity of containment was shattered by the Vietnam experience, it was replaced in the Nixon-Kissinger years by an emphasis on balance-of-power diplomacy centering on the Soviet-Chinese-American triangular relationship. Once again, either the United States failed to hold explicitly defined regional policies or they appeared merely to be derivative of a global division among the great powers. To the extent that more specificity was offered during the Nixon and Ford administrations, it concerned the concept of "regional hegemones." In this approach the United States sought to place the responsibility for carrying out its own foreign policy objectives within a region on the shoulders of the state that both had a pro-Western orientation and would likely be the dominant regional force (e.g., Iran in the Persian Gulf). But Mr. Nixon's unexpected fall from power, the weakening of the office of the Presidency, and then the subsequent debacle in Iran itself seemingly has discredited this approach.

More recently it has been fashionable to offer laundry lists of objectives which, in toto, constitute American foreign policy. Former Secretary of State Cyrus Vance, for example, suggested shortly before he left his post that three of the principal aims of American foreign policy were controlling the spread of nuclear weapons, confronting the global energy crisis, and seeking peaceful solutions in troubled regions.[17] Such a presentation, of course, leaves open the difficulties of integrating and advancing a foreign policy some of whose elements seem clearly to be in contradiction with others.

---

[17] Mr. Vance's testimony before the U.S. Senate Foreign Relations Committee was summarized in the *New York Times,* 28 March 1980.

In fact American behavior suggests that the United States has emphasized several common objectives in its approach to a wide variety of regional settings. The first has been to assist in the preservation of the territorial integrity of pro-Western regimes clearly threatened by external aggression. Originally this objective was achieved in the most direct fashion possible: the conclusion of formalized mutual security pacts and the stationing of American combat troops and the establishment of naval and air bases on the territory of the state to be defended. Security assistance in the form of military and economic aid and diplomatic and political support has been the cornerstone of American policy within specific regional settings and has continued long after it was no longer feasible or desirable to formalize defense arrangements or to maintain an American military presence.

A second objective has been the maintenance of a stable military balance between the principal protagonists in a region. In instances where the United States has been on reasonably good terms with two states that are regional rivals, arms supplies have been provided to both sides to preserve a military equilibrium and to reduce the incentives for either state to initiate military hostilities.

Third, the United States has sought where feasible to minimize Soviet presence and the strength of procommunist elements within the states of each region and has criticized techniques of political subversion and propaganda as well as overt military, economic, and political instrumentalities in support of this objective.

Fourth, the United States has emphasized peaceful resolution of regional conflicts. As a guarantor of the status quo within regions the United States has found that, virtually without exception, its interests are preserved if local differences are settled through peaceful means rather than by force of arms. It is also the case, however, that there is a strong sentiment within the American body politic for conflict avoidance and termination even when the dispute involves parties or issues far from U.S. interests.

Fifth, the United States seeks within regions to maintain access to markets and ensure the continued flow of raw material for itself and its closely allies. Because of the intrinsic wealth of the United States, this classical economic motivation behind regional policies has been less central than for resource-limited colonial powers of the past.

Sixth, the promotion of democratic forms of government and the weakening of authoritarian rule has at times been influential on America's policy orientation within given regions. But since democratic governments in developing societies are an extremely rare political commodity, these considerations have had a limited direct bearing on concrete American policies.[18]

Seventh, the United States, in an increasingly complex world, has sought to enlist states in one region to adopt positions or take action in support of

---

[18] An exception are some of the initial efforts by the Carter administration to link human rights policies to military assistance programs.

American policies in another region. This is a particularly demanding task because the variegated relationships among states in the contemporary international system enhance the prospects that a state in one region may have very different interests from the United States with respect to a state in a distant region.

But it is increasingly obvious that the international setting in which America's regional interests are to be pursued during the next three decades will be markedly different from the last three. Most conspicuously, the United States is unlikely to play as dominant a role in world affairs in the future as it has in the past. It is becoming a truism to note that the United States was in a unique position to dominate international military, political, and economic life at the end of World War II, but that this exceptional period is rapidly drawing to a close with the growth of competing military and economic power centers and the emergence of significant economic and political domestic constraints on American policies.[19] Besides the relative decline in American power, real and perceived, the future, unlike the past, will be increasingly sensitive to the problem of energy security and to the pronounced heterogeneity of interests within the community of developing countries and between these states and the industrialized world. A direct consequence of these developments is that American leverage is becoming increasingly limited on the course of energy and security policies adopted by developing countries— policies that have a direct bearing on the likelihood that such countries would acquire nuclear weapons. Yet, if America's international position does continue to weaken, its sense of vulnerability will increase and its desire to arrest or counteract nuclear proliferation will not be commensurate with its capabilities to satisfy such objectives.

Moreover, the pace of nuclear proliferation might not be as leisurely in the future as it has been in the past, and should proliferation chains develop, it would be more difficult to insulate American foreign and defense policies from such a process.[20] Such chains would likely produce more pairs of contiguous nuclear rivals—Israel and Syria, Egypt and Libya, India and Pakistan, North and South Korea, Argentina and Brazil, the People's Republic of China and Taiwan—increasing both the incentives for preemption and the likelihood of nuclear weapon use in the escalation of a conventional war. Contiguity has always been a useful indicator of conflict likelihood in international relations and there is no reason to suspect that it will not be an important determinant of nuclear conflict as well.[21]

---

[19] The changes are examined at length in the author's "Toward an American Conception of Regional Security," *Daedalus* (Fall 1980).

[20] George Quester in this volume argues precisely the opposite—namely, that the pace of nuclear proliferation is likely to slow down in the future.

[21] It could be argued, of course, that contiguity would be a deterrent to nuclear weapon use if it was appreciated that destruction of thy neighbor led through radioactive fallout patterns to destruction of thyself.

Consider the following prospective list of new nuclear weapons states categorized according to their political relationship with the United States:

Category 1: major ally
Federal Republic of Germany
Japan

Category 2: potential or actual regional ally
Pakistan
South Korea
Taiwan
Yugoslavia

Category 3: neither ally nor adversary
Argentina
Brazil
South Africa

Category 4: adversary of regional ally
Iran
Iraq
Libya
Syria

If West Germany or Japan determine the need to acquire nuclear weapons as a consequence of dramatic changes in either their domestic affairs or in international conditions, it is vitally important that the United States make every effort to retain strong political relations with both states. The most decisive setback to America's international position, aside from a Sino-Soviet rapprochement, would be the military, economic, and political loss of a nuclear-armed Germany or Japan. To be sure, the acquisition of nuclear weapons by either state would seem unnecessary and undesirable from most American perspectives, no matter how dramatically international conditions had changed. But if nuclear weapons acquisition takes place nonetheless, there are no inherent barriers to prevent this transition from producing as few adverse effects on American policy as did the British and French cases.

Failure to accommodate such transition would have profound consequences not only on international political alignments but on all facets of American defense posture. A nuclear-armed Germany or Japan in an adversarial relationship with the United States would surely stimulate a major growth in U.S. offensive nuclear forces, ballistic missile defenses to protect nuclear retaliatory forces and possibly even population centers, renewed emphasis on air defenses and civil defense programs, in addition to an enormous impact on the deployment patterns of general purpose forces.

If any of the states in category 2 acquire nuclear weapons, American foreign policy is more likely to be affected than U.S. defense programs. An Indian-Pakistani nuclear standoff would challenge American diplomacy to avoid unnecessary interference, limit Soviet influence in the South Asian region, and assist, if possible, in forestalling nuclear weapons use should conventional war break out. A South Korean nuclear force could rupture its security arrangement with the United States, since a persuasive argument could be made in Washington that the deterrent value of the weapons would obviate the need for a continued presence of American troops on the Peninsula. Nuclear weapons possessed by Taiwan or Yugoslavia would raise serious problems for the United States. While few Americans would wish to risk nuclear war with China over Taiwan or nuclear war with the Soviet Union over Yugoslavia, there is strong support in the United States for the maintenance of the sovereignty of both states. Indeed, closer technical cooperation between the new nuclear state and the United States could well follow in the form of American advice about permissive action links and other methods of command and control as well as measures for nuclear weapon physical security.

If states in category 3 acquired nuclear weapons or emulated the Israeli model of fostered ambiguity, there might be minimal effects on U.S. security policy. Bilateral relations would probably worsen in the short-term, with the United States being tempted to "punish" the new nuclear state through the imposition of economic or political sanctions. But American leverage in each of these cases is in fact quite limited. If it were appreciated that American regional interests, particularly trade and economic investment and the containment of Soviet influence, were not directly jeopardized by such proliferation, the United States would probably adjust with limited difficulty.

Nuclear proliferation among states in category 4 would pose fundamental problems for American policymakers. The likelihood of nuclear weapon use would be perceived to have increased dramatically, the survival of Israel and possibly of Egypt would be in jeopardy, connections would be appropriately drawn between a renewal of the Arab-Israeli armed conflict and the vulnerability of Persian Gulf oil, and the specter of nuclear terrorism might rapidly lose its sense of fantasy. The incentives for the United States to become directly involved in the region in ways it has never been before—stationing of troops, formulation of explicit security guarantees, even contemplation of preventive strikes against nuclear storage depots or delivery vehicles—would materialize. Most dangerously, such actions would raise the prospect of a Soviet-American confrontation in the region. There seems little doubt, therefore, that a group of nuclear-armed rivals in the Middle East would have a far greater effect on U.S. security policy than have Israel's moves alone down the nuclear path.

States have many possible incentives to acquire nuclear weapons, including the enhancement of their security, and to serve a variety of foreign policy goals and domestic needs.[22] But it is not at all clear that the traditional set of U.S. regional security objectives cited above is consistent with reducing these incentives or, more broadly, with U.S. nonproliferation policies. If U.S. nonproliferation policy initiatives successfully deny states access to nuclear

---

[22] These incentives are well presented in Yehezkel Dror, "Nuclear Weapons in the Third World," presented at the Annual Conference of the International Institute for Strategic Studies, Villars, Switzerland, September 1979.

weapons, it would appear that such success could be a mixed blessing in terms of American regional interests. Preservation of allied territorial integrity would be strengthened if the effect of the nonproliferation policy was to deny nuclear weapons to its adversary. But it would reduce allied confidence if its only effect was to deny the state a nuclear deterrent that was considered necessary to avoid war. Successful nonproliferation policies tend to reinforce existing military balances. Where such balances are relatively stable or in regions that are presently free of nuclear weapons, both the maintenance of stability and the promotion of peaceful conflict resolution could result. Alternatively, where existing disparities are already in place, successful nonproliferation could tend to undermine the achievement of both objectives.

Nonproliferation policies aggressively pursued could stimulate adverse responses by threshold states toward closer ties with the Soviet Union or to the adoption of policies to deny the United States access to markets or raw materials. It could also stimulate nationalist feeling that would tend to strengthen authoritarian regimes, although such governments could be weakened if the net effect of American policy was to deny a prestigious accomplishment needed for domestic consumption. Moreover, nonproliferation policies could generate resistance within states to cooperate with U.S. policy initiatives in other regions.

In sum, the impact of nonproliferation policies on U.S. regional security interests is highly sensitive to the existing military balance in a region and to the foreign policy orientation of the states most directly affected by the policies.

In all respects, therefore, the relationship between nuclear proliferation and American security policy is changing. The intensification of the superpower rivalry and specific developments in their nuclear weapons and doctrines, the decline of American power more generally, and the characteristics of nuclear threshold states all serve to stimulate nuclear proliferation. It will be increasingly difficult in the future for American security policy to be as insulated from this process as it has been in the past.

11

Preventing Proliferation:
The Impact on International Politics

George H. Quester

When the question of the impact of the nuclear proliferation problem is discussed in the literature, it usually becomes an analysis of what *actual* nuclear proliferation would do to international diplomacy. Dire predictions are offered by most observers,[1] amid more optimistic predictions advanced by a few.[2] We will not devote much space to this version of the question, generally accepting as a premise the pessimistic view, as outlined in the introduction to this volume.

The more important form of the question, to which the bulk of this article will be devoted, may concern the impact on international politics of the continuing *threat* of nuclear proliferation, as the threat is perhaps generally fended off, but as the barriers necessary to achieve this themselves impose some important changes on the way nations do business with each other.

The primary barrier to nuclear proliferation may thus be none of the factors listed below, but rather the view of reality attributed to most reasonable

---

[1] For broad-ranging discussions (mostly pessimistic) of the impact of actual nuclear weapons spread on the international system see Stanley Hoffmann, "Nuclear Proliferation and World Politics" in *A World of Nuclear Powers?*, Alastair Buchan, ed. (Englewood Cliffs, New Jersey: Prentice-Hall, 1966) pp. 89–122; Richard Rosecrance, ed., *The Future of the International Strategic System* (San Francisco: Chandler, 1972); and Albert Wohlstetter, et al., *Swords From Plowshares* (Chicago: University of Chicago Press, 1979) especially pp. 126–50.

[2] For considerably less pessimistic analyses of the impact of actual proliferation, see Kenneth N. Waltz, "What Will the Spread of Nuclear Weapons Do to the World" in *International Political Effects of the Spread of Nuclear Weapons,* John Perry King, ed. (Washington: U.S.G.P.O., 1979), pp. 165–97. See also Hedley Bull, "Rethinking Nonproliferation," *International Affairs,* 51, 2 (April 1975): 15,175–80, 187–9.

observers at the very outset, namely, that actual widespread proliferation would be a disaster for the world, a disaster even for those nations which acquired such weapons (precisely because their neighbors would have acquired them too).

The generally bad consequences of widespread nuclear proliferation may in fact keep it from happening, leading states to draw back from a plunge into a world of many nuclear powers. Without offering any certainty or high probability, the prognosis is advanced that only a few more nations will acquire nuclear weapons in the next two or three decades, and that the major predictions of change in the international system over this time must stem not from nuclear proliferation, but from the devices and adjustments which head such proliferation off.

The changes outlined will largely be the consequences of success in the antiproliferation effort, or concomitants of such success, rather than the basic sources of such success. What causes nuclear proliferation to slow down will at the same time cause some other changes in the international system, and those changes are the theme of this essay.

Dilutions of sovereignty

A first prediction about the impact on international politics is that the nonproliferation effort will produce, as it already has, a certain dilution and diminution of sovereignty. Nations, as they become parties to the Nuclear Nonproliferation Treaty, or as they adhere to other international agreements renouncing nuclear weapons, will be renouncing what used to be thought of as an inherent part of the prerogative of nations: the right to manufacture weapons. In 1968, critics of the NPT were already decrying it as the "first unequal treaty of the twentieth century," because it is far from fully reciprocal, permitting five countries to possess nuclear explosives and requiring all other parties to renounce them and to submit to international safeguards to assure that such renunciation is actually adhered to. Yet a great number of nations have accepted the provisions of this treaty, however unequal it might seem, and public opinion in most of these countries has indeed accepted this apparent compromising of the equality of nations and national sovereignty.

Strictly speaking, nations have thus far surrendered their nuclear weapons option as a matter of national choice, freely and voluntarily accepting international safeguards on a basis of national independence. If the treaty is "unequal," it is still a treaty. Some other nations have not signed the NPT, but have accepted IAEA safeguards over specific projects simply as part of the purchase agreement for the reactors or fuels in question; this similarly amounts to working from a base of equal international sovereign prerogative, since the seller of equipment presumably has always had the right to put any conditions he wants onto the sale as part of *his* inherent sovereign prerogatives.

Where states have decided to accept safeguards in such situations, this may then still seem to show nothing at all about trends of international legitimacy. The purchaser could accept them without any swallowing of national pride, still looking forward to a day in the near future when it can build its own reactors or process its own fuel, and thus avoid entering into such contractual requirements.

Yet the mood of world opinion on international legitimacy is moving faster than this. The reason that so many nations signed and ratified the NPT, without any obvious quid pro quo or exchange of concessions (perhaps it is thus indeed an "unequal treaty"), was that world moral pressure against further weapons spread had grown considerably by the end of the 1960s and has grown even further a decade later. We will soon see the day when most of the world thinks it normal that all but the five major nuclear weapons states should have renounced such weapons, and thinks it unseemly that any "nth" state should try to assert its national sovereignty by proliferation. We will similarly see the day when it is thought normal and correct that every nation engaged in peaceful nuclear activities must submit to total "full-scope" international safeguards, so as to reassure its neighbors that no nuclear warheads are being produced.

As noted, the submission to safeguards has up to the present been handled and negotiated as a straightforward exchange between two commercial powers, or then, in the ratification of the NPT, as the voluntary commitment of a nation choosing on its own to accede to an international agreement. Even where a state has declined to sign or ratify the NPT, however, and is becoming self-sufficient in nuclear matters, we will now see an international consensus that it should submit to full-scope safeguards, that it should be denied further purchases of nuclear equipment from abroad, or even of other kinds of equipment, if it does not accept this international requirement.

Skeptics about the NPT itself often point to its provisions for withdrawal in Article X, specifying that "each Party shall in exercising its national sovereignty have the right to withdraw from the Treaty if it decides that extraordinary events, related to the subject matter of this Treaty, have jeopardized the supreme interests of its country."

The history of this clause is somewhat bizarre, since it is identical to Article IV of the 1963 Partial Test-Ban Treaty.[3] The clause was inserted into the earlier treaty at the insistence of the United States, in some part in the illusory hope that it might lead the USSR to put strong pressures on Peking not to acquire nuclear weapons (in the face of the threat that the United States

---

[3] The text of the Nuclear Test-Ban Treaty of 1963 can be found in United States Arms Control and Disarmament Agency, *Documents on Disarmament: 1963* (Washington: U.S.G.P.O., 1964), pp. 291–3. The text of the Nuclear Nonproliferation Treaty of 1968 can be found in *Documents on Disarmament: 1968* (Washington: U.S.G.P.O., 1969), pp. 404–9.

might then avail itself of the withdrawal prerogative in this clause, because a Chinese detonation amounted to "extraordinary events, related to the subject matter of this Treaty").

What was intended to provide some antiproliferation leverage almost two decades ago vis-à-vis the People's Republic of China may have backfired, ironically giving potential proliferators some undesirable leverage in escaping the obligations they have undertaken in the NPT. Every so often one encounters this kind of political cleverness, which produces very much the opposite of what was intended.

Yet it would be altogether too pessimistic to assume that it will be very easy for parties to the NPT to exploit this clause to escape their commitment. To begin, one might insist that the phrase "related to the subject matter of this Treaty" must have some real meaning, or else it would not have been included, and that its meaning could only refer to nuclear proliferation by some other state. If one's neighbor has violated the NPT by acquiring nuclear warheads, one might well be justified under the treaty in withdrawing and also acquiring such weapons. Such is the logic we have already noted of chain reactions—a logic which worries us a great deal. Yet, if the neighbor can be prevented from making this move, the entire chain may be kept from proliferating, and this is our hope.

Apart from such tight legal quibbling, the more general political and psychological hope would be that the world will increasingly convert this withdrawal clause into a dead letter, as it goes unused by any of the parties year after year, and as the taboo against its invocation grows (along with the taboo against nuclear weapons spread in general, along with the demand for full-scope safeguards even where nations have not even signed the NPT).

What we wish to achieve is a progressive lessening of any strength the potential "nth" nations may see in legal loopholes or in traditional sovereign prerogatives. The model might be supplied by West Germany and Japan, each of which sent its lawyers into the NPT negotiation process to explore every possible legal foothold for later demands and each of which has since felt itself and the world, settling into an uncontested decision that Bonn and Tokyo are never to become possessors of nuclear explosives.

The world will thus see a greater moral opposition than before to the national acquisition of the very latest and deadliest of weapons. It of course could make this new opposition consistent with a full equality among nations by applying similar moral pressures against everyone, even the present holders of nuclear weapons.[4] The prediction, however, would be that this will occur only in moderation, that more of a new "double standard" will thus emerge in world legitimacy than most of today's diplomats would like to admit.

To make the ban on nuclear weapons total, applying to all the current nuclear weapons states, even to the United States and the USSR, would be to undertake and predict a very much more fundamental change in the entire

---

[4] For a good illustration of such arguments, see William Epstein, *The Last Chance* (New York: The Free Press, 1976).

international system. We are not predicting that the world's horror at nuclear proliferation and warfare is going to produce world government, or general and complete disarmament (even if Article VI of the NPT indeed, as window dressing, calls for "negotiations in good faith on effective measures relating to cessation of the nuclear arms race at an early date and to nuclear disarmament, and on a Treaty on general and complete disarmament under strict and effective international control"). We are instead predicting that the world's horror in contemplating nuclear warfare will lead to a truncation of a portion of nations' sovereignty—a truncation of the right to nuclear weapons.

There will be some pressure for "consistency" with respect to nuclear states, but not a great deal. We may see a part of such pressure directed at India, slowing delivery of various important nuclear imports or other imports, perhaps to assure that New Delhi does not openly proclaim itself as having a bomb and does not repeatedly detonate nuclear explosives in tests, and perhaps so that India in the end would submit to total international safeguards, giving up whatever bomb potential it has laid away. We might see some similar pressure over the years to induce either Britain or France to give up their independent nuclear forces, since a "reduction" in the number of nuclear weapons states would surely seem to be a major contribution to staying the momentum towards proliferation.

Yet the nature of some of the unfairness of the nuclear proliferation problem reappears here, for we must guess that pressure on Argentina and Brazil will at all points be stronger than pressure on Britain and France, and that pressure on Pakistan or Taiwan will be greater than pressure on India. It is indeed unreasonable that those who got nuclear weapons early should find life easier than those that queue up later. But the world, for the very practical concerns cited at the outset, may well have to make such unfairness a central part of its accommodation to the destructive power of such weapons.

Finally, what of pressure on the United States and the USSR, now that the SALT agreement seems to be in very deep trouble at the end of the first Carter administration, in apparent noncompliance with Article VI of the NPT? Threats will periodically be voiced that key NPT adherents may now choose to regard any renewals of the Soviet-American strategic arms race as freeing them of their nonproliferation obligations; the public opinions of a few countries can surely be bent in this direction by any obvious slowdown of détente.

Yet the most important argument for accepting a nonproliferation regime, even if only a few diplomats ever admit it, will not be that the superpowers are somehow matching this with restraints of their own, or that national equality and fairness are being restored, but rather that most of the states involved have their own interest in avoiding such proliferation. The dire logic of the nuclear proliferation chain reaction does not yet have to be fully in effect. The sense that "everyone else is getting the bomb, so why don't we" is not yet in place. For the moment, the logic will still more normally be "if we get the bomb, others will follow us," a difference of sequence which may make all the difference in results.

The workings of domino chains in the nuclear proliferation field have not, thus far, been inexorable and have not been the whole of the picture. Rumors of German work on the atomic bomb undoubtedly stimulated the United States to develop it, and the American bomb in turn surely did not decrease Soviet desires for the weapon. Yet it is less clear that the British and French bombs followed in any strategic chain sequence from the Russian or American bombs. Similarly, it is not obvious whether the Chinese bomb should "link" more to the American or Russian in the chain. India's bomb can be tied to China's, but Israel's would be more tied to the inherent possibility that the Arab states might someday try a grand tank assault intended to push the Israelis into the sea. Rumors of Iraqi or Libyan bomb projects clearly tie to the rumors of an Israeli stockpile; yet, as will be discussed, the situation is not symmetrical here. An Arab nuclear arsenal would hardly undo or cancel out the impact of an Israeli nuclear weapon.

Coming back to a more plausible link, the Pakistani impetus for reaching for the bomb certainly stems from India's decision to detonate. But South Korean or Taiwanese bomb aspirations would stem rather from the politically and militarily exposed positions of these regimes, and less from the mainland Chinese bomb, or from any rumors of North Korean nuclear aspirations.

All of this is meant to suggest that no pattern of predetermined nuclear proliferation chain-linkages has really come into being yet. Such a pattern does not explain the pattern of the first six nuclear weapons possessors, and it is not yet so far along that we cannot head it off. If proliferation goes very much further, however, then such a more pronounced pattern may emerge and "the dominoes may fall."

Where a pattern of matching one's opposite number has shown itself, it has sometime been primarily strategic, as in the Soviet Union's following the U.S., or in Peking's decision to follow either Washington or Moscow, and sometimes a matching in terms of prestige (an Arab "matching" of Israeli rumors would be mainly effective in undoing the prestige one-upsmanship the Israelis might extract from their bomb). Prestige is not always tied-in with countering the actions of a specific other nation, however. While Indians sometimes point to China's bomb as the justification for their "peaceful nuclear explosive," it was probably intended to win India prestige across the entire globe, rather than simply to be a response to China. The French and British bomb projects play much the same role.

There is a logical link between predicting that we cannot (or will not) go down to zero nuclear powers, and in noting that the pattern of nuclear proliferation has not thus far simply been a chain reaction. For, if the pattern of past proliferation were all a reaction of dominoes falling, we could hope to make the dominoes pile up in the opposite direction again, as if avoiding the seventh nuclear weapons state led to the elimination of the sixth and fifth, and then the fourth, etc., etc. Yet it is a sad fact that nothing might be more likely to induce a country like Australia or Brazil or Sweden or Japan to become a nuclear weapons state than the total nuclear disarmament of the existing weapons states.

Despite our world's intuitive taste for equality and fairness, states are converging increasingly in seeing nonproliferation as a desirable accomplishment in its own right, while wanting some moderation or reduction of the superpower arms confrontation, yet drawing back from the idea of general and complete disarmament. I would predict that the world will not be serious about pressuring the United States and the USSR to disarm and will decreasingly use threats of upsetting the nuclear nonproliferation regime as a prod to superpower concessions on this front. Even the nonweapons states will increasingly recognize and acknowledge that they have just about as much interest as the weapons states in preventing further proliferation.

If the compromising of sovereignty and weapons prerogatives is going to occur, as outlined above, it is going to focus mainly on nuclear proliferation beyond the basic five or six, or the basic two, and will not go further to try to make the leap to world government or total disarmament. This may disappoint those who would agitate for more. The straightforward advocate of disarmament would argue that zero nuclear weapons states would be the best number of all, so that each increase thereafter is undesirable: $0 > 1 > 2 > 3 > 4 > 5 > 6. \ldots$

The advocate of a priority and a saliency for nonproliferation might agree that five is better than six, four better than five, etc., but might rather claim that two nuclear weapons states are better than one for holding the world in balance, and that a "zero" which was widely feared or rumored to be a clandestine one would then be far worse than two. A little bit of uncertainty would persist on whether the Chinese bomb played a real role in stabilizing threats from Moscow or Washington, but the array of preference would run as follows: "0" $= 1 < 2 < ?3 > 4 > 5 > 6. \ldots$

Our discussion is meant to be mainly an exercise in prediction rather than prescription. Yet our guesses as to what the world will do must at times seem to endorse this as sensible and wise. Like it or not, the prediction might be that the world will become resigned to two, or three, nuclear arsenals for Washington, Moscow, and Peking, tolerant but unconvinced of their necessity for London, Paris, and New Delhi, and firmly resistant to such weapons for most other regimes.

In a paradoxical way, the sheer devastation that nuclear proliferation can cause will thus induce international accommodation to head it off. This adverse impact of the destructive possibilities of nuclear weapons is, of course, somewhat of an old story, as this is how we often interpret the balance of mutual deterrence and mutual assured destruction. Some supporters of nuclear proliferation would have contended that this is why they indeed advocate it, that the spreading of destructive potential will keep it from ever coming into use. The bulk of the world will now, however, work through this paradox along a different path opposed to proliferation, not just limiting wars because nuclear war would be too horrible, but crimping the prerogatives of nation states for acquiring nuclear weapons, precisely because this also could be too horrible.

There are hardly any signs that the world is ready to renounce more generally the prerogatives of sovereignty and national independence.[5] If a tendency to compromise such prerogatives on the narrow front of nuclear energy and nuclear weapons options seems to be developing, this is probably the outer limit of what one can anticipate in changes in international legitimacy. Yet this may well show the strength of our prediction that nuclear proliferation is indeed a uniquely menacing problem, such that unique departures from the earlier style of international arrangements are in order.

Just as the earlier "worry list" which included Japan and Italy and West Germany has been replaced by a newer list, most of the nations on the newer list may thus graduate to the category of countries deciding to forego an acquisition of nuclear weapons.

One or two failures will occur in the rest of the century, but the trick will then be to make these look to all concerned as exceptional cases, without any domino impact, without any necessary precedent or stimulus for other nuclear weapons programs. The possibility also exists, as noted, that a state might actually leave the ranks of the nuclear weapons states in this period, to keep the "trend" from appearing to go in one direction (although one would not want to base any large part of the antiproliferation effort on this).

Multinational institutions

As another development to be anticipated in international relations, the resistance to nuclear proliferation may after a time produce some breakthroughs in more meaningful international management of nuclear industry.[6] The track record of such international or multinational projects to date has been the object of considerable skepticism. The prognosis has sometimes been advanced that only considerations of economic return can now have very much impact in the nuclear field, so that multinational projects which might be effective as proliferation barriers will be vetoed whenever they are not conducive to a material profit for all concerned. But the 1980s and 1990s may see this "iron law" disproven; the state apparatus may become effective at subsidizing and promoting and managing such operations, even where they seem second-best by some material standards, because the arms control return will have come to be seen as a very material gain in its own right.

A second kind of skepticism about any multinational business arrangements stems from memories of their past accomplishments in other

[5] See Richard Falk, "Nuclear Weapons Proliferation as A World Order Problem," *International Security*, I, 3 (Winter 1977): 79–93.

[6] For a reasonably optimistic interpretation of the possibilities of multinational approaches here, see Myron B. Kratzer, *Multinational Institutions and Nonproliferation: A New Look,* Occasional Paper No. 20 (Muscatine, Iowa: Stanley Foundation, 1979).

industries, namely, that they conduce to the profits and to the continued technological advantage of the most advanced state joining in them, and in effect stunt, rather than help, the development of the partner that began at an economic or scientific disadvantage. The breakthrough we could look forward to here would be in the development of internal management and capital-development procedures which reversed this tendency.

Some nations will thus very honestly seek to invest in separate pilot plants of plutonium reprocessing or uranium enrichment for civilian purposes (even though such investments suspiciously resemble weapons projects, arousing the concerns of neighbors), simply out of the fear of being left still further behind as the world moves into higher technology. The goal of developing new forms of multinational partnership in these areas would be to reduce such fears of "missing the boat," to allow for the economies-of-scale and multinational reassurance against weapons diversion that larger facilities can offer, while also stimulating a fuller sharing of scientific experience.

The skeptic might note how proposals for such new arrangements have tended to be much more numerous than concrete responses to such proposals. The multinational facilities for the handling of nuclear fuels might thus seem doomed to remain on the drawing boards, as the concrete intentions of the separate countries again and again take precedence. Yet the trend will probably be in the other direction. Such trends develop slowly, but the growth of nuclear industry, and of the nuclear weapons proliferation problem, has also come along more slowly than predicted, so that the good might still get out in front of the bad.

The Scandinavian Airways System may not be a persuasive model[7]: we have a long way to go before international cooperation between Brazil and Argentina, or Egypt and Israel, can be as meaningful as the cooperation of Sweden and Denmark. Yet such models nonetheless meaningfully contradict the pessimistic assumption that sovereignty is an insuperable barrier, and that active corporations will always have to be meaningful "national," and only superficially "multinational". The multinational corporation (MNC) may already in truth have gotten across such boundaries in search of profit; similar crossings of the boundary may be possible for the purposes of avoiding nuclear weapons spread.

Related to this is a prediction that the International Atomic Energy Agency (IAEA) will rise, rather than fall, in stature and preeminence in the next decades.[8] While fears will often be voiced that the safeguards provided by the Agency cannot be materially airtight, the safeguards may work politically, together with the other social and psychological factors noted, to

---

[7] For a discussion of the analogies here, see Atlantic Council of the United States: Nuclear Fuels Policy Working Group, *Nuclear Power and Nuclear Weapons Proliferation,* Volume II (Boulder, Colorado: Westview Press, 1978), pp. 39–63.

[8] A good overview of the prospects and problems of the IAEA can be found in Stockholm International Peace Research Institute, *Safeguards Against Nuclear Proliferation* (Stockholm: Almqvist and Wiksell, 1975).

achieve the kind of de facto nonproliferation with which we can be quite content. The sheer political impact of submitting to such international inspection should not be discounted, in reminding the scientists and ordinary citizens of the country in question that it has indeed renounced nuclear weapons, in accelerating the legitimacy of a nonproliferation regime which then would be brought to bear against other countries. A nation which has submitted to full-scope safeguards will be prompted, by the regular visits of IAEA personnel, to become a stronger exponent of full-scope safeguards as the "normal" pattern in any other nonweapons state.

There are at least two reasons why much of the world may come to defend more staunchly the IAEA. First, the Vienna Agency is declared by its charter to be not just a policing agent over the uses of nuclear energy, but also a conduit for the sharing of such technology. A strong endorsement of the IAEA as the preeminent international actor in this field will thus be consistent with trying to enhance such sharing as an important part of the mix.

Second, there will be Congressmen and others in the United States demanding a shift to still tighter safeguards on the premise that those of the IAEA are not sufficient. Countries questioning this premise will then rally to the Agency's defense, because the Agency is indeed enshrined by the NPT as the verification instrument designated to assure that materials are not diverted to weapons from peaceful nuclear activities.

Skeptics about the chances of preventing proliferation might take a defense of the IAEA as a sign that LDCs and other nonweapons states are not very serious about the problem, supporting an ineffective agency which is likely to let materials get diverted. If one shares the premise that IAEA safeguards can be effective, however (the U.S. Congress has at points been overly cautious and misguidedly pessimistic), then the greater preeminence accorded the IAEA might reflect sentiments which are less feigned and more genuine.

It is likely that international activities such as the INFCE and even the London "Suppliers' Club" will increasingly be pulled under the IAEA's wing. It is also likely, as time moves along, that the day-to-day stature of the IAEA will grow, as publics and government bureaucracies in general come to understand its function and to be more aware of the proliferation aspects of nuclear energy. The worst demeaning of the IAEA's position in the 1970s probably did not come from U.S. Congressional staff reports that were critical of it, but when customs inspectors at some frontiers had never heard of the agency and would insist on trying to impose duties on its monitoring and testing equipment. The prediction is that this will happen far less often as we move through the 1980s.

The IAEA may never quite become a household word like the UN, but the trend of international politics will be to raise its stature, along with the general stature of international approaches to the managing and monitoring of nuclear energy, along with the world's endorsement for an imposition of safeguards over peaceful nuclear activity anywhere.

A part of what would support our prediction that multinational arrangements will grow in prominence and effectiveness is simply the guess that governments and peoples around the world will continue the process of becoming better at integrating political and economic considerations. Just as the "pure" profit curves of industry are now more regularly adjusted for their comparative impacts on pollution and environment, by having the state intervene to force a meaningful assessment of the social costs imposed on the community as a whole, so will the impact of alternative arrangements on nuclear proliferation also be taken into account more and more.

One of the genuine accomplishments of the International Nuclear Fuel Cycle Evaluation (INFCE),[9] despite the shortcomings one might find in its actual substantive product, was that the national representatives involved generally acknowledged the need to become accustomed to integrating such considerations. As such it was something of a closing of the European-American gap illustrated in the Nye and Lellouche chapters. The question of whether "some ways of handling the nuclear fuel cycle are excessively proliferation prone" was perhaps brushed off too lightly at INFCE, but it has at least now generally been dignified as a question of high priority and legitimacy. This is likely to sink in around the national capitals of the world in the decades ahead—in the discussions of projects to be undertaken, in the attitudes adopted about the projects of other countries.

The redemption of "pariah states"

A third major prediction about how the international political system will respond to the threat and possibility of nuclear proliferation is that the so-called "pariah states" will gradually escape this status, as the mere rumors and possibility of their acquiring nuclear weapons slowly bring around the neighbors who had aspired to their total defeat and annihilation. The "pariah state" might straightforwardly be defined as follows: a regime winning little or no sympathy in the outside world, while being threatened with an imminent military conquest by neighbors. Israel long was in this category, and now is moving out of it, perhaps very much as a by-product of the nuclear proliferation possibility. South Africa and Taiwan have fallen into this category. South Korea has come close to it, as perhaps has Pakistan.

The Israeli model, in many ways now copied by the others, is illuminating.[10] Nuclear weapons are not test-detonated, and no public statement is ever made explicitly claiming a weapons program. Yet rumors of the manufacture of nuclear warheads are allowed to leak out, never to be

---

[9] See Peter Clausen, "Nuclear Conference Yields Potential New Consensus," *Arms Control Today*, 9, 6 (June 1979): 1-4.

[10] A full discussion of what we might be able to know about the Israeli nuclear weapons program can be found in Robert E. Harkavy, *Spectre of a Middle Eastern Holocaust* (Denver, Colorado: University of Denver Monograph Series in World Affairs, 1977).

categorically or convincingly denied, and no international safeguards are accepted which could disprove the rumors once and for all. Sometimes the rumors are in fact launched and spread by the very enemies of the pariah state, on the mistaken assumption that this will increase the world's hostility or indifference to the regime in question. Rumors about Israeli nuclear programs thus emerge from Arab sources, and about South Africa from Black African states. At other times the rumors are launched by the quasi-proliferating pariah state itself.

Regardless of the source, the rumors over time work to the advantage of the beleaguered regime, for they complicate and upset its enemies' "fondest dream." The fondest dream for the Palestinian Liberation Organization has been to defeat Israel totally, to deport or annihilate most of the Jews living in Palestine today. Yet when that dream must also contemplate the last-gasp retaliation that would be directed against Cairo and Damascus and Mecca, it no longer amounts to such a pleasant reverie. The proliferation possibility has the same impact on Black African dreams of forcing the white oppressors of South Africa to go back to Europe, or Peking's dreams of a forcible reunification with Taiwan, or Pyongyang's aspirations to conquer all of Korea. The mere prospect of a manufacture of nuclear weapons, and of their use in a last-gasp retaliation, serves to divert the thoughts of the irredentists to other things, to a compromise and accommodation of sorts with the status quo. If much of the outside world might otherwise have been content to see South Korea liquidated, as easily as South Vietnam, it similarly would have its attitudes changed somewhat here by the nuclear proliferation risk, by what we might generally style as "quasi-proliferation".

Some of such effect thus will depend on states getting close to this credible base from which the "bomb in the basement" could be manufactured. When the bombs are never detonated and never openly proclaimed, until now they seem to have been less stimulating to further proliferation; yet they nonetheless also induce some of the stabilization that Gallois predicted twenty years ago. The stabilizing effect may require time; the impact on the Arab states (Egypt arguably being the visible example) was spread over a decade or more. Some of the effects will also of course depend on help from background factors, or at least from the absence of background developments greatly exacerbating the very hostilities with which we are burdened.

There will be instances where the political background will not cooperate on this, where the underlying disagreements between neighbors will worsen, so as to push the irredentists toward threatening to obliterate an existing regime. Yet there is really no broader reason why such a tension-increasing trend should be a general rule; the more general tendency may now be as suggested— that the worldwide digestion and appreciation of the nuclear weapons proliferation possibility will take the edge off such feelings, making it seem generally less and less reasonable for any state to indulge in threatening a pariah state with extinction.

Israel may have to surrender the West Bank to the Palestinians, but in the end it will be relieved of the threat that it must surrender all of the old Palestine Mandate. The white South African regime will similarly probably have to surrender much more land to black rule than its current nominal offer of some "Bantustan," but it may not have to consider being pushed into the sea, forced to return to Europe.

Nonuse of nuclear weapons

Still another prediction will hardly seem startling in the wake of all that has happened since World War II, but it would have looked quite dangerous and foolhardy in 1945. As we move ahead in an international system where the possessors of nuclear weapons generally share an aversion to further proliferation, nuclear weapons will not be used in combat by any of the states that possess them.[11]

It has been noted several times that the acquisition to date of such weapons has not by and large produced any particularly flamboyant or radical behavior. The picture is, of course, a little mixed. The United States, as the first nuclear weapons state, proceeded to use its bombs against Japan, at the end of World War II. Yet the United States did not really try to apply its monopoly thereafter against other likely enemies—i.e., the Soviet Union did not try to maintain the nuclear monopoly by force. The Russians behaved provocatively in Iran in 1945 and around West Berlin in 1948, before they had the bomb; but they then also apparently countenanced the invasion of South Korea in 1950, in what was widely seen as their showing interest in military aggression after their acquisition of A-bombs. It is not really until the middle 1960s that the world began to see the USSR as having moderated its behavior in détente, and the end of the 1970s revealed a pessimistic revision of this assessment. Britain and France did not become wilder after acquiring their nuclear weapons in 1952 and 1960 respectively, and may indeed have receded from world power roles in these years (although the most recent French decision to try to be a counterweight to Cuban and Russian influence in Africa might seem the resurgence of a great power role). The first four nuclear weapons states thus do not confirm any tendency to become aggressive or irresponsible once nuclear weapons have been added to its arsenal. Rather, they might more generally be seen as having been made more responsible and cautious.

This generalization might hold all the more for China and India, in the wake of their detonations of nuclear devices in 1964 and 1974. Peking, once feared as a possibly very irrational and warlike possessor of such weapons, has made the most forthcoming pledges of all about its arsenal—that it will never

---

[11] For a broad discussion of the value of holding back the use of nuclear weapons, see Richard Ullmann, "No First Use of Nuclear Weapons," *Foreign Affairs,* 50, 4 (July 1972): 669–83.

use nuclear weapons unless some other state uses them first.[12] India, despite the participation in government of the ultra-nationalistic Jan Sangh party after the election defeat of Mrs. Gandhi, similarly has been relatively circumspect in its foreign policy since 1974. Its seemingly hypocritical definition of its nuclear explosive as "peaceful" might indeed now amount to the functional equivalent of a no-first-use statement, even a nonbrandishing statement.

But what if there came to be some exceptions to this pattern of nonuse and moderation in the countries that might acquire nuclear weapons in the future? Just as Russian and American handling of nuclear weapons has not always been as moderated as it is at present, the assurance is hardly there that Libya or Pakistan or the two Koreas would behave so satisfactorily.

Precisely the worry that moderation could not be counted upon amounts to the strongest incentive against continued proliferation. We would otherwise have to entertain a strong argument in favor of continued nuclear weapons spread, in that this would lead to better behavior by all concerned.

We are thus in a situation where the rule is reinforced by the anticipatory fear of exceptions. If the world disciplines itself enough, and girds itself strongly enough against the further spread of such weapons, Libya and Iraq and Argentina and Taiwan may never get them. A continuation of the elementary moderation that has held so far may well be a part of the general package of attitudes and deportments required to keep further proliferation from happening.

The obverse is easy to show. If nuclear weapons were to be brandished much more openly and regularly by the countries currently possessing them, then the barrier to proliferation would become very weak indeed. Nothing might be quite as traumatic for the world, and as damaging for the effort to resist proliferation than to have another warhead used in anger, to have the taboo of thirty-five years broken.

What if some prospective nuclear power were then to be easily identified from the outset as prone to breaking such tradition, to violating the nuclear taboo, and to putting its new explosives into use as weapons? We have not yet seriously discussed the possibility of preemptive military attacks in order to keep such a power from acquiring warheads. Despite all that has been said about the world's shifting of legitimacies on proliferation, it has not yet come really close to endorsing unilateral military action to prevent such a weapons project.

Yet two and two might be put together in a way which still left the world intact. If a truly glaring case of prospective international irresponsibility (Amin's Uganda or Qaddafi's Libya perhaps being apt models) were to move close to nuclear weapons, the world might be ready to tolerate and even approve such an intervention. If "tough cases make bad law," "clear cases" should make "good law."

---

[12] The particularly fastidious Chinese policy on no-first-use of nuclear weapons is discussed in Jonathan D. Pollack, "China as a Nuclear Power," in *Asia's Nuclear Future,* William H. Overbolt, ed. (Boulder, Colorado: Westview Press, 1977), pp. 35–66.

The lack of international outrage at the sabotaging of the French nuclear equipment consigned for delivery to Iraq may thus already illustrate the beginning of the world's new attitudes. We are approaching an age where there will be greater outrage at the manufacture of nuclear weapons, and less outrage at some forms of intervention to prevent this.

Much might depend on how rapidly and expeditiously and surgically such an intervention could be carried through. It might, for reasons of avoiding side-damage to civilians (and especially of avoiding the precedent of nuclear usage) have to be carried out entirely with conventional weapons. The pinpoint accuracies which are of such concern on the strategic balance between the United States and Soviet Union might thus one day be put to a use which would be much easier to defend, destroying a reprocessing or enrichment facility without doing great damage to those around it.[13]

The use of new Soviet and American missiles may be more generally constrained. The apparent breakdown of Soviet-American strategic arms control and SALT II has seen a frightening increase in the discussion of new ballistic missile and cruise missile options, and of "war-fighting" scenarios. The superb accuracies of the new missiles will offer more options of striking at enemy military forces, rather than simply at large cities (as was the apparent pattern of "mutual assured destruction"). In many ways this can be destabilizing, increasing the risks of World War III.

Yet the same accuracies that might threaten the survivability of an underground missile silo have also now led some strategic analysts to contemplate the use of conventional warheads instead of nuclear, for possible future wars on the European central front, or wars elsewhere. Consistent with all that we have been discussing in this article, the prediction will thus be advanced that the newest in cruise missiles will not be fired in anger with nuclear warheads, but with conventional. Just as the B-52 in the end only saw combat delivering TNT bombs in Vietnam, rather than the H-bomb it was designed for (because of fears of escalation, and respect for the "nuclear taboo"), so the latest in strategic weapons will similarly remain constrained in use.

Soviet-American cooperation

We might turn now to a fifth prediction which, after the invasion of Afghanistan and the apparent breakdown of the SALT negotiations, might strike many readers as decidedly swimming against the tide—namely that Soviet-American cooperation in international matters will continue to grow, specifically because of Moscow and Washington's shared aversion to nuclear proliferation.

The handling of the NPT negotiations from 1967 to 1968, and the han-

---

[13] A good overview of the warfare uses (including conventional) of cruise-missiles, which may become possible with their extreme accuracy, can be found in Kosta Tsipis, "Cruise Missiles" in *Scientific American*, *Progress in Arms Control* (San Francisco: Freeman, 1979), pp. 171–81.

dling of proliferation matters since then, might substantively and procedurally be viewed as almost the ideal of how smoothly Soviet-American dealings could run. At meetings of the IAEA, or in the NPT Review Conferences, or at sessions of the UN General Assembly on the proliferation topic, it apparently has been typical for Soviet delegations to compare strategy and tactics very closely with the United States, indeed sometimes (where the Soviet delegation had not had the time to make its own assessment) even letting the American delegation decide how some other nation's proposals should be responded to. American and Soviet participants in such gatherings are old friends and comrades, radiating a trust and commonality of purpose which occasionally also shows up at UNCTAD or Law of the Sea discussions, but otherwise has been startlingly special for all the years since 1946.

But why should anyone count upon a spreading of such superpower cooperation, given the obvious issues which now seem to divide them elsewhere? As the U.S. government has cut off grain sales, and withdrawn from the Olympics, because of events in Afghanistan, can one count upon Soviet-American cooperation to persist?

One reason to have expected a slight expansion of this cooperation over time would have been a certain "multiplier effect" or "spinoff," as the personnel on each side who had become accustomed to Soviet-American cooperation and conspiracy on nuclear proliferation were perhaps promoted or moved to other tasks, where their new instincts of trust continued to generate good feelings rather than bad. But won't the managers of projects more in conflict with the United States also get promoted?

A more tangible reason to expect such growing cooperation would instead have been that the nuclear proliferation risk will itself grow in importance. Yet doesn't the Soviet invasion of Afghanistan, and the vehemence of the American response thereto, show that both the superpowers have other goals which they care about more than nonproliferation? And if these are likely to be goals on which Moscow and Washington come into conflict, what does this do to any prediction of greater cooperation?

If one had tried five years ago to project how the use of increased Soviet military power would be reconciled with the greater Soviet need for cooperation with the United States on nuclear proliferation, the prediction might have been that the superpowers would try to channel their comparisons of clout into zones relatively far removed from nuclear proliferation. Angola and South Yemen might have been up for grabs and productive of contest, but the SALT process, and the regions most prone to proliferation, would at the same moment have seen greater cooperation. Such clearly was not ordained to be the pattern.

How then is one to relate the events in Central Asia to the prediction that greater Soviet-American cooperation will still be the rule? As Soviet troops move through Afghanistan to approach the borders of proliferation-suspect Pakistan, one can of course interpret this simply as an exception to the rule. But one can also even first make a half-hearted try at interpreting their advance as consistent with the rule. No one has been inclined to offer so benign an explanation of the brazen Soviet invasion of Afghanistan as that this might indeed be the Russian contribution to dissuading Pakistan from acquiring nuclear weapons. Other factors clearly dominate this in importance, including the future of the Islamic minorities within the USSR, and the vested interest the Russians had acquired in the Marxist regime in Afghanistan—a regime which seemed headed for a defeat quite embarrassing to Moscow.

Yet Americans should remember the Pakistani issue which had gripped them most before the Soviet troops invaded Afghanistan, or at least before the embassy in Islamabad was burned by mobs blaming America for unrest in Mecca. The primary issue for Americans was the uncovering of a Pakistani clandestine attempt to acquire a uranium enrichment facility, after American arguments had persuaded the French government not to go through with selling Pakistan a plutonium reprocessing plant. The major issue, in short, was nuclear proliferation.[14]

Skeptics about any cooperation with the Russians might, of course, gleefully contend that most of the "nth country" bombs would be aimed at the USSR. It surely is more likely that any Pakistani bombs would be used against a Russian target than against an American, by reasons of geographical proximity, as well as likely political alignment. (If this were not always true, critics of the Soviet invasion of Afghanistan would suggest that this invasion made it true.)

Yet, as fears of "Islamic bomb"-Pakistani nuclear cooperation with Iraq or Libya suggest, the superpower concern about nuclear proliferation can hardly be so one-sided.[15] The same people who burned our embassy could one day be threatening to burn down one of our cities. The proliferation risk for most countries in the world may sooner or later acquire an element of "all-azimuth."

The impact of the Soviet forward move in central Asia can also not be so one-sided. It draws Pakistani fear and hostility more toward the USSR; but the threat posed by Russian forces on the Pakistani frontier may also inhibit Pakistani application of hydroelectric power to the manufacture of nuclear weapons.

Perhaps one can thus salvage the forecast that the Soviet Union will attach high priority to the prevention of nuclear proliferation by finding this to be consistent with moving troops into and through Afghanistan, so as more directly to intimidate Pakistan, despite the American reactions this has produced. Perhaps not. We in any event must develop a somewhat more complicated model, and not simply one where the appearance of superpower détente is maintained whenever the risk of nuclear weapons spread rears its

---

[14] A valuable discussion of the threat of Pakistan's acquiring nuclear weapons can be found in Zalmay Khalilzad, "Pakistan and the Bomb," *Survival*, XXI, 6 (November/December 1979): 244–50.

[15] For an Indian discussion, see Major-General D. K. Palit and P. K. S. Namboodiri, *Pakistan's Islamic Bomb* (New Delhi: Vikas Publishing House, 1979).

ugly head. Perhaps no one should expect that the two superpowers will place nonproliferation ahead of all other considerations in the deployment of their military forces and the use of their other power assets. Yet the prediction will remain that proliferation will claim some very significant part of the policy budget, and typically will still pull the superpowers together more than apart.

We opened speculation in the introduction on the more general impact of the threat of nuclear proliferation on existing alliances, and some more should also be said here on the impact of "quasi-proliferation" where it occurs.

Will alliances now normally harden, pulling the United States and the USSR more into hostile confrontation with each other, as a nuclear protegé of one side faces the nuclear protégé of the other?[16] Or will alliance ties be loosened as a result? The alliance leaders might have wished to discipline proliferators by moving away from them, but our worst fear is that they will not be able to do so, and will have to become even more entangled in the local conflicts which now are nuclearized.

The real and major tensions between the two superpowers have to date generally occurred at greater remove from such proliferation. Since Britain and France have gotten their bombs, the Soviet military threat to these U.S. alliance partners has actually faded; since China got its bomb, the USSR has in no way become more entangled in the alliance with Peking, while the United States, once the clearest enemy for Peking, has also switched roles.

The important exception, perhaps, has been the case of Israel, where Israel's asymptotic approach to nuclear weapons has been marked by a more and more explicit alliance identification with the United States while the Russians went further and further toward an open military identification with the Arab side. Yet even here the alliance polarizations have been thrown into disarray in the wake of Egyptian shifts in attitude since 1975.

What then happens as nuclear weapons spread into a region free of the veto of Moscow or Washington? Are the threats from the outside lifted, as happened for both Peking and Tel Aviv? Are the superpower guarantees lifted, as happened for Peking, or are they strengthened as happened for Tel Aviv?

If the threats are in effect lifted faster by the impact of proliferation than the superpower guarantees can be lifted in any demonstrated retaliation, the entire exercise can become a relatively empty one. Has the United States or the USSR become less reliable as a defender of India, in retaliation for the Indian nuclear detonation? The question might go unanswered, as the response would rather be "But who is threatening to attack India these days?"

We have been assuming that most of the world will see neither the detonation of actual weapons nor quasi-proliferation. But if this is to be, what will continue to be the international prerequisites and consequences of this?

If nuclear proliferation is to be avoided, the superpower participation in this can simply not be of the bipolar intensity of the old Cold War days, for a

---

[16] See Lewis A. Dunn, "Aspects of Military Strategy and Arms Control in a More Proliferated World," in King, *International Political Effects of the Spread of Nuclear Weapons*, pp. 145-64.

certain amount of coordination among the superpowers will have to occur, wherever a potential "nth" power could otherwise play one off against the other. Yet would it then instead amount to the superpower condominium that the smaller states often used to say they feared, as the United States and the USSR divided the world and parceled out who will dictate policy to whom? Almost certainly, it again would not.

"Condominium" is simply too strong a label for an arrangement where the predominance of Washington and Moscow is concentrated so largely in this field of nuclear arms control. Preventing the spread of nuclear weapons will not just be the better half of the loaf for the less developed nations (as they privately come to attach high priority to this—while they must at the same time tolerate a lack of superpower arms reductions, and even perhaps some very active superpower political and military competition in many corners of the globe). The same half of the loaf will be of preeminent value to the superpowers, such that they become ready to appease the West Germans or the East Germans, or the Japanese or the Cubans, on other questions, as the price of winning in exchange an assurance against further nuclear proliferation.

Even where the Russians and Americans agree, therefore, the world will not become unipolar instead of bipolar or multipolar. Because Moscow and Washington agree on the nuclear weapons question, they will collude somewhat on it, but they both will have to make concessions to the national desires of other countries on other questions. To make things more confused, moreover, where the Russians and Americans disagree on other questions, these will occasionally be given a priority ahead of the proliferation concern, all the more erasing any neat image of "condominium."

Where in the end could one look for the Soviet Union to demonstrate this predicted growing commitment to preventing nuclear proliferation? One might surely anticipate that countries recently subjected to Marxist takeovers, such an Angola and Ethiopia and South Yemen (and Afghanistan) will become "as Catholic as the Pope" in endorsing nonproliferation at international gatherings. Where non-Marxist LDCs still make speeches stressing economic development and energy production ahead of nonproliferation, the Russian-dominated countries will speak or vote on the opposite side. East Germany today is already perhaps the model of what the IAEA could expect in national compliance and cooperation in the nuclear safeguards field. The East German model may appear in all the countries over which the Russians wield such influence. Cuba, of the states allied with the Soviet Union, has shown the most recalcitrance on the nuclear weapons question, rejecting both the NPT and the Latin American Nuclear Free Zone Treaty, but Havana also might be induced to fall into line within the decade.

With regard to South Asia, the Russians might similarly be counted upon to join with the United States in discouraging any new detonations of nuclear explosives by the Indian government, both under Mrs. Gandhi (who might be fairly regarded as closer to the Russians) and under any other regime able to unseat her again in later elections.

As noted, the crucial issue for Americans may be one of keeping Pakistan from acquiring nuclear weapons to match India. One might thus finally hazard a prediction that Soviet forces, if kept on the frontiers of Pakistan, will be handled moderately so as to maintain incentives against Pakistani nuclear weapons, rather than casting the Islamabad regime once again into the role of a pariah state, and stampeding it into proliferation.

Traffic in conventional arms

A sixth prediction to be advanced is that the traffic in conventional arms will continue to be tolerated, if not expanded, as part of preventing nuclear proliferation.

This at times may simply amount to making the best of a bad bargain, as selling advanced weapons to a state like Pakistan or South Korea and Cuba will be the price of assuring their superpower patron that nuclear weapons will not be sought. Yet a deeper logic of comparison might turn again to the costs and likelihood of wars. We are dealing with a generally known commodity in the spread of conventional weapons, even if their technological elegance and power is growing each year by leaps and bounds.[17]

Reasonable people can debate whether various new forms of such weaponry increase or decrease the likelihood of sneak attacks and preemptive wars. It is hardly certain that upping the conventional arms traffic increases the stability of regions, but it is also not so certain that this stability is decreased, for some modern weapons may indeed incline toward making battlefield confrontations more defensively-oriented and stable again.

The clearer comparison with nuclear weapons comes in the costs of wars when they occur. As noted above, it is widely and probably correctly assumed that nuclear weapons would indeed increase the costliness of wars, imposing far greater casualties and physical damage. By contrast, the introduction of the very latest in tanks or jet fighters or naval vessels has even sometimes brought down the level of civilian casualties and economic damage in wartime. The Middle East and South Asian areas are important illustrations of this.

However we might strike this balance ourselves, an important part of the entire picture will be how it is struck by the powers that matter. There is evidence that this is a conclusion on which the nuclear weapons states and the Third World may agree: that efforts to constrain the arms trade in conventional arms can generally be taken less seriously than nuclear non-proliferation.

Compared to the serious Soviet-American coordination on the nuclear proliferation problem, we have seen only the most tentative beginnings of any superpower effort to restrain the conventional arms traffic, with the United States and Soviet Union being principal offenders as suppliers.

---

[17] A very thoughtful analysis of the conventional arms trade problem can be found in Anne Hessing Cahn, Joseph J. Kruzel, Peter M. Dawkins, and Jacques Huntzinger, *Controlling Future Arms Trade,* Council on Foreign Relations 1980s Project (New York: McGraw Hill, 1977).

The speeches of other states, at UN General Assembly sessions or in any other forum, have similarly tended to deprecate the appropriateness of any efforts to hold back modern arms. One must, of course, stipulate that the same LDCs have often expressed skepticism about nuclear proliferation as a menace. Yet there are reasons to suspect that the indifference to nuclear proliferation is indeed more feigned, that the fears there are more real, while the fears are in truth missing on conventional arms, for all the reasons noted.

The spread of advanced electronic military equipment of jet fighters is not as likely to threaten immediately the safety and well-being of all within any region. This spread is typically seen as in part reflecting a new-found affluence or economic leverage in the Third World. Why should not some other states, besides the traditional superpowers, have a turn at handling the very latest and fine-tuned of weapons?

In part, this is thus simply a substitution of the glamour or prestige of one new kind of weapon for another, of conventional for nuclear, for the LDCs as well as for the superpower donors. Yet neither side flipped a coin as to which kind of weapon to promote and which kind to try to avoid. Each may share the view that the spread of conventional weapons is at worst a mild curse, and at times even a help.

Diplomatic distortions

The next prediction may hardly be news at all to those who have seen the same pattern in a host of other international questions, but it still bears repetition on the nuclear proliferation issue. It is that the issue will be discussed amid a host of diplomatic misstatements and overstatements of position by all the countries involved.[18]

Some other countries which indeed share the Soviet and American opposition to nuclear weapons spread will over and over again pretend to be not so particularly concerned here, amid statements that energy development and a fairer division of the world's economic pie should be given a much higher priority. Charges will regularly be trotted out that the superpowers are supporting bars to nuclear proliferation simply out of their own selfish power-political interest, and such charges unfortunately will still be accepted by some observers as serious statements of the national goals and perceptions of the countries making them.

As with everything else on the nuclear question, a great deal of this will be theatrics, in this case with the intent of winning concessions on other issues, as part of the general exchange of effort on proliferation. While there will thus be a great deal of apparent anguish about a double standard, by which horizontal proliferation is halted while "vertical proliferation" continues, the truth, as noted earlier, is that much of this double standard is indeed being

---

[18] A valuable survey of the issues presented in the negotiations of the NPT and in the years since can be found in Enid C. B. Schoettle, *Postures on Nonproliferation* (New York: Crane and Russak for the Stockholm International Peace Research Institute, 1979).

accepted and internalized around the globe. While the LDCs will stake a serious claim on the future by feigning a grievance in being denied the benefits of nuclear power, most of them have perceived that this technology is at present hardly well designed or tailored to their needs. The United States would do well to understand that the supposed equanimity of much of the world with the threat of nuclear proliferation is very much overstated; over time Washington will probably come back to matching such diplomacy with subleties of its own.

The beginnings of major Congressional intervention in nuclear policy came after the Indian detonation of 1974,[19] and this was followed by the election in 1976 of a Carter administration committed to a more straight-forward American resistance to nuclear weapons spread. Given some of the trimming back of the visibility of this straightforward resistance since then, critics might intervene to claim that this was all a bad idea—that the indirect approaches of previous administrations had been better tuned to the subtleties and complexities involved. Defenders of post-1976 policy could counter that the United States was doing nothing more than being clever as a bargainer, demanding more restraints on sensitive technology than it could hope to get, so as to settle with at least a better position in the ultimate "compromise."

Whichever interpretation is adopted for the events of 1974 to 1980, the likelihood as we move ahead in the 1980s is that American nonproliferation policy will shift to something again a little more soft-sell and low-key; this may not reflect any reduction whatsoever in the priority attached to the topic, but rather a conclusion that this should at least *now* be carried through with less visible confrontation.

Just as other states will be more opposed to nuclear weapons spread than they admit, the United States may now occasionally hedge on the intensity of its own commitment, if for no other reason than to thrust some of the burden elsewhere, and thus to smoke out the real priorities of others.

Public sophistication

One could move from this into an eighth prediction—namely that the peoples of the world will show an increasing sophistication now about nuclear matters.

A great number of countries will indeed acquire a large part of the competence needed for the manufacture of nuclear warheads, as the exact details of bomb assembly become less and less a "secret" and the possession of weapons-grade fissionable material spreads despite American objections. Yet the number of sensational magazine articles about "X is close to the bomb" will subside since all of this is no longer big news: the publics that matter will relax a little bit, as long as their neighbors are not detonating, or announcing, or

[19] See Frederick Williams, "The United States Congress and Nonproliferation," *International Security,* 3, 2 (Fall 1978): 45–66, for details of the Congressional involvement in a more explicit approach to halting nuclear weapons spread.

brandishing such weapons. A certain "live and let live" may settle in about being "near-nuclear," in a form much stronger than we have anticipated thus far, entirely comparable to what at this moment perhaps applies between West Germany and Sweden, or Canada and Japan.

We already have signs of this in the public's tendency to stay at much lower levels of alert where no nuclear weapon has yet been test-detonated. A skeptic about the public's sophistication might argue that this simply shows how the man-on-the-street is unaware of the real weapons-production capabilities that have spread around the world—how he is trapped in an ignorance which can be dispelled only by photographs of a mushroom cloud. A more generous interpretation of the public's attitudes would be that a country such as Israel or South Africa or Argentina has not done anything irrevocable or so fully menacing until a bomb has been detonated, and that the world public knows this.

A great deal of the proliferation impulse we worry about is based on a possible chain reaction of public anxiety and response. The public's determination not to credit Israel fully with a bomb, until it explodes or claims one, might then be a very welcome symptom of a barrier to such chain-reaction anxiety.

Perhaps even more interesting than the world's disinclination to become visibly excited by rumors about Israel, or South Africa, or Taiwan, has been the evident nonexcitement with the possible late-1979 reconnaissance satellite detection of a nuclear explosion in the southern hemisphere. Until the explosion is proven as definite, and is tied by proof or admission to some definite "nth" state, the public's response seems to be much the same as if it had never happened.

North Americans and Europeans may look upon the military-dominated governments of Latin America as the very opposite of the modernity and progress we seek in the world. Yet the manner in which Argentina and Brazil have handled their possible nuclear competition is in many ways to be commended. While outsiders write of "historic rivalries" and "incipient nuclear arms races," Brazilians and Argentinians (with exceptions) have shown little alarm, or sense of racing. The local discussions of the possibilities of nuclear explosives have seen little of the leering innuendo about weapons possibilities that we find in South Africa or the Middle East, and even in India.

One could enter into a interesting debate about whether this reflects some special characteristics of Latin American international political style, reflecting a tradition at variance with much of European diplomacy and arms confrontation. Argentina and Brazil have simply not been traditional rivals in the same way as Germany and France, or Britain and Russia, or the United States and Japan. This of course may have very little to do with modernity or any new sophistication. We are accustomed to scoffing at Latin America's "parade-grounds armies," and at investments in aircraft carriers which never are equipped with airplanes. Yet would the world have preferred that Latin American armies and navies be more real and functional over these years, or that these countries actually use forces in wars, rather than simply apparently wasting money on them?[20]

What has been true for armed forces in the past may be true for nuclear weapons potential in Latin America in the future, and might also be increasingly true for nuclear weapons potential in other countries around the world. The public may become more relaxed in the presence of unrealized or unused potential—more accustomed to the possibility of independently "sitting on the brink." This, after all, is what the superpowers have done with the battlefield use of nuclear weapons ever since 1945. It is what many countries may now do just as naturally with the manufacture of such weapons.

One can already see some of the differences here, in comparing the attention and excitement accorded the Chinese detonation of 1964, and the Indian nuclear detonation of 1974. While nuclear weapons are clearly very destructive and dangerous, they will be viewed less and less as an accomplishment of glamour or prestige (and as a result they will produce less public pressure for "keeping up with the Joneses," less invidious demand that "if they can do it, we can too").

Fifteen years ago it might have been predicted that an Indian nuclear detonation would capture imaginations in Japan or Italy or Australia. What has happened to pro-nuclear-weapons popular feeling in such countries is indicative of what may grow generally—a decrease in the apparent scientific and economic accomplishment that is assumed when nuclear explosives become possible, a decrease in the possibility that any regime could bail itself out of domestic troubles by detonating a nuclear device.

The tools of nonproliferation

Finally, as a ninth and last prediction about the international system's handling of the nuclear proliferation threat, we might focus a little on what the tools of the containment effort will be. As suggested, occasions may arise where military force is directly utilized to prevent a state from acquiring such weapons. Ideally this would take place without using nuclear weapons in the preemptive effort—thus avoiding the worst possible precedent. Most probably, it would occur only when the potential nuclear weapons state had become widely notorious for irresponsibility and aggressiveness, so that the rest of the world quietly approved of an intervention which would have had no legitimacy under older standards of international law.

Looking far down the road, one or two such situations where "an easy case makes good law" might in fact be welcomed by the antiproliferation coalition, simply for the precedent this sets for deterring other erstwhile possessors of nuclear weapons. This may all be a little like the problem of the

[20] For an authoritative Latin American statement on the prospects of avoiding nuclear weapons spread in the region, see Alfonso Garcia Robles, *The Latin American Nuclear-Weapon-Free Zone*, Occasional Paper No. 19 (Muscatine, Iowa: Stanley Foundation 1979).

traffic policeman trying to enforce a 55-mile-per-hour speed limit when everyone is driving 57; when someone comes along at 80 miles per hour, it is easy to pull him to the side, and the example of seeing him arrested may then even slow everyone else down.

Much more significant than the possibility of military intervention, however, will be the threat (explicit or implicit) of withholding advanced technological exports from any nation that has not done what is expected to assure against weapons manufacture. Getting the members of the London Suppliers' Club to coordinate behind a demand for full-scope safeguards has not been easy, and the coordination may always seem a little tenuous and fragile. Nonetheless, a great deal has been accomplished, both in policy and in the development of a legitimating philosophy behind that policy. Rather than argumentively referring to such coordination among suppliers as a "cartel," more and more of the countries with whom they do business will acknowledge the need for full-scope safeguards, or for other assurances against weapons manufacture.

It will thus simply be too pessimistic to throw up one's hands and conclude that any country denied purchases from the Americans or Canadians will find the same sensitive equipment and materials available from France or Germany. Many of the loopholes will be closed; where a loophole remains, moreover, it will still require that the purchaser will have to pay more and will have to settle for equipment which is less than his first choice—i.e., that some important economic price will have had to be paid for retaining the weapons option.

Such channelings of economic leverage will sometimes be exercised through explicit pronouncements and widely-declared policy. In other cases, they may be handled more effectively by subtle and less explicit forms of economic discrimination. Nations that accept a full program of safeguards over their peaceful nuclear industries will simply find it easier to get their purchase orders processed, while those who do not will often see their contracts mishandled or delayed and will find themselves too often asked to step to the back of the line.

Such indirect enconomic pressure is closely linked to the form of leverage we have been betting on most highly in this prognosis: political pressure. The United States, together with the other major opponents of proliferation, will now find it possible to let the arguments against nuclear weapons spread be voiced more and more by other states, by industrialized nonweapons states, and even by less developed countries. As the shared interest in preventing the horizontal proliferation of nuclear weapons is more generally admitted, the political pressures against nations seeking such weapons will be more difficult to ignore.

There will be occasions when the opposition to proliferation seems quite well coordinated, as all the powers that matter regularly compare notes with each other. But we will sometimes also see the significant states approaching the matter from substantially different perspectives, perhaps when disagreement about other issues and goals makes coordination on the agreed goal of nonproliferation more difficult. As the United States and the Soviet Union enter the 1980s, this may become the pattern of their "joint" antiproliferation effort, as the demise of détente makes closer cooperation less possible. Coordinated policy is (almost by definition) usually more effective than uncoordinated policy. Yet the effectiveness of this effort may still be great, simply because the different actors each put some substantial effort into it and attach high priority to it.

As with all aspects of halting nuclear weapons spread, it would be a mistake to try to wrap up the problem "once and for all" in a single policy sweep. Attempts at great clarity and decisiveness can produce excessively blunt and explicit policy approaches that will then be counterproductive. The global system to prevent or to contain nuclear proliferation must rather amount to a patchwork of international and national measures, some of them clear and fair, while others are murky and unfair. Some of them will be military or materially economic, while others are merely political or philosophical; some of them will be coordinated and some uncoordinated, some will work for decades, others will merely patch gaps for a few years at a time.

Our stress on the role of economic sanctions, implicit or explicit, stems from an assumption of increasing world economic interdependence. Despite the rhetoric about the evils of "dependencia" and the need for a "new economic order," the reality of the future is that states trying to break out of economic poverty most probably will find international trade the means to do so. Both the United States and Brazil will benefit from such trade. Rather than getting into a moral argument about which benefits the most, it will be more relevant for the practical questions at hand to guess which of these trade partners will find it less easy to give up such trade; in this century, this is very likely to be Brazil.

A government which bases its hopes of advancing to affluence on continued access to the high-technology exports of the United States and Western Europe will then have to think twice before it detonates a nuclear device. India overrode such considerations, but other regimes may hold back before breaking the proliferation taboo. Economics may thus help to solve our proliferation problem, in that it makes many of the potential "nth" nuclear weapons states so dependent on international trade that a deterrent to proliferation will emerge.

Economics, on the other hand, is also an important source of our proliferation problem, in that the urgent world need for energy justifies the investments that bring many states so precariously close to the bomb. Since some of such dual-purpose nuclear activities will definitely have to be tolerated, our final economic input might then turn to the hopes noted above of multinational or transnational institutions. The threat of economic trade cutoffs, as punishment for a weapons program, would be reinforced by the day-to-day involvement of foreigners in many of the sensitive peaceful nuclear operations that may become operational in this century.

The very nature of nuclear industry requires that a fair amount of "multinational" management will have to emerge, even if this is never made very formal or explicit. The producers and users of nuclear fuels will have to take considerably more interest in each other's welfare and economic viability than is normal for the sellers and buyers of more conventional items. The esoteric and fragile quality of nuclear technology would have dictated this, even if weapons proliferation had never arisen as an issue.

Advocates of "fuel independence" in foreign countries might understandably be suspect of wanting this as a cover for seeking weapons options; yet in some cases they have simply been nostalgically yearning for the past when other industries allowed such independence. Such nostalgia will be overcome. The United States, on its side, has similarly indulged in displays of national independence that now may be inappropriate and will be overcome. American treatment of uranium enrichment policies under President Nixon are indeed responsible for some of the difficulties which we have experienced since then in developing a coordinated antiproliferation policy. The post-1974 Congressional intervention, culminating in the 1978 Nuclear Nonproliferation Act, may reveal an approach that was too national, rather than systemic.

As we move toward the 1990s, an effective nuclear power program, in virtually any country of the world, will require close ties with industry people from abroad, in a transnational pattern dictated by technology as much as anything else. An undesirable form of "spinoff" is that an elementary competence at weapons assembly will move from country to country, no longer really letting itself be contained or hemmed in. But another spinoff is the kind of working relationship which should amplify the deterrent to the making of bombs, even where people know how to make them.

A summary of expectations

Much of what has been suggested might strike the reader as optimistic, as "too good to be true." Yet the alternative of allowing a widespread increase in the number of separate nations controlling nuclear weapons is very convincingly bad, so that the world is not really so likely to resign itself pessimistically to such proliferation. If the world chooses to avoid nuclear proliferation, therefore, much of what has been outlined here may happen—may indeed have to happen, as the price of such arms control.

The world is not itching to move into dilutions of sovereignty, or expansions of multinational management, or tolerations of obnoxious neighbors, simply for their own sake. The expectation of an expanded conventional arms trade surely shows the limits of the reasonableness we are anticipating. Soviet-American rivalry may persist on numerous fronts, and statements of national purpose will be offered in duplicitous forms by all concerned. What we are predicting is not some general trend toward internationalism and peacefulness. Rather we are projecting a degree of reason-ableness which will have been tailored for the nuclear proliferation problem in particular.

What is required to contain these most threatening weapons may thus be conceded, and not very much more. This might seem to be attaching an enormous amount of importance to a particular "gimmick" in military technology, overriding much broader, and historically better grounded, tendencies of sociology, economics, and politics. Yet the entire balance-of-terror system that has governed international politics since 1945 is based upon a similar gimmick. A political analyst looking ahead in 1945 might have felt very uneasy about attributing so much of the future to the influence of so little; yet he or she would have been wise to do so.

The same unexpected logic which (since Nagasaki) has kept nuclear weapons from being used in anger by those who have them, may keep such weapons from being built in the future, by those who have the ability to make them. One foregoes the use of nuclear weapons in today's limited wars because other powers have such weapons too. However attractive the prospect might be of winning victory through a unilateral use of nuclear weapons, the prospect goes down in relevance, because for one side to use such weapons would be for two to use them. So it may be with the acquisition of such weapons. The attractive prospect of being the last state to get away with ac-quiring such weapons loses its relevance, for the word is out that one's neighbors could follow, and would follow, with nuclear weapons procure-ments of their own.

This is hardly, however, to deny that some of this "proliferation chain" will continue to plague us—as a nuclear Korea is more likely to produce a nuclear Japan and a nuclear Brazil very possibly would lead to a nuclear Argentina. The existence of such linkages is both a large part of our problem and a portion of our solution; for it is the fear of being followed into the nuclear weapons club that will supply some of the deterrent to entry. Yet the linkages may (as noted) also be less close than in the past, less continually discussed and central to people's consciousness.

Two problems of tendency may seem to blur together when we come to look back on events at the close of the century. The logic of proliferation chains is indeed stronger for having a fifteenth nuclear weapons state produce a sixteenth, and less that a seventh must produce an eighth; it is plunging into this abyss of continual and unchecked domino chains of proliferation that we most want to avoid. Yet any of such connections, between eighth and seventh, or sixteenth and fifteenth, may be less tight in the 1980s than in the 1970s, and may be less tight again in the 1990s. If we can keep the forward motion of proliferation from achieving too rapid a pace, therefore, time may still be on our side.

Index